AUTOBIOGRAPHY AND QUESTIONS OF GENDER

Autobiography and Questions of Gender

Edited by
SHIRLEY NEUMAN
University of Alberta

FRANK CASS

First published in 1991 in Great Britain by
FRANK CASS & CO. LTD.
Gainsborough House, Gainsborough Road,
London E11 1RS, England

and in the United States of America by
FRANK CASS
c/o International Specialized Book Services, Inc.
5602 N.E. Hassalo Street, Portland, Oregon 97213

British Library Cataloguing in Publication Data
Autobiography and questions of gender.
I. Neuman, Shirley
809.93592072

ISBN 0-7146-3422-0

Library of Congress Cataloging-in-Publication Data

Autobiography and questions of gender/ edited by Shirley Neuman.
    p.   cm.
    "Essays first appeared in a special issue ... of Prose studies,
vol. 14, no. 2"—T.p. verso.
    ISBN 0-7146-3422-0
    1. American prose literature—Women authors—History and
criticism. 2. Women authors, American—Biography—History and
criticism. 3. Autobiography—Authorship—Sex differences.
4. Autobiography—Women authors. I. Neuman, S.C. (Shirley C.)
PS366.A88A93 1991
810.9'49207—dc20   91-32766
                                                   CIP

This group of studies first appeared in a special issue on "Autobiography and Questions of Gender" of Prose Studies, Vol. 14, No.
2, published by Frank Cass & Co. Ltd.

Typeset by Regent Typesetting
Printed in Great Britain by
Antony Rowe Ltd, Chippenham, Wiltshire

Contents

Acknowledgements

Much of the work of assembling this collection was enabled by a McCalla Research Professorship from the University of Alberta awarded to the editor. She is most grateful for this support.

The editor also wishes to thank those who helped: Deborah Wills, who brought a keen eye to the checking of citations and references throughout the collection; Flora Pavich, who typed it with a cheerful patience that never flagged before authors' corrections and changes; and Don Anderson, who proofread with promptness and care.

Autobiography and Questions of Gender: An Introduction

SHIRLEY NEUMAN

The intense scrutiny given autobiography during the last thirty-five years, and particularly scholars' attempts to theorize it in terms of genre, must be read at least partly in the context of a larger "crisis" of referentiality and of the representation and self-representation of the subject. For our elaboration of various poetics of autobiography coincides with that historical moment when the notion of an internally coherent and stable "self" – developing and changing to be sure, but nonetheless, in some fundamental sense, the same, self-identical – has been called into question by theories of the subject as constructed in and by discourses, as both the historical site and the product of a nexus of cultural discourses. The development of a poetics of autobiography has been one response to a moment of cultural contestation about the "self." Indeed, in arguing that *Roland Barthes by Roland Barthes*, "In its grappling with representational and philosophical dilemmas glimpsed and repressed by Wordsworth, . . . makes clear how far modern self-reflexive texts have evolved in response to problems first raised by the Romantics – and anticipated long ago by Augustine," at least one critic, Paul Jay (38), intimates that the problems in self-representation encountered by autobiographers have long prefigured post-structuralist theories of the subject as decentred, unstable, in process, multiple.

Theorists of a stable, coherent and unified self, which, they hold, autobiography discovers and represents, have themselves represented that self in the transcendent and universalizing terms of the traditional metaphysics of western literatures. But theorists of a destabilized, decentered subject-in-process who hold, with Michael Sprinker, that autobiography can only be a "writing where concepts of subject, self, and author collapse into the act of producing a text" (342), have also presented us with subjects of autobiography more generalized than particularized. In both instances, the subject of autobiography has been theorized without self-consciousness about, or differentiation of, what in western cultures is a fundamental aspect of our "identity" or "subjectivity": our identity as a man or a woman. These poetics assume a male subject of autobiography: consequently, gender remains unproblematized and unreflected in them for, as Susan Stanford Friedman succinctly put it, "A . . . man has the luxury of forgetting his . . . sex. He can think of himself as an 'individual.' Women . . ., reminded at every turn in the great cultural hall of mirrors of their sex . . ., have no such luxury" (39).

Indeed, the politics of identity of the recent women's movement has complicated the "crisis" of representation and self-representation by making it turn on the problematization of questions of gender at least as much as on post-structuralist theory. It has given rise to an "other" poetics developed by women readers who found, in the words of Estelle Jelinek's introduction to the first (1980) collection of essays on women's autobiography, that the "objective theories" of most critics "are not applicable to women's life studies" (5). Over the last dozen years, questions of gender in autobiography have been raised almost exclusively around women's writing, in the context of the assertion of a politics of identity resistant to the deconstruction of "self," and on the foundations of a model of gender difference which is extended to genre difference, or what Domna Stanton, playing on etymologies, terms "genderic differences" (11). The most generally accepted thesis of gender difference in autobiography has been Mary Mason's that, where men stress their individualism in their autobiographies, women define their identity in terms of their relationship with others. Other "genderic differences" frequently put forward hypothesize the discontinuity and fragmentation of women's autobiographies as opposed to chronological, linear and coherent narratives by men; the personal, intimate subject matter of women's autobiographies as opposed to the public, professional matter of men's; and the "split subject" of women's autobiographies written against a cultural "injunction against [women's] writing" (Stanton 14–15; cf. Benstock 29). The very qualities critics such as Georges Gusdorf claimed were *not* significant in the autobiographical self – qualities such as "*identification, interdependence,* and *community*" were seen to be "key elements in the development of a woman's identity" in autobiography as in life, Susan Stanford Friedman argues in an essay that theorizes women's autobiographical identity in terms of feminist delineations of female psychosexual development (38). In the name of these differences, a good deal of important description of women's autobiographies has been carried out, much of it gathered in edited collections such Estelle Jelinek's *Women's Autobiography: Essays in Criticism*, Domna Stanton's *The Female Autograph: Theory and Practice of Autobiography from the Tenth to the Twentieth Century*, Shari Benstock's *The Private Self: Theory and Practice of Women's Autobiographical Writings*, and Bella Brodzki and Celeste Schenck's *Life/Lines: Theorizing Women's Autobiography*.

A range of women's texts has been brought into the autobiographical canon and previously excluded subject-matter has been introduced in discussions such as, for example, Carolyn Heilbrun's and Joanne Braxton's about the representation in autobiography of women's anger. In many ways, the collection before you continues this work of "collective restoration" (Brodzki and Schenck 13) of women's texts, women's representations, and "genderic differences" into the autobiographical canon.

Domna Stanton, however, points out the theoretical limitations of the model of difference that has been assumed in discussions of gender and women's autobiography, observing that it is predicated "on a preselected corpus of male autobiographies [a canon] and a preestablished set of common traits" (11), and that what is often hypothesized "as a fundamental female quality" was in fact the product of "cultural norms" (12–13). T.L. Broughton, in her essay for this collection, notes the difficulty of maintaining these distinctions for autobiographies "generated within ever-fluctuating discursive worlds, ever-changing possibilities of meaning and values." Other critics have come up with numerous examples of women who did write in the "masculine" mode of the coherent, linear, narrative describing an individualized self or, for that matter, of men who wrote autobiographies in discontinuous modes about a fragmented or "split" subject. Increasingly, critics have argued for the need to anchor generalizations about "genderic differences" in an analysis of specific historical and cultural circumstances. T.L. Broughton and Sidonie Smith, for example, both warn in their essays here against the ease with which enumerations of gender difference become generalities which efface differences *between* women. And the first chapters of Sidonie Smith's important *A Poetics of Women's Autobiography: Marginality and the Fictions of Self-Representation* looks at the cultural history which defined the autobiographical subject as male and examines the strategies women have found to write within that historical tradition. She describes, for example, the double bind of the woman autobiographer: given that the autobiographer has been generically constructed as a public figure with access to public discourses, the cultural and material circumstances of women have, until recently, made autobiographical subjectivity unavailable to them; however, to the extent that they do adopt the "masculine" mode of the genre, they speak as "men" and not as "women." "We recognize," she sums up, "the repression of sexuality in either the transvestism of the soul or the silence of the mouth" (37). In such circumstances, the question is how the woman autobiographer can achieve agency, rather than self-silencing, through autobiography, how she "speaks to her culture from the margins" (Smith 176).

The answer for many recent critics is the adoption of a theory of the

subject that accepts neither ontological nor post-structuralist positions
but negotiates a space and a "subject" between them by acknowledging
the specific "epistemologies" behind the speaking/writing "I." Paul Smith
puts the position:

> . . . what is taken to *be* the "subject," the "I" that speaks a given
> discourse, reflects, as it has always been taken to reflect, specific
> epistemologies. Wherever the "I" speaks, a knowledge is spoken;
> wherever a knowledge speaks, an "I" is spoken. This is the dialecti-
> cal mechanism of a certain *presumption* of the "subject": that is, a
> "subject" is presumed to exist, indexed as an "I" and loaded with
> the burden of epistemologies, wittingly or not. (100; cf Butler 144–
> 5)

Behind the formulations of both Sidonie and Paul Smith, lies a body of
work which has developed out of Foucault's argument that sexuality is
produced by social discourses and "technologies" and the relations of
power and knowledge that they embody. Gender theory steps into a gap
in Foucault's argument, observing, as he did not, that sexuality is
constructed differently on male and female bodies. However, since these
"technologies" are multiple and interactive, the ideology of gender does
not figure the subject in isolation but at the nexus of several discourses –
"a subject constituted in gender, to be sure," Teresa de Lauretis remarks,

> though not by sexual difference alone, but rather across languages
> and cultural representations; a subject en-gendered in the exper-
> iencing of race and class, as well as sexual, relations; a subject,
> therefore, not unified but rather multiple, and not so much divided
> as contradicted. (2)

For this representation of multiple subjectivities in autobiography,
Gloria Anzaldúa uses the metaphor of *travesía*, or crossing over, while
Françoise Lionnet develops the "aesthetic concept" of *métissage* in order
to

> illustrate the relationship between historical context and individual
> circumstances, the sociocultural construction of race and gender
> and traditional genre theory, the cross-cultural linguistic
> mechanisms that allow a writer to generate polysemic meanings
> from deceptively simple or seemingly linear narrative techniques.
> (29)

In the context of social discourse, then, gender is both ideology and
representation, which autobiographers will be complicit with in varying
degrees, and which interacts with other ideologies and representations,

all of them the product of political, cultural, and material factors at particular historical moments. The ideology and representation of gender, in autobiography as elsewhere, remain subject to the limitations of the social discourse(s) constructing it. Teresa de Lauretis has been our most astute theorist in this respect, arguing that if there is a "space represented by/in a representation, by/in a discourse, by/in a sex-gender system," there is also a "space not represented yet implied (unseen) in them" (*Technologies* 26) or, as she put it in the title of another essay, a space to which they are indifferent. Those spaces within the representation of gender of near-to-complete invisibility and indifference remain large and numerous in the theory of autobiography. Most obviously, the self-representation of the autobiographical subject at the intersection of discourses of race and class as well as of gender has received comparatively little attention. Almost nothing has been done to examine the ways in which gender intersects with the ideological construction of the working class in autobiographies, although Carolyn Steedman's *Landscape for a Good Woman* marks out worthwhile directions and Regenia Gagnier's *Subjectivities* (1991) has recently addressed the topic in a more sustained way. In the area of "collective restoration" of black women's autobiographies to criticism of the genre, one points primarily to Sidonie Smith's discussion of Maya Angelou in *Where I'm Bound*; to William Andrews' discussion in *To Tell a Free Story* of Harriet Jacobs as constituted by the interaction of racial and gender ideology and to his *Sisters of the Spirit*; to essays by Jean Yellin on Harriet Jacobs and Nelly McKay on Zora Neale Hurston; to the introductions to autobiographical narratives published in the *Schomburg Library of Black Women Writers of the Nineteenth Century* (1988); and to Joanne Braxton's argument, in *Black Women Writing Autobiography: A Tradition within a Tradition*, "for a redefinition of the genre of black American autobiography to include the images of women as well as their memoirs, reminiscences, diaries, and journals – this as a corrective to both black and feminist literary criticism" (9).

Where what is "invisible" in our social constructions of gender exists on what Judith Butler has analyzed as a continuum between the heterosexual poles of masculinity and femininity, the space of silence and indifference grows even larger. There are two important essays on lesbian self-representation in autobiography, by Catharine Stimpson and Biddy Martin. Two further works, Gloria Anzaldúa's *La Frontera/Borderlands* and Minnie Bruce Pratt's "Identity: Skin Blood Heart," blur the boundaries between autobiography and cultural history and theory to construct a "self" at the intersections of lesbian sexuality and racial "difference." There is even less available on the self-representation of gay men in autobiography. And for all the emphasis in feminist theory of autobiography on the gender difference of women's autobiographies, the maternal remains practically unaddressed as a gender issue; the notable exception is the section of four essays on "Maternal Legacies/Mythographies" in *Life/Lines*.

Finally, and paradoxically, one of the major gaps in our theorizing of a poetics of gender in autobiography is the category in relation to which "genderic difference" has implicitly been defined: masculinity. As I will argue in my own essay in this volume, gender ideology in western cultures not only constructs certain subjects (women, racial "others," homosexuals) in terms of their invisibility, it constructs men as the only visible category and, therefore, one that need not be represented because it is always known to be there. This is as true of criticism of autobiography as it is of autobiographical representations of the male subject as transcendent and, therefore, beyond a category constructed on the sexed body such as gender.

The essays in *Autobiography and Questions of Gender* intervene in the "crisis" of representation and self-representation at many junctures on the continuum from ontological to post-structuralist theories of autobiography and in the problematization of gender within the genre and its critical theory. Susanna Egan's and T. L. Broughton's continue the work of "restoration" of women's works to the autobiographical canon. Egan's "From the Inside Out" reads Mary Meigs' *Lily Briscoe a Self-Portrait* by attentiveness to the mother–daughter relationship, among others, and by examining the ways in which fictional(ized) "others" serve the autobiographer's self-representation. T.L. Broughton stresses the "interconnected histories" which lead to a woman's " 'finding a voice' " in autobiography: "how the author acquired or came to do without a room of her own; how she came to command an audience rhetorically, ideologically and socio-economically." Her "Women's Autobiography: The Self at Stake?" brings these concerns to a reading of Annie Besant's autobiography, examining the gendered character of models of religious conversion and of the ideal of Christian self-sacrifice and going on to show how a contemporary concept of "activism as self-sacrificing motherhood" provided Besant with a subject position which her interest in theosophy, with its "metaphysics of maternal activism," enabled. In Besant, Broughton argues, we have an example of the inter-relationship of gender and genre in which both are structured around the "discourses of identity" available to the autobiographer at a particular historical juncture.

Attentive to the ways in which gender and genre inter-relate, several essays here discover new genres by addressing the ways in which women's relationships to others constitute not only the thematics of their auto-biographical self-representations but also the structural principles of their use of the genre. Lynn Bloom exuberantly announces the birth of auto/bio/history, a genre in which a scholar decodes, selects, annotates and presents in its historical and personal contexts an earlier diary which, because it was written so entirely for private consumption and because only the scantiest information about its writer is available, would remain literally unreadable were it not for the collaboration of the scholar. In *The Basement* representation of an other and self-representation, autobio-graphy and biography, "refract" each other as Kate Millett documents and absorbs the sexual torture and murder of sixteen-year-old Sylvia Likens, and makes it part of her own self-representation as a woman in her particular culture. Jeanne Perreault lays out this process of repre-sentation of an other which is also self-representation – "registering difference and asserting sameness from within" –, and which she christens "autography," in an essay that goes on to show that Millett's work is also gender-representative insofar as Sylvia's death is a threat potentially faced by all women in her culture of sexual violence.

Susanna Egan and Leigh Gilmore demonstrate the ways in which presenting the self through the mediation of an other enables the auto-biographical representation of lesbian sexuality in a genre founded on heterosexual assumptions. Egan suggests that Mary Meigs's self-repre-sentation through metaphors of fictional characters such as Virginia Woolf's Lily Briscoe and Mary McCarthy's Dolly Lamb is a technique of opacity that is also a technique of illumination, allowing Meigs to come to terms with, and come out in autobiography about, her lesbianism. Like Egan reading Meigs, Leigh Gilmore, in "A Signature of Lesbian Auto-biography," finds the oblique strategies of *The Autobiography of Alice B. Toklas* enabling the autobiographical representation of lesbian sexuality. Adapting Teresa de Lauretis' theory of the subject as a network of identities rather than a coherent "self," Gilmore presents Stein's "Gertrice/Altrude" doodle as emblematic of her ambivalence about the self as a unified figure, of her approach to autobiography, and of the "irreducibility" for Stein of "identity, sexuality and self-representation . . . either in identity politics or in autobiography." When the writer represents the self through the other and the "other" is a lesbian woman, Gilmore concludes, we are looking at a "re-framing" of autobiography and its readers.

Rebecca Hogan turns from autobiography to the diary, furthering the arguments of those who have held that women have found diaries more congenial than autobiography to self-representation. She sketches a poetics of the diary, defining its formal and generic features and linking them to what our culture has constructed as feminine. Cynthia Huff also turns to women's use of the intimate genres of the diary and the letter. Where Lynn Bloom uses the metaphor of midwifery for the process by which one woman makes accessible an earlier woman's diary, Huff asks what women's personal accounts of childbirth reveal about its cultural construction, about the relations that construction enacts between physical and artistic creativity and between ideological and textual constraints on women. Crucial here is the intervention of male medical practitioners; by comparing the accounts of two Victorian women diarists and a series of anonymous letters written by women in 1958 to the *Ladies' Home Journal* about their childbearing experiences, Huff illustrates how, over the intervening century, changes in the practices of delivery had had the effect of making the "body of the autobiographical text of creation . . . the province of the physician who had excised the text of the mother by inscribing her body with his story."

The gaps in gender studies remain so large that, just as women were once *the* sex, they are now in danger of becoming *the* gender. Not the least of the paradoxes of the study of gender at this moment is that we need *both* to step outside the heterosexual polarity of masculine/feminine, as de Lauretis and Butler suggest, in order to be able to conceptualize subject positions along a sexual continuum, *and* we need to look at how masculinity is constructed in order to understand it in itself but also to understand the social construction of femininity as its opposite and "other." Cynthia Huff's discussion begins with this assumption, paying attention to the male physician's as well as his woman patient's role in delivery in childbirth and in textual delivery of narratives about childbearing. Three other essays focus on the gendering of autobiographical self-representations as masculine. Both Roger Porter and I turn to texts in which the male subject represents his body as the site of gendering and gendered (self)representation. This atypical representation in a genre largely defined in terms of a spiritual tradition perhaps accounts for the fact that both of us have independently taken as our examples the same autobiographies and that one of them is written by an hermaphrodite. Roger Porter, by way of an excursus through Michel Leiris and Edward Dahlberg, reads Herculine Barbin's *Memoirs* as an instance in which the absence of a clear sexual identity leads to an attack on the body and an absence of the self. By way of an excursus through Barbin's *Memoirs*, contextualized by the medical discourse which constructs "his" masculinity, I examine the cultural values and the historical events at stake in Michel Leiris' self-representation as unmasculine and in the counter-gesture by which he reclaims masculinity for himself by the act of writing autobiography. In Leiris' hands, to borrow a term from Cynthia Huff, autobiography becomes androbiography and a definitive masculine act. If it is somewhat unusual to include two essays on the same authors in collections such as this, readers may find the decision not entirely inappropriate insofar as the unfolding of these essays points to the ways in which critics, like writers, occupy gendered subject positions productive of different readings.

Joseph Fichtelberg also turns to the representation of men more threatened than enabled by the cultural codes of masculinity and shows how questions of gender intersect with those of racial and cultural difference and oppression in Maxine Hong Kingston's *China Men*. Through the relations of her China men to "a murderous discourse" of patriarchy, he argues, Kingston demonstrates that they must learn how to redeem themselves by a "writer's faith that language can save," by traversing rather than merely reversing cultural meanings. Fichtelberg argues that this "guerilla writing" ruptures and then reabsorbs differently such meanings into a Kristevan *chora* underlying all discourses and grounding not only poetic but also gender revolution.

"Poet and Patriarch in Maxine Hong Kingston's *China Men*" points to autobiography's role in emancipatory politics and it is this role which Sidonie Smith's "The Autobiographical Manifesto: Identities, Temporalities, Politics" takes up. Outlining autobiographical strategies by which those "marginalized" by "history, representational imprints, and self-representational politics" can assume agency by working both within and against the rules of genre, Smith goes on to read three autobiographical manifestos as a "staging" of autobiographical practices and agency within them. In each instance a *travesía* – of "sociality and the language of the body" (Hélène Cixous), of different cultural, linguistic, gendered and generic spaces (Gloria Anzaldúa), of human and machine, individualism and engenderment (Donna Haraway) – dislodges the "sovereign self" to make room for a subject constructed in terms of "interdependencies of identities." Smith shows us a use of autobiography that is not retrospective but projective, not only a representation of the socially constructed self, but a strategic assumption of agency by means of alternate and multiple constructions of gender and the subject.

Certainly no single collection can even touch on, let alone resolve, all the issues raised by a problematizing of gender within autobiography. This collection aims to extend the work of those which have preceded it by continuing to expand the autobiographical canon through a re-thinking of earlier exclusions effected by constructions of gender and by re-reading the canon in terms self-conscious about the effects of gender construction. It also aims to suggest ways in which the tensions gender introduced into genre lead to new autobiographical forms, to further the

discussion of gender beyond women's autobiography and beyond heterosexual polarization, to bring a gender-conscious reading to men's autobiographies, and to complicate the discussion of autobiographical subjects by pointing to some of the ways in which gender intersects with
racial, sexual and class "identities." Finally, it aims to intimate by the
issues its essays open up, as well as by those it has been unable to raise, at
least some of the work on gender and autobiography which remains to be
done.

WORKS CITED

Andrews William L. *Sisters of the Spirit: Three Black Women's Autobiographies of the
    Nineteenth Century*. Bloomington: Indiana UP, 1986.
——. *To Tell a Free Story: The First Century of Afro-American Autobiography, 1760–1865*.
    Urbana: U of Illinois P, 1986.
Anzaldúa, Gloria. *Borderlands/La Frontera: The New Mestiza*. San Francisco: Spinsters/
    Aunt Lute, 1987.
Benstock, Shari. "Authorizing the Autobiographical." *The Private Self: Theory and Prac-
    tice of Women's Autobiographical Writings*. Ed. Shari Benstock. Chapel Hill: U of
    North Carolina P, 1988. 10–33.
Braxton, Joanne M. *Black Women Writing Autobiography: A Tradition Within a Tradition*.
    Philadelphia: Temple UP, 1989.
Brodzki, Bella and Celeste Schenck, eds. *Life/Lines: Theorizing Women's Autobiography*.
    Ithaca: Cornell UP, 1988.
Butler, Judith. *Gender Trouble: Feminism and the Subversion of Identity*. New York,
    London: Routledge, 1990.
de Lauretis, Teresa. "Sexual Indifference and Lesbian Representation." *Theatre Journal* 40
    (1988):155–77.
——. "The Technology of Gender." *Technologies of Gender: Essays on Theory, Film, and
    Fiction*. Ed. Teresa de Lauretis. Bloomington: Indiana UP, 1987. 1–30.
Foucault, Michel. *The History of Sexuality: Volume I: An Introduction*. 1976; Trans. Robert
    Hurley. New York: Vintage, 1980.
Friedman, Susan Stanford. "Women's Autobiographical Selves: Theory and Practice." *The
    Private Self: Theory and Practice of Women's Autobiographical Writings*. Ed. Shari
    Benstock. Chapel Hill: U of North Carolina P, 1988. 34–62.
Gagnier, Regenia. *Subjectivities: A History of Self-Representation in Britain, 1832–1920*.
    New York and Oxford: Oxford UP, 1991.
Gusdorf, Georges. "Conditions and Limits of Autobiography." 1956; Trans. James Olney.
    Autobiography: Essays Theoretical and Critical. Ed. James Olney. Princeton: Princeton
    UP, 1980. 28–48.
Heilbrun, Carolyn G. *Writing a Woman's Life*. New York: Norton, 1988.
Jay, Paul. *Being in the Text: Self-Representation from Wordsworth to Roland Barthes*.
    Ithaca: Cornell UP, 1984.
Jelinek, Estelle C., ed. *Women's Autobiography: Essays in Criticism*. Bloomington: In-
    diana UP, 1980.
Lionnet, Françoise. *Autobiographical Voices: Race, Gender, Self-Portraiture*. Ithaca: Cor-
    nell UP, 1989.
Martin, Biddy. "Lesbian Identity and Autobiographical Difference[s]." *Life/Lines:
    Theorizing Women's Autobiography*. Eds. Bella Brodzki and Celeste Schenck. Ithaca:
    Cornell UP, 1988.

Mason, Mary G. "The Other Voice: Autobiographies of Women Writers." *Autobiography: Essays Theoretical and Critical*. Ed. James Olney. Princeton: Princeton UP, 1980. 207–35.

McKay, Nellie Y. "Race, Gender, and Cultural Context in Zora Neale Hurston's *Dust Tracks on a Road*." *Life/Lines: Theorizing Women's Autobiography*. Eds. Bella Brodzki and Celeste Schenck. Ithaca: Cornell UP, 1988. 175–88.

Pratt, Minnie Bruce. "Identity: Skin Blood Heart." *Yours in Struggle: Three Feminist Perspectives on Anti-Semitism and Racism*. By Elly Bulkin, Minnie Bruce Pratt, and Barbara Smith. Brooklyn: Long Haul P, 1984. 9–63.

Smith, Paul. *Discerning the Subject*. Minneapolis: U of Minnesota P, 1988.

Smith, Sidonie. *A Poetics of Women's Autobiography: Marginality and the Fictions of Self-Representation*. Bloomington: Indiana UP, 1987.

——. *Where I'm Bound: Patterns of Slavery and Freedom in Black American Autobiography*. Westport: Greenwood P, 1974.

Sprinker, Michael. "Fictions of the Self: The End of Autobiography." *Autobiography: Essays Theoretical and Critical*. Ed. James Olney. Princeton: Princeton UP, 1980. 321–42.

Stanton, Domna C. "Autogynography: Is the Subject Different?" *The Female Autograph: Theory and Practice of Autobiography from the Tenth to the Twentieth Century*. Ed. Domna C. Stanton. 1984; Chicago: U of Chicago P, 1987.

Steedman, Carolyn Kay. *Landscape for a Good Woman: A Story of Two Lives*. 1986; New Brunswick: Rutgers UP, 1987.

Stimpson, Catharine R. "Gertrice/Altrude: Stein, Toklas, and the Paradox of the Happy Marriage." *Mothering the Mind: Twelve Studies of Writers and their Silent Partners*. Ed. Ruth Perry and Martine Watson Brownley. New York: Holmes & Meier, 1984. 122–39.

Yellin, Jean Fagan. "Texts and Contexts of Harriet Jacobs' Incidents in the Life of a Slave-Girl: Written by Herself." *The Slave's Narrative*. Eds. Charles T. Davis and Henry Louis Gates, Jr. Oxford and New York: Oxford UP, 1985. 262–82.

Auto/Bio/History: Modern Midwifery

LYNN Z. BLOOM

Let us now celebrate the birth of auto/bio/history, fledgling offspring of
the close collaboration between the author of an autobiographical document and the scholar who completes the original text with a complementary and equivalent text of her own. May the arrival of this healthy and
promising new genre be greeted with joy and hope for a long and
meaningful life.

The birthrate of auto/bio/history, a label I will use until a more elegant
alternative emerges,[1] has increased rapidly in the past decade, many,
though not all, of the recent works involving collaboration between
women. This paper aims to define this new genre, or hybrid of genres – a
distinctively though not uniquely female, if not feminist, creation; to
explain how and why it came into being; and to identify some of its major
characteristics through examining Laurel Thatcher Ulrich's exemplary *A
Midwife's Tale: The Life of Martha Ballard, Based on Her Diary, 1785–
1812.*

In auto/bio/histories the original author, often unknown outside her
circle of intimates, kept a diary, wrote letters, or composed an ab-
breviated autobiography, narrating isolated incidents or presenting a
fragmented self-characterization. These documents, however, often
written without the concept of an external audience that a professional
writer would keep in mind, are so elliptical, private, context-specific, or
remote in time that most readers, unfamiliar with the author, cannot
understand them.

But a particular sort of reader, usually a literary or historical scholar,
can crack this often unintentional code. She knows how to do the research
and is willing to expend the often considerable effort in order to make the
sparse, workaday prose of the original documents not only comprehen-
sible to an external audience, but to transform the raw materials of
history into a narrative of literary distinction. She can envision what such
a skeleton text would look like fleshed out, its author fully alive, a real
person whose work, character, point of view, culture, or experiences
would be of great interest to contemporary readers. Although a pom-
pous pedant could entomb her subject beneath a mass of uninterpreted
details, when the scholar is herself a good writer, the subject can be
reborn with even greater vitality than she had during her days on earth.

If we consider the author of the initial text as the mother, we can regard the author of the complementary text as a combination of co-author and midwife. It does not matter whether the original author lived long ago or more recently, even contemporaneously with the scholar, or whether they ever actually met. The latter comes to know her unwitting collaborator intimately in the course of the re-creation of a new life, and consequently, so do her readers. Because the work of one collaborator could not meaningfully exist independently of the other, the original work cannot be considered primary and the later work secondary. Together these two authors have given birth to a new text, the auto/bio/history whose parts are symbiotically integrated and must be read together for either to be understood.

These works have different shapes, depending on what the midwife-author chooses to emphasize – and she has the last word. In some, the "auto" is more prominent; in others, the "bio" or the "history" outweighs the "auto"; and in still others the emphasis is evenly distributed (for examples, see below). But in all these works the later author *writes in her own words a significant segment of the body of the text itself*, and her words are *distinct and clearly discriminated from the original author's material*.

I am hereby defining auto/bio/history as a literary genre distinctive in its own right. Though a hybrid form with variations (as any form has), this genre is quite distinct from scholarly editions of diaries or collections of letters. In scholarly editions the editor commonly provides an interpretive introduction, perhaps a preface and epilogue, and abundant notes. All of these are subordinate and not integral to the original text, which in many (but not all) instances could exist in its own right, independently of the scholarly apparatus.[2]

Auto/bio/history is also different from conventional historical writing, even social history, because it foregrounds the experiences of single individuals or extended families (which might be considered as a collective autobiographer) as a way of approaching the normative experiences of the larger society. Representative works, all published in the 1980s, include: *Far From Home: Families of the Westward Journey*, a volume composed of the auto/bio/histories of three families, by Lillian Schlissel, Byrd Gibbens, and Elizabeth Hampsten; Shannon Applegate's *Skookum: An Oregon Pioneer Family's History and Lore*; and J.S. Holliday's *The World Rushed In: The California Gold Rush Experience*. Schlissel's *Women's Diaries of the Westward Journey* and Hampsten's *Read This Only to Yourself* combine extended historical and literary analysis of a variety of diaries and letters with separate chapters on the lives and private writings of individual authors. Unfortunately space does not permit additional analysis of these works here. Given this blurring of genres, it is not surprising that the authors who give history a human face include historians (Ulrich, Holliday), literary scholars (Hampsten, Gibbens), specialists in American Studies (Schlissel), and others who transcend disciplinary boundaries.

But why would a scholar be willing to devote significant portions of her own life, five to twenty years is not unusual,[3] to re-creating the life and times of a person unknown when she began her work and likely to remain unknown even after the work is published? Can any of us, for instance, remember the name of even a single member of the three families portrayed in *Far From Home*? If we do better with *Skookum*, it is because nearly everyone in the book is named Applegate. Martha Ballard, Revolutionary War midwife, will never become a household word, despite her prodigious delivery of 816 babies in her hometown of Hallowell, Maine.

On the contrary, Joan Givner's enormous efforts expended to research and write a biography of Katherine Anne Porter, and Deirdre Bair's comparably thorough examination of the life of Simone de Beauvoir, have some predetermined results. Biographies of distinguished or well-known people, even bad biographies – and Givner's and Bair's are superb – are guaranteed reviews in respectable places, an audience of readers, a reputation (for better or worse) for the biographer, and very likely, a royalty check that will provide some recompense for love's labors. Because no biography is definitive, but only a definition, there will always be a wealth of well-known women whose lives warrant definition or reinterpretation. So why not praise famous women, and count on some recompense? What is the payoff for the extraordinary commitment of time, energy, and expertise that auto/bio/histories represent?

The scholar-midwife's activity in such cases is not as self-effacing as it may appear, for we remember these books and their contemporary authors, the scholars, even if we do not remember the subjects. But scholarly recognition is merely a by-product of the compelling reason for such labor-intensive research, the desire of contemporary feminist scholars to understand the meaning of women's experience on women's own terms, rather than those of men. Carroll Smith-Rosenberg's "Hearing Women's Words" offers a philosophical and social justification for examining the private papers, largely unpublished letters and diaries of eighteenth- and nineteenth-century women, in order to understand women's experiences "as the women themselves described them, not as men attempted to direct them" (28). She explains that in these documents "women's discussions of the normal events of every day permitted us to endow census data with the warmth of emotional reality. Now we could test the accuracy of [male-determined] prescriptive materials against the reality of what people actually did" (29).

In reconstructing what it was like to be a woman in times past through deconstructing women's private writings, Smith-Rosenberg, Schlissel, Hampsten, Stanton, and a host of other researchers in the past decade have discovered, as Smith-Rosenberg says,

> the existence of a female world of great emotional strength and complexity ... a world of intimacy, love, and erotic passion [in which] uniquely female rituals drew women together during every stage of their lives, from adolescence through courtship, marriage, childbirth and child-rearing, death and mourning. (28)[4]

Auto/bio/history thus becomes an inevitable consequence of such historical focus. Scholars, primarily women, in literature and other disciplines or combinations of disciplines become committed to studying the newly-significant private writings of ordinary women, however cryptic and allusive, to understand the lives of their particular authors both as individuals and as representatives of women's experiences more generally.

Concern for minorities and people of less privileged classes has intensified this interest. Today everybody, as Gertrude Stein observed in the prescient opening sentences of *Everybody's Autobiography*, marches in the parade of autobiography, majority and minority, old, young, and middle-aged, privileged and bourgeois and working-class. Everyone has a story to tell, and if the teller has left a record of any substance, her life will prove of intense interest to a scholar who can embed it in time and culture and publish it in a book.

Proof of the increasing opportunities for these diverse voices to be heard is the groundswell of published autobiographies in the past forty years. Kaplan's *Bibliography of American Autobiographies* identifies some 6,400 works published from colonial times to 1945, 5.5 times more by men than women. Briscoe's sequel identifies over 5,000 works, nearly as many published in the following thirty-five years (to 1980) as in the preceding three hundred; the ratio of books by men and women has dropped to 2.8:1. And the interest in women's autobiographical writings continues to escalate. To take the publications of just one press as an example, the University of Nebraska Press has recently published or re-issued forty-eight volumes of American pioneer women's vigorous and colorful letters, diaries, autobiographies, oral histories, and auto/bio/histories, ranging from Anne Ellis's mining-camp autobiography, *The Life of an Ordinary Woman* (first published in 1929), to the best-known volume, Elinore Pruitt Stewart's *Letters on an Elk Hunt* (first published in 1915). Whereas only three were in print before 1970, forty have been published in the past decade – an explosive 1200 per cent increase.

So *A Midwife's Tale* is a work whose form and substance are indeed timely. Let us now examine the text to determine some of the formal characteristics and methodology of auto/bio/history and in the process to understand the collaborative relationship between the original author and the scholar/midwife.

Martha Ballard, as a diarist, is both an author and the primary subject of *A Midwife's Tale*. Although Ulrich explains that "few New England women of her generation left writing in any form," Ballard, of Hallowell, Maine kept this diary for over 27 years, making this not only the most extensive midwife's diary of the Revolutionary War era, but an exceedingly rare and full document (9). Its structure "derives from two workaday forms of record-keeping," the daybook, "used to keep running accounts of receipts and expenditures," sometimes supplemented by "short notes on important family events and comments on work begun or completed"; and "the blank pages bound into printed almanacs," on which early diarists kept "their own tally on the weather, adding brief entries on gardening, visits to and from neighbors, or public occurrences of both the institutional and the sensational sort" (8).[5] Ballard's entries, following this culturally-dictated format, are invariably concise, often a few short sentences, and seldom more than a hundred words. She is writing only for herself; consequently, her observations are elliptical and usually uninterpreted, as in these typical entries for August, 1787, when Ballard was 51, married and the mother of nine children, six of whom were still living:

> 14 Clear and hott. I pikt the safron. Mrs Patten here. Mr Ballard & I & all the girls attended funeral of William McMaster. Their other Children are mending. James Howard very low. I drank Tea at Mr Pollards. Calld at Mr Porters.

> 15 Clear morn. I pulld flax the fornoon. Rain afternoon. I am very much fatagud. Lay on the bed & rested. The two Hannahs washing. Dolly weaving. I was called to Mrs Claton in travil at 11 O Clok Evening.

> 16 At Mr Cowens. Put Mrs Claton to Bed with a son at 3 pm. Came to Mr Kenadays to see his wife who has a sweling under her arm. Polly is mending. I returnd as far as Mr Pollards by water. Calld from there to Winthrop to Jeremy Richards wife in Travil. Arivd about 9 o Clok Evin.

Birth Mrs Clatons son

17 At Mr Richards. His wife Delivered of a Daughter at 10 O Clok
morn. Returned as far as Mr Pollards at 12. Walked from there. Mrs
Coy buryd a dafter yesterday. Mr Stanley has a dafter Dangirous.
William Wicher 2 Children also.
Birth Jeremy Richard dafter. (18)

Smith-Rosenberg has explained why contemporary feminist scholars
would care about these records of births and deaths and illnesses, and
why they would want to know about the "domestic chores and pastimes"
that the few male historians who knew the diary found "trivial and
unimportant" (Ulrich 8–9). Yet to read 9,965 uninterpreted entries like
these would be a daunting enterprise for even the most committed
readers. Ulrich, as auto/bio/historian, presents the diary in a form so
fitting that it seems inevitable, beginning each of the ten chapters with a
month-long representative segment of the diary, of some three or four
pages. In the rest of each 25–30 page chapter Ulrich provides the full
orchestration for Ballard's descant, without which the author would
remain a shadowy presence in an account terse and coded. Each chapter,
while focusing on the life of Ballard and her family, is devoted to an
aspect of social, cultural, and medical history in which women were of
particular prominence: midwifery, domestic economy (particularly
weaving), litigation (including rape), marriage and illegitimate births,
childbirth practices, housework, seduction, murder, indebtedness, and
gardening. Thus although the forty diary pages occupy less than ten
per cent of the text, Ulrich's subsequent analysis makes the diary come
alive with a narrative thrust and historical texture only hinted at in the
original.

To fully understand only the entries quoted above requires far more
interpretation than even highly sophisticated readers are capable of. Who
are all these people? Why is it noteworthy that "the two Hannahs" were
washing and "Dolly weaving"? Are two deaths in four days unusual in this
small town? If so, are these the result of the epidemic of "canker rash"
that afflicted six people specifically mentioned in Ballard's August
entries? What is "canker rash" anyway? What ails another dozen identified as sick whose illness is not identified? Can we assume that because
the context of "Their other Children are mending" (8/14) clearly indicates
that these particular children are recovering from an illness, that "Polly is
mending" (8/16) means the same thing? Given the references to "washing" and "weaving" on 8/15, might Polly instead be sewing? (Not likely,
because on 8/7 she is identified as being "very ill with the Canker," which
also rules out the possibility that Polly is recuperating from a broken

heart.) How are we to interpret the labors of Ballard, who "pikt safron," "pulld flax," and spent two consecutive nights delivering two babies in different households and had to walk part way home after the second delivery? No wonder that she was "very much fatagud," given the heavy demand for her services not only as midwife but as a "social healer" (Ulrich's label derived by analogy with "social medicine," [61]) during the epidemic. Were such effort and skill commonly demanded of women of the time? of women Ballard's age? Or was Ballard a rare embodiment of energy, expertise, and enterprise? Given her other responsibilities, of what significance is the "bland sentence" (65) that Ballard "drank Tea at Mr Pollards"?

Ulrich must have asked all these questions, and more, of Ballard's text, for she supplies all the answers, providing synthesis, analysis, and context for the raw material. Indeed, her overriding concern is to interpret every item in the diary in the contexts of the time, with particular emphasis on its relation to women. Thus she approaches the August, 1787 entries from several angles, "as a case study of an epidemic, as an exemplar of Martha's therapies, and as a window into the broader system of social medicine" (66). Ulrich explains that between August 3 and 24 Martha Ballard

> performed four deliveries, answered one obstetrical false alarm, made sixteen medical calls, prepared three bodies for burial, dispensed pills to one neighbor, harvested and prepared herbs for another, and doctored her own husband's sore throat. In twentieth-century terms, she was simultaneously a midwife, nurse, physician, mortician, pharmacist, and attentive wife. Furthermore, in the very act of recording her work, she became a keeper of vital records, a chronicler of the medical history of her town. (40)

Though Ulrich has become an intimate of her subject during her long years of research, she does not give Ballard undue privilege in the community of healers, a remarkable but necessary act of scholarly restraint.[6] Citing Florence Nightingale's claim that "every woman is a nurse," Ulrich comments on differences in "the breadth and depth of their commitment" to healing. Several women in every community "went farther, stayed longer, and did more than their neighbors." "It would be a serious mistake," says Ulrich,

> to see Martha Ballard as a singular character, an unusual woman who somehow transcended the domestic sphere to become an acknowledged specialist among her neighbors. She *was* an important healer, and without question the busiest midwife in Hallowell

during the most active years of her practice, but she was one among many women with acknowledged medical skills. (62)

"Furthermore," Ulrich continues, "her strengths were sustained by a much larger group of casual helpers" (62), whom Ulrich identifies by name and an explanation of their roles, "reaching beneath the story of the August 1787 epidemic" – "canker rash" was scarlet fever – "for clues to Martha's herbalism" (hence her cultivation of saffron) and "to her relations with the town's other healers, male and female" (48). To be a midwife required an extensive period of informal apprenticeship: as a single woman "doing nursing as well as housework for her relatives or neighbors," as a young housewife "perfecting the gardening and cookery that were so closely associated with herbal medicine," and keeping watch with sick neighbors and assisting at births. Finally, in midlife, "with her own child-rearing responsibilities diminished," Ballard had the time and experience to become "a more frequent helper and eventually a healer and midwife" (64). Thus it is not surprising that Martha Ballard performed her first delivery at the relatively advanced age of 43. And it is not surprising that this chapter of Ballard's diary reflects the competent, hardworking, well-organized, managerial, and sympathetic midwife in her maturity.

Even as apparently innocuous an activity as tea-drinking warrants contextual interpretation. Says Ulrich, "There is no need to sentimentalize this 'female world of love and ritual,' to use Carroll Smith-Rosenberg's now famous phrase, to understand that birth, illness, and death wove Hallowell's female community together." Drinking tea was important as "continuations of meetings at the bedsides of gravely ill children." Ballard's social visit following the death of an infant "cannot have been a casual one. Was it a practical errand that brought her there, or a deeper need to consolidate the experience she had shared a few hours before" by extending sympathy after a "profoundly disturbing" nightwatch "to a young mother still new to the circle of matrons?" "Female healers," asserts Ulrich, "identified with the patients they served in ways that male physicians could not," as friends, confidantes, mothers themselves (65).

This chapter epitomizes Ulrich's meticulous, thoroughgoing interpretation of a diary, a person, a life in a community with a particular culture. Two questions, however, remain concerning her method as auto/bio/historian. The first is, how can we be sure that in selecting only three per cent of Ballard's total entries Ulrich is accurately representing the diary's author and her major concerns? The consistency of events, details, language, and point of view throughout the twenty-two years the diary spans imply a representativeness. Although accounts of only ten months of this time oversimplify a work that "introduces more stories than can easily be recovered and absorbed" (25), such sharpening of focus is an inevitable consequence of the transformation of a work of life into a work of art.

The other question concerns Ulrich's credibility – a problem for any auto/bio/historian of any time, any place. How do we know that her interpretations are always right? If there were only a single correct and invariant way to understand the evidence of a person's life, there might be only a single, "standard" biography of writers such as Poe, Dickinson, Hemingway, and Plath – not to mention a uniform account of most political figures of any time, any place. But in any climate that permits the free play of inquiring minds, this is not possible. Thus the "right" interpretation of a primary text essentially means that the analysis is fitting, accurate, and appropriate to the extent of what is relevant and known; it makes contextual sense. Consider, for instance, Ulrich's explanation of the phrase "up in arms" from the entry for 15 January 1796, when Ballard was 60:

> I was at Mr Mathews. His wife was delivered at 6 hour morning of a fine daughter after a severe illness. Her first Child. I received 9/. Made a present of 1/6 to the infant. I returnd home and find my house up in arms. How long God will preserve my strength to perform as I have done of late he only knows. ... (206)

Whatever does this curious phrase mean? Has Ballard's post-revolutionary family suddenly decided to rise in mutiny against their aged mother? Not at all. Ballard uses similar language two years later when, again without a domestic servant, after five days away performing deliveries she returns home "to find my house alone and Everything in arms." Thus "up in arms"

> suggests an attitude. A house could be an adversary. Turn your back, and it rippled into disorder. Chairs tipped. Candles slumped. Egg yolks hardened in cold skillets. Dust settled like snow. Only by constant effort could a woman conquer her possessions. Mustering grease and ashes, shaking feather beds and pillows to attention, scrubbing floors and linens into subjection [information derived from a variety of other documents] she restored a fragile order to a fallen world. (219)

This could be a passage from a modern novel, or a treatise on the dilemma of today's working wife, returning exhausted from her job, her daughters grown and married with "no one to preserve order at home" (218–19). If her husband and sons had been there at all, they would have "gotten their supper and breakfast themselves, leaving their platters and mugs, un-made beds, and stiffening socks behind them" (219). Thus Ballard is praying "not for ease or for release from her burdens, but for strength, for the physical ability" to combat not a human enemy but her very house (218). Ulrich's explanation is utterly convincing, for contemporary readers live there too.

Another characteristic instance of Ulrich's ability to crack the code of custom as well as language is apparent in her interpretation of Ballard's entry for 23 October 1791. The midwife was summoned to Sally Pierce: "Because this was going to be an illegitimate birth, she knew what she had to ask. She also knew what Sally would say. 'Shee was safe delivered at 1 hour pm of a fine son, her illness very severe but I left her cleverly & returnd ... about sun sett. Sally declard that my son Jonathan was the father of her child'" (147).

Ulrich here focuses not on the implied human drama but on whether there was a social and legal double standard governing illegitimate births. She rejects the perspective suggested by novels of the period: "There is no evidence that in rural communities women who bore children out of wedlock were either ruined or abandoned." Nevertheless, it was impor-tant to determine the identity of the "reputed father" so he would pay child support: "The assumption was that a woman asked to testify at the height of travail would not lie" (149). Although heroines of sentimental novels "died rather than confront their betrayers," in Hallowell, says Ulrich, "betrayed women collected cash payments" in court, "then went on to marry other men" (159–60). In substituting realism for romance, Ulrich's straightforward interpretation reinforces Ballard's own direct-ness of expression and behavior.

Without Ballard's diary "her biography would be little more than a succession of dates" (5), notes Ulrich, her birth in 1735, her marriage in 1754, the births of nine children (1756–79), the deaths of three in 1769, and her own death in 1812, commemorated by a one-sentence obituary: "'Died in Augusta, Mrs. Martha, consort of Mr. Ephraim Ballard, aged 77 years'" (5). Yet without such an incisive auto/bio/history, Ballard's diary itself, full of coded language, lacunae, repetition, and lack of interpretation, would be hard to understand – and so sparse as to be boring to read. The insight, elegance, and eloquence of *A Midwife's Tale* enables us to know and care about Martha Ballard because Ulrich shows us why she is important, an extraordinary ordinary person whose life history expands and enriches our understanding not only of her times but our own. Ulrich's scholarly midwifery has set an impeccably high stan-dard for such collaborative works, and in the process has given birth to a splendid member of this new genre.

NOTES

1. An alternate name I have rejected is *symbiography*. Although this has appropriate connotations of *symbiosis* and *biography*, because there is very little known about the lives of the original authors of many of the letters and diaries consulted, it would be impossible to write individual biographies of most of them. I would appreciate alternative suggestions for a concise label of fewer than the seven syllables of *auto/bio/history* or, for that matter, the six syllables of *autobiography*.

   Blended labels such as *auto/bio/history* appropriately reflect the blurring of genres that Geertz discusses in examining the contemporary "refiguration of social thought." Such "genre mixing" reflects the trend of social scientists to turn away from "a laws and instances ideal of explanation toward a cases and interpretations one, looking less for the sort of thing that connects planets and pendulums and more for the sort that connects chrysanthemums and swords" (19).

2. Such self-contained works, by authors such as Samuel Pepys, James Boswell, Alice James, Anaïs Nin, and Virginia Woolf, are sufficiently well-known to need no elaboration here.

   Other diaries, notebooks, and collections of letters that would not be self-explanatory without extensive editiorial apparatus may be written by famous people about whose lives every scrap of information, however trivial, is of interest. Thus George Washington's elliptical surveyor's diaries, which often focus primarily on the weather and on distances traveled are valuable according to both these criteria (though they barely sketch a narrative) and warrant the extensive scholarly apparatus of the Jackson/Twohig edition.

   Autobiographical writings of less well-known people whose roles or activities are of significance may also require the efforts of a scholarly editor to endow them with sufficient shape or substance to be both readable and self-contained. The two diaries I have edited represent different editorial problems and typical scholarly solutions. The original typescript of Natalie Crouter's *Forbidden Diary: A Record of Wartime Internment, 1941–1945* was, like Martha Ballard's diary, too long to encourage perusal of its 5000 pages. In reducing the original manuscript to a readable 10%, I tried to retain the *Diary*'s major themes, its author's perspective, and the pace and texture of daily life without re-creating the monotony of, for instance, the daily diet which consisted mostly of camotes, beans, or rice. A soupçon of those portions of the narrative conveys the essence of entire meals and other repetitive events (xxv–xxvi).

   On the other hand, Margaret Sams's *Forbidden Family: A Wartime Memoir of the Philippines 1941–1945* told the fast-moving, self-contained story of the author's extramarital love affair in internment, her resulting pregnancy and childbirth, and efforts to establish and preserve a new, illicit family. My editorial work consisted of adding punctuation, correcting misspellings, providing "Tagalog or Spanish terms for transliterated native words in the original text," supplying occasional clarifying footnotes, and writing a preface and afterword to set the memoir in its human and military contexts (xii–xiii).

   That some editors, not only in Romantic and Victorian times but our own, significantly but silently alter the body of the autobiographical text as well, through bowdlerizations and other unacknowledged emendations that intentionally misrepresent the subject, does not affect either the conception or the practice of auto/bio/history.

3. Ulrich spent seven years researching and writing *A Midwife's Tale*, nearly 25% of her adult life; and that work itself built on her previous research for *Good Wives*, a study of women in early colonial America. Applegate devoted 17 years to *Skookum*, including the careful and loving examination of

   > literally thousands of family documents, which include letters, journals, recollections, manuscripts ... as well as sketchbooks, and a truly vast array of camera works ... cherished and protected by the generations of female relatives before me ... for long years stored in chests of aromatic cedar and Douglas fir. (10)

4. This premise is so well-established in contemporary scholarship that it is surprising to see it articulated as recently as this 1985 quotation, though, as Ulrich's work makes clear throughout, it is a point that cannot be impressed too often on many male scholars.
5. This form has not changed over the centuries, appearing throughout the eighteenth and nineteenth centuries and today, as well, whether in the line-a-day diary format or as an extension of the lawyer's ubiquitous Filofax. Thus the form of this typical entry from an anonymous Michigan farm wife in 1949 does not differ significantly from Martha Ballard's:

> Monday, January 31, 1949 – 3 eggs.
> A nice day. 20 up [above zero]. I washed but hung all but three pieces inside. all is dry. We went to see Mable about 3:00, came back at 5:15 Jack had to hurry out to feed his chickens. Got a letter from Mrs. Clark. I put the wrong number on the package of butter. and got these little shoes from Eva. Jack just went to bed. I didn't get any mail out to-day. I sent a card to Sister Clair for gas I took Mable a loaf of bread. We went back to bed after breakfast got up at 11:15.

The diarist keeps accounts, notes the weather, and identifies work – and by whom – , visits, mail sent (or not sent) and received and contents duly noted. That this farm family sleeps unusually late even for January is left for interpretation to external readers, for the farmer's wife herself never makes it or any comparable analyses. The diarist is using a page-a-day preprinted memorandum book and never exceeds the daily allotment of space, though she sometimes writes less. Whether or not she feels constrained by this format, she seldom provides interpretive commentary more elaborate than "nice folk's" when she meets someone or "ever one say's my hair [with a new home permanent wave] looks nice. I think so too" (9/4/50).
6. Such distancing from one's subject requires an extremely level head, as anyone aware of the absorbing process of writing a biography or editing autobiographical texts will realize. The researcher ordinarily develops a profound, if one-sided, affection for her subject which justifies both the effort and its consuming intensity. The writing of biography and auto/bio/history can be extremely seductive, for the author or co-author spends long periods of time absorbed in the most intimate details that comprise the recreation of another's life and its ethos. Devotion leads all too easily to valorization.

WORKS CITED

Anon. Diary of a Michigan Farm Wife 1949–53. Typescript, collection of the author.
Applegate, Shannon. *Skookum: An Oregon Pioneer Family's History and Lore.* New York: William Morrow, 1988.
"Books By and About Women." (Catalog). Lincoln: U of Nebraska P, 1989.
Briscoe, Mary Louise, Barbara Tobias and Lynn Z. Bloom. *American Autobiography 1945–1980: A Bibliography.* Madison: U of Wisconsin P, 1982.
Crouter, Natalie. *Forbidden Diary: A Record of Wartime Internment, 1941–45.* Ed. Lynn Z. Bloom. American Women's Diary Series, Vol. 2. New York: Franklin, 1980.
Ellis, Anne. *The Life of an Ordinary Woman,* 1929; rpt. Boston: Houghton Mifflin, 1990.
Geertz, Clifford. "Blurred Genres: The Refiguration of Social Thought." *Local Knowledge: Further Essays in Interpretive Anthropology.* New York: Basic, 1983. 19–35.
Hampsten, Elizabeth. *Read This Only to Yourself: The Private Writings of Midwestern Women, 1880–1910.* Bloomington: Indiana UP, 1982.
Holliday, J.S. *The World Rushed In: The California Gold Rush Experience.* New York: Simon and Schuster, 1981.
Kaplan, Louis. *A Bibliography of American Autobiographies.* Madison: U of Wisconsin P, 1961.
Sams, Margaret. *Forbidden Family: A Wartime Memoir of the Philippines 1941–1945.* Ed. Lynn Z. Bloom. Madison: U of Wisconsin P, 1989.

Schlissel, Lillian. *Women's Diaries of the Westward Journey*. New York: Schocken, 1982.
——, Byrd Gibbens, and Elizabeth Hampsten. *Far From Home: Families of the Westward Journey*. New York: Schocken, 1989.
Smith-Rosenberg, Carroll. "Hearing Women's Words: A Feminist Reconstruction of History." *Disorderly Conduct: Visions of Gender in Victorian America*. New York: Knopf, 1985. 11–52.
Stewart, Elinore Pruitt. *Letters on an Elk Hunt by a Woman Homesteader*. 1915; rpt. Lincoln: U of Nebraska P, 1979.
Ulrich, Laurel Thatcher. *A Midwife's Tale: The Life of Martha Ballard, Based on Her Diary, 1785–1812*. New York: Knopf, 1990.
——. Telephone conversation with author, 5 August, 1990.
Washington, George. *The Diaries of George Washington. Vol. 1, 1748–65*. Eds. Donald Jackson and Dorothy Twohig. Charlottesville: UP of Virginia, 1976.

Refracting Selves:
Kate Millett's The Basement

JEANNE PERREAULT

I

Writing of her fourteen-year obsession with the torture and murder of sixteen-year-old Sylvia Likens by Gertrude Baniszewski and a group of teenagers, Kate Millett makes her first gesture in *The Basement: Meditations on a Human Sacrifice* a linking one – of herself and Sylvia Likens. They "touch" with Millett's voice as Millett names for the silent Sylvia the crimes against her: "Your body had been hideously mutilated and with the words 'I am a prostitute and proud of it' engraved upon the abdomen" (11). It is the first of the thousand repetitions of those events. Millett's opening meditation, addressing Sylvia Likens, rehearses her own repetitions: "In how many sad, yellow hotel rooms have I spoken to you, writing these words before me on the wall" (11). The overall structure of this book is also a repetitive one in that *The Basement* is arranged into three segments or "parts," each telling the same story. The movement is not chronological, but rather spirals inwardly, seeming to look for a center to the puzzle, to the horror and mystery, and finally even to the experience, Sylvia's and Gertrude's.[1] With each turn of the spiral Millett moves into a greater intimacy with Sylvia Likens.

The private nature of this obsession, this conversation with a dead girl, is undone as Millett draws her circle to include all women: "You have been with me ever since, ... my own nightmare ... of growing up a female child, of becoming a woman in a world set against us, a world we have lost and where we are everywhere reminded of our defeat" (11). She investigates her own relation to Sylvia Likens as icon and as independent, historical person and brings into question the textual status of Sylvia Likens: "That you endured it at the hands of a woman, the hardest thing in the fable" (11). With the word "fable," Sylvia Likens is not merely another dead girl, but the fleshly echo of a literary lesson. It is when Kate Millett's "sick fascination," "horror," "anger," and "fear especially, an enormous fear," grip her that she asserts, "I was Sylvia Likens. She was me. ... she was what 'happens' to girls. Or

can. Or might ... if you are sixteen, or ever have been or female and the
danger is around you. Women, the corpses of women, surfacing in
newsprint" (14). Millett's "I" becomes "you" and then "we," and the
personal is exposed as public, and shared. She says, "We all have a story
like this, and I had found mine" (14). Feminist consciousness (not
analytic here, but deeply associative) charges Millett's emotional
reaction with a deep identification with Sylvia Likens. It is the blurring
of the boundary between Millett and Sylvia Likens, and the subsequent
challenge to other boundaries, that make this account of a horrible and
bizarre crime, and this "fable," a form of self-writing.

The "self" that is written here is in no way a sovereign presence.[2]
Rather, Millett's textual enactment of selfhood finds voice only by
abandoning sovereignty. My aim is to examine the ways in which
Millett's account of a specific event, her ideological perspectives and
her inclusion of her own responses, both in her own person, and
through the figures of Gertrude, Sylvia, and her younger sister, Jenny,
come together to comprise a specifically feminist autography, or self-
writing. "Autography" makes "self" a textual act, but one not bounded
by the text alone. The cultural conditions that Millett painstakingly
examines are embodied in the mutilations on Sylvia Likens' corpse,
in Millett's relentless voice, and in the intersections of recognition
and response the reader brings to this text. Drawing upon shared
experience, Millett makes the basement torture scene thinkable, even
familiar. She elaborates on the kinds of "fun" Sylvia provided. Millett
reminds us of the sexual energy of childhood basement games, and the
forbidden sense of power we enjoyed in our master–slave, captor–
captive fantasies, but against this familiar picture of childhood fantasy
and shared experience, the real events rise. From the generalities and
abstractions Millett selects details to demonstrate the kind of fun, play,
power the "basement theatre" allowed: "laughter ... as Johnny hits
upon the brilliant idea of shoving Sylvia down the basement steps ... .
The 'good times' of group enterprise, the chumminess .... And for wit
they forced Sylvia to insert a Coca-Cola bottle in her vagina. They had
fun" (21).[3] Distanced by revulsion, we are drawn back again, this time
by Millett's socio-historical speculations: "the public relished this case
... special appeal ... enacting the forbidden ... . Always there is the
thrill of identification" (22). "Identification" suggests complicity, and
this is precisely what the text requires us to acknowledge. Millett
names, for example, the inclusive categories of adults who have ever
struck a child or wanted to as those who may well identify with Gertrude
(22). The torturers are humanized by their likeness to us.

The characters or people (both appear here) inhabiting this text are representations of bodies with little access to language. Gertrude suffers from skin afflictions[4] and Sylvia from the cigarette burns, the scars, the words carved into her skin. And Kate Millett, herself, with no access at first to words, builds cages, dozens of them, each cage, she tells Sylvia, "an oblique retelling of your story" (12). Now a writer, the focussing lens of social obsession, she speaks the troubling and troubled desire of all who hear of such a "case": the "sick" or at least conflicted desire to know, to understand, to imagine, to feel. To suppress that desire is to deny it language, and thus to deny the self its mirror. Yet, this text is no monotonous Sadean "fable," in which sexual suppressions find a particularly theatrical outlet.[5]

Millett explores the atrocity as an outrage and a mystery, "You think, why the hell did they do this?" (14), but the answer she gives implies that there is no mystery at all about "why":

> And then you see the line about being a prostitute and you know, though you can hardly think – in the sense of conceptualizing it – you know, it is for sex. That they killed her for sex. Because she had it. She was it .... . Because nubile and sixteen she is sex to the world around her and that is somehow a crime. For which her killing is punishment. Execution. A sentence carried out. Upon Shame. (14)

The forcefulness of this broken syntax suggests that only a small piece of this knowledge can enter at one time. Millett asks the logical questions, the ones inevitably asked about battered wives, abused children, – why didn't she tell the teachers, the pastor, why didn't she run away? In short, "Why did she let them do it to her?" (14). Millett answers the questions, "It was not only the body that must have been broken, but the spirit. And that is the whole meaning of shame" (15). She concludes her first chapter with reference to another story: "In Kafka's Penal Colony the sentence is carried out upon the flesh, written thereon so that it will enter into the soul. Here too" (15). In this sentence "here" is multiply ambiguous. "Here," in Sylvia's life, was her sentence (in words and in punishments) inscribed on her flesh. "Here," in this culture, is sexual shame inscribed on women's lives. "Here," in this text, is Sylvia Likens' body repeatedly undergoing its sentence(s) of death.

The hysteric body of this text, inscribed compulsively in Sylvia Likens' suffering and Kate Millett's identifications, is not only hysteric, playing out on the textual screen configurations of some personal trauma that Millett never brings to the surface of this writing. The "story" here is the objective correlative for the internalized fear and shame of femaleness in our culture. Seeing that story as a cultural "fable" is the product (and producer) of a feminist consciousness. The story speaks rage as well as guilt and reason as well as desire. Its rhetoric/language(s) make a writing of self that incorporates self and other, victim and tormentor, reader and writer in an articulation of feminist interrogations. The female self/subject here, then, is both subject as agent of selfhood and subject as topic – as passive, as written upon – , this text a fragmented and refracting mirror of female selfhood and cultural superstructures.

II

Sylvia was forced to say the word "whore." From Sylvia's interior monologue: "I say whore for them. Over and over, they wanna hear it all the time. And they say it. If they say anything" (263). In this chanting of that word, humanness is emptied out, Millett insists – a kind of purity of abstraction displaces any remote human connection. To grasp how destructive this repetition of that word could be we might contrast Sylvia's experience with that of Jacobo Timmerman during his imprisonment and torture in Argentina. Timmerman's torturers chanted the word "Jew" as they beat him (61, 132).[6] Timmerman could take on the word: he was a Jew, and inhabited that identity with pride, using their hatred for strength and affirmation and community. No such possibility could exist for Sylvia with the word "whore." With the branding of the words "I am a prostitute and proud of it," Sylvia Likens' body speaks against her in an explicit accusation, the flesh no longer merely a metaphor for guilt, but a referent for the sign it carries. When the body is so articulate, its power to communicate inwardly must be at least as strong as the messsage it communicates outwardly. The purpose and function of the writing, or even of the mere word "whore," is its effect in breaking through to the sexual guilt and shame that is the not-so-submerged heritage of most females in patriarchal society.

Making a social context for this ideological position, Millett links Sylvia Likens' murder to the astonishing case of Richard Speck. Millett does not, at first, focus on the facts but rather on the reaction of the woman reader to those facts: "It's the impotence we feel, reading how Richard Speck, alone and unaided and without a weapon, murdered eight student nurses, one by one, going from room to room, tying and strangling them, the one next to die hearing the dying scream" (69). Millett understands this devastating passivity as the necessary requirement "to be feminine," and that means to be "already defeated in fear by ... carefully conditioned certainty that there is no point in struggling, that the moment the enemy comes, the aggressor puts a hand on the doorknob, is the moment one dies" (70). The best women can hope for then, she says is

> not to be raped .... Not to be tortured first .... To cooperate, to assuage, to hold out the hands to be tied. To beg quietly .... To mimic every gesture of submission even as in animals, the dog rolling on its back. Even as in women. To be "feminine." (70)

Barely suppressed rage is in the rhythm and structure of these passages, the blending of factual details (the student nurses did indeed obediently hold out their hands for Speck to tie them) with conjecture and surmise, and with our reduction to bestial forms of submission.

These elaborations, meditations, work towards the large project of this book: Millett writes her self, Sylvia, Gertrude and Jenny, but she also writes the self of female self-hatred, submission to that hatred, and destruction by it in this culture. A reader of an earlier version of this article reacted with deep indignation, not at the crime against Sylvia Likens, but at Kate Millett for telling the story in the way she did – to make it our own. For that reader, the book was a violation of her sense of self-in-the-world: individual, autonomous, private. The bodies of women "surfacing in newsprint" may have lost their privacy, but not their uniqueness. To her, they signified nothing but bad luck.

For Millett, nothing that touched Sylvia Likens escapes signification. She attends to the specific details of everyday life in Gertrude Baniszewski's household, examining them for whatever shards of meaning can be invested in or divested from them. Millett explains that "Finally, it is not even faces one studies, but artifacts. The pictures of *things*" (54). We recall that Millett sees Sylvia's mouth has become "artifact" (42), her whole self "their thing" (293). The inversion of person into thing, meaningless in itself, to itself, or for itself, that took place in the process of destroying Sylvia, parallels the infusion of the power of signification into the objects that inhabit this text. In her description of the New York Street house, the poverty and depression that characterize it, Millett considers, for example, the spoons: "Gertrude had nine persons to feed and one spoon to do it with" (55). Millett notes that Gertrude could afford a lawyer, a doctor, a television, a stereo. "So that the question of spoons is not simply poverty, but poverty of a special kind, a kind of disorganization hard to imagine in someone responsible for nine children" (57). Of course the spoon reappears as an aspect of Sylvia's torment, when she is denied its use (252).[7] The spoons (we could also consider Millett's treatment of soap, or toast, or cigarettes or pop bottles) become emblems both of Sylvia's suffering and of a particular kind of disorder, invested with a significance that Naomi Schor discusses in her study of the aesthetics of the detail and its relation to "the feminine." She notes that "to read in detail ... is to invest the detail with a truth-bearing function, and yet ... the truth value of the detail is anything but assured. As the guarantor of meaning, the detail is ... constantly threatened by falsification and misprision" (7). Millett is very much a reader in this text, and as such she seems textually to turn the objects and people this way and that, each angle of attention to each detail imbued with possible meaning, yet, discarded and laid aside or held suspended in the movement to the next detail. The stressed object/person/figure acquires a patina of significance and with each layer of attention its power as an inflictor of humiliation or pain upon Sylvia Likens, or as a clue to this mystery is intensified. Millett often speaks of this as a "mystery" giving the word its popular fiction connotation as well as the more grand and sacred suggestiveness that "meditations on a human sacrifice" call for. For example, "Because she would die here, everything in this house held a mystery for Sylvia" (58). Clearly in this sentence, Millett conflates herself with Sylvia entirely. It is she, Millett, for whom everything holds a "mystery" in that house. The "truth-bearing function" of the textual detail has in actuality had its significance established in its historical usefulness as an instrument of Sylvia's torture. The emotional or cultural or political significance of the detail for us, however, is acquired by Millett's treatment of it.

III

The last third of this book is dominated by the dialogue, or rather, the parallel monologues of Gertrude and Sylvia, the interior language of Sylvia in the basement experiencing her own dying, and Gertrude pacing and thinking above her. The slow repetitive registering of these minds, of Millett's infusion of personhood into them, mesmerizes, long after the reader's identification with the "characters" has been burned away by the extremes of Sylvia's pain or Gertrude's cruelty. We watch and listen and wait. There we find another part of ourselves (in Millett's mirror) with Jenny Likens, the crippled younger sister, a brace on her leg from polio, sharer of the early, naked, paddlings, and gradually a silent, helpless, present observer of her sister's slow murder. Only after Sylvia is dead, bewildered police wandering around the house, does Jenny say, "If you get me outa here I'll tell you everything" (269).

Millett wonders if Jenny's courage was the result of her fear that with Sylvia dead, she would be next, or if at last she sensed some weakness in Gertrude's omnipotence. Jenny is

> the very common denominator we dislike most to admit. The ordinary soul in extraordinary circumstances who cannot accomplish the heroic, who tries and tries and still can't get up the nerve. Closer to all of us than we care to acknowledge. And how we hate cowardice in others, feeling it so pervasively in ourselves .... The knowing against knowing that the enemy is inside ourselves, that we are our own undoing, that at bottom, we are despicable. And therefore we cannot act – because we have not acted. (269)

All action as repetition: just as part of Gertrude's actions can be explained by repetition (she can do this because she has done this), so Jenny's passivity is explained by the absence of precedence.

Again the "we" makes this writing an inscription of us all, this text a kind of everyone's story; only the circumstances are exceptional. As a cultural reflection, this text writes the reader, not in idiosyncratic wretchedness but in the familiar movements of dominance and submission, sexual excitements and anxieties, the worn smooth archetypes of political power and mythic potencies. Despite being precisely located in time, space, class, economics, racial and national habits, and gender orientations, this story dismantles those particular historical boundaries. The gags used on Sylvia are "medieval"; her inability to make tears (after some hours of beating and burning) witch-like (306); Gertrude, too, is a witch figure, distorted by the loss of ancient female power:

> once the wicca, or wise woman, denigrated to the evil female of fairy tales .... A warning, a notification to females; the news of their defeat ... the great goddess no longer protects us, we must fear one another. As all must fear the female. For the male, who has changed everything, fears these old images most of all: Kali ... Ishtar, Hecate – all words to fear.
> ... Now in the very evening of patriarchy, sacrificing the maiden with whose murder this age dawned long ago. (315–16)

Associating Gertrude with the inversion of the protection once afforded women by female power (at least mythically) embeds this crime in a kind of racial memory of loss that must be enacted repeatedly. The individuals become emblematic of an ancient power struggle, and the forces working within and against them take on an impersonal and inexorable energy.

Alongside this visionary comprehension of the characters and events, Millett articulates the instability of her individual consciousness and the complexity of her insight – registering difference and asserting sameness from within, from close-up. These shifts from exterior to interior, from remote to immediate, form the parameters of this autography. Millett speaks:

> I become Gertrude. I invent her, conceive her, enter into her, even into the long afternoons of her end, the habit of torture, its urgency, its privacy, the same obsession growing in me like cancer. Like a pregnancy. I am pregnant with Gertrude – and I am a fraud. My Gertrude never the real one, if there was one. For it was all secret. And remains so. (290)

Millett as "fraud" is confessed. Her Gertrude is made of language, but the "real" Gertrude cannot be contained or discovered in words, for they were not her medium. The everydaynesses of domestic life, the demands that fragment the attention of every mother, displace in Millett's understanding of Gertrude the kind of coherent self-knowledge that she associates with language. Millett's movement here: to make Gertrude, to unmake her, and then to recreate her, all this a virtuoso performance, in the inscription, not of Gertrude, or not only of Gertrude, but of Kate Millett. The Gertrude (like the Sylvia) she makes is a mask for Millett.

And her explanation for Gertrude seems close enough to Millett's descriptions of her own experience of obsession to be unnerving. We recall her words "I go further into fantasy, as far as delusion, even full-fledged possession, becoming Sylvia or Gertrude as day becomes the next day" (105). She declares,

> One does not say: "I will torture this child to death." Torture was surely not a word Gertrude permitted herself . . . . She was "correcting" the child, "disciplining" . . . . All terms that she must have begun with and then lost sight of later. When it became secret. Secret even from herself. When it began to step beyond what she could explain in any familiar terms she understood, if not to say aloud, then in the wordless flux of her mind . . . . Then it became a mystery. Something she did, something that came over her, something that happened . . . the great tent of it coming to a form whole and perfect around her just as it did to Sylvia, engulfing her in misery as it engulfed Gertrude in a wild new forcefulness, interest, vitality. (290–1)

A "full-fledged possession" overtakes Millett, and a "wild new force-fulness, interest, vitality" engulfs Gertrude. For the written Millett and the written Gertrude, the power of the experience (and the experience of power) is allowed to develop because a discourse provides a frame in which it can be represented, but which, finally, does not contain it. Gertrude has been limited or licensed (Millett imagines) by the rhetoric of authority to which her Christian fundamentalism gave her access (259). The ambivalent "vitality" that invades Millett ("like cancer," "like a pregnancy" [290]) also has its source in the authority of discourse – the right of the writer to determine what the text designates as the "mystery," the "secret."

The tension at work here has its source in Millett's sense that "these are not characters but inarticulate historical persons" (105). To make the inarticulate articulate is necessarily to falsify, to distort, and the only way to atone for the distortion, to make some truth possible, is to admit the "fraud." By so doing, Millett's text writes an articulate historical person, herself.

Millett resists the question of how much of the "I" in *The Basement* is fraudulent. She makes herself available in details that require us to know her as subject, as "I." We must feel her situation as she reads the volumes of court transcripts, for she makes herself present as and in a body. Sometimes this seems startlingly banal: when she first sees the photograph of Sylvia Likens' mouth, "both lips ... chewed almost in half" (the image that would drive her "mad," she says), "I wished I had a cigarette" (25). In each of the three photographs of Kate Millett that lie on my desk she is holding a cigarette. The apparently superficial response that she has to the devastating image is in fact an expression of her deep addiction and need and desire. That is, Kate Millett, not merely her mind but her body, the person, with her particular require-ments, is at work in these "meditations."

It is the existence of this person that Millett insists on when she says,

> I have lived a long time with these photographs, laid over and elaborating the mental picture I made standing before the real house, because I have been Sylvia dying or Gertrude tormenting ... and have inhabited that place in imagination and feeling so long, I almost know the inside of that house .... (54)

Yet she inscribes her refusal to take her body where her imagination lives: "The house at 3850 New York Street. I have seen both the house itself and its photograph; they are different .... I could never enter the house itself, the present house" (54). It is as though Millett will submit her mind (imagination/emotion) to any degree of torment, but her body she will protect from a complete yielding to the New York Street house. (This is a point at which she is precisely *not* Sylvia Likens.) The years separating the horror from the house, the new paint job, these do not erase the "taint of what has occurred here ... an aura permanent now ... imbued now indelibly over the indifferent paper of police and news documents" (55). That "indifferent" writing has been written over, and the submission in the text to the obsessive power of this "story" has been interfered with by Millett's resistance to the final submission of her body to that place.

Sylvia Likens' voice also offers a site of resistance. Contrasting it with the ease with which Millett finds herself "being" Gertrude ("One's own bullying yell not that hard to summon" [99]), she attempts to explain this difficulty:

> But you are harder, Sylvia, the figure bowed before Gertrude is harder to be. Or is one simply more ashamed finally, not very paradoxically, to remember this, the taste of every humiliation or defeat, the moment one is so despised, one despises oneself. (99–100)

Millett's generalized self, the "one" she slips into, assumes a shared response – that "one" is more easily a bully than a victim of bullying. This assumption makes Sylvia's experience more intensely mysterious. Inscribing the elusiveness of Sylvia seems a necessary part of Millett's own mysterious process. It appears that Sylvia's elusiveness is Millett's. And, finally, uncomfortably, the textual hunt for Sylvia Likens seems to parallel the obsessive need/lust that Kate Millett's Gertrude exhibits in her desire to dominate, fix, control Sylvia. Millett says, "I read and read again the descriptions ... each time more anxious to locate you somewhere in them .... Sylvia, victim and center of the whole legend – how you escape me, grow shadowy. How I lose touch with you, becoming the others" (100). The rhetorical flourishes here (the "hows," the use of apostrophe rather than of a dialogic mode of speech) seem to stretch the literary and the emotional between them. Since the puzzle Millett wants to find the key to is the reason for Sylvia's "complicity," Sylvia's "resistance," her recalcitrance in the face of Millett's hunger for her, is suggestive. Millett is perplexed by a statement Gertrude made when she was arrested – " 'Sylvia wanted something from life. But I could not find out what it was' " (131) –, a statement which echoes Millett's sense that Sylvia "escapes" her. One might feel disturbed by the textual hunt for, capture, and possession of Sylvia Likens. Millett's need to "locate" Sylvia in words, even in the cage of her own fantasy of Sylvia's words, to force Sylvia to speak her experience, makes an uncomfortable parallel with Millett's observation that tormentors (whether of political prisoners or Christian heretics) want "far more than 'information' ... . They want conversions. They want belief" (83). Bodily submission, external control, these are not sufficient. The similarities of and differences between Millett and Gertrude, Millett and Sylvia, Millett and the reader, establish the complicity of everyone in our time and place with this ideology of power.

What distances Millett from the mere will to power or hunger for domination is her respect for Sylvia, for the fact of her as a separate and independent being, with a life and a death of her own. Millett, despite her (exposed) frustration with Sylvia's elusiveness, constructs or evolves her knowledge of self with her acceptance of the limitations of textual power. She says to Sylvia, to the reader, and to herself,

> sometimes I feel I know you and have been conversing with you for years. And especially now, trying to re-create your world. As if I knew it. Yet I think I know. Or perhaps merely remember – as one remembers a collective nightmare. Or I guess. Or I imagine. But the thing is – I have no certainty whatsoever ... . How many months now I have hesitated even to write the smallest passage in your voice, to "put down" your thoughts – as if I knew what they were or had any insight into your own particular language. Fraud. The tricks of bookwriters. The glory of Faulkner's Benjy. Was that he was Faulkner's Benjy. But you are Sylvia. I did not make you up, you happened. And what you experienced, therefore would be of particular validity – if we knew it. (104–5)

Elaine Scarry, writing about political torture, describes Amnesty International's attempts "to restore to each person tortured his or her voice" before "a deluge of voices speaking on behalf of, voices speaking in the voice of, the person silenced." Her description of the effect of these voices "giving the pain a place in the world" (50), a place denied by the power of silence and invisibility, could describe Kate Millett's *Basement.* This writing of an unbounded feminist self has revealed the unspoken webbing of connections that makes Sylvia and Gertrude and Kate and the reader (male and female) participants in a culture of sexual hatred. The "particular validity" of Sylvia's actual experience can never be known, but Kate Millett's incursion into (and re-creation of) those people and events explores and exposes the cultural construction of female sexuality that makes such violence possible. It is the presence in this text of Kate Millett's own voice in all its variations that makes *The Basement* a work of feminist ethical autography.

NOTES

1. I am reminded of the way the horror stories of war are told and retold. The obscenity of the trenches or the jungle treks have become obsessive icons of manhood in Western culture. Perhaps Kate Millett's is the female version of the male war story. That is, each kind of story tells what it *really* means to be a (white?) man or woman.
2. For an elaborated discussion of sovereignty, see Perreault, "'that the pain not be wasted.'"
3. The following report appeared in the University of Toronto's student newspaper:

   > Several campus groups are up in arms over a September 8 incident involving some male engineers and a female inflatable doll.
   > The doll episode occurred during the U of T's Engineering Society's 1987 orientation. Several engineering students used beer bottles to simulate various sex acts in what several witnesses called a gang rape ... . Engineering Society Vice President (Activities) Keren Morehead said, 'It's not supposed to be a gang rape .... It's supposed to be fun.'"

4. The disease of hysterics. See Hélène Cixous and Catherine Clément 34.
5. One of the similarities may be the monotony of torture. The word Millett makes Sylvia repeat endlessly as she nears death is "monotony" (277), while Roland Barthes says, "Sade is *monotonous*" (36).
6. This book read parallel with *The Basement* illuminates the kinds of civil rights and privileges Timmerman was allowed to which Sylvia had no access. Nevertheless, the hatred of his Jewishness and the hatred of Sylvia's femaleness are close. We cannot assume this similarity is merely the ideological "reading" provided by Millett and Timmerman. The torture and the words were both real.
7. Elaine Scarry discusses the commonplace transformation of everyday objects into instruments of political torture:

   > in the conversion of a refrigerator into bludgeon, the refrigerator disappears: its disappearance objectifies the disappearance of the world (sky, country, bench) experienced by a person in great pain ... when it is the very essence of these objects to express the most expansive potential of the human being, his ability to project himself out of his private, isolating needs into a concrete, objectified, and therefore shareable world. The appearance of these common domestic objects in torture reports of the 1970s is no more gratuitous and accidental than the fact that so much of our awareness of Germany in the 1940s is attached to the words "ovens," "showers," "lampshades," and "soap." (41)

WORKS CITED

Barthes, Roland. *Sade/Fourier/Loyola*. Trans. Richard Miller. New York: Hill and Wang, 1976.

Cixous, Hélène and Catherine Clément. *The Newly Born Woman*. Trans. Betsy Wing. Minneapolis: U of Minnesota P, 1986.

Millett, Kate. *The Basement: Meditations on a Human Sacrifice*. New York: Simon and Schuster, 1979.

Perreault, Jeanne. "'that the pain not be wasted': Audre Lorde and the Written Self," *a.b: Auto/Biography Studies* 4.1 (1988): 1–16.

Scarry, Elaine. *The Body in Pain*. New York: Oxford UP, 1985.

Schor, Naomi. *Reading in Detail: Aesthetics and the Feminine*. New York and London: Methuen, 1987.

Timmerman, Jacobo. *Prisoner Without a Name, Cell Without a Number*. Trans. Toby Talbot. New York: Vintage, 1982.

Varsity: The Undergraduate Newspaper (University of Toronto), 1 Oct. 1987: 1.

From the Inside Out:
Lily Briscoe a Self-Portrait:
an autobiography by Mary Meigs

SUSANNA EGAN

INTRODUCTION

In the course of unravelling a complex situation, Mary Meigs provides, in *The Medusa Head*, an image that encapsulates her distinctive approach to autobiography. "I remember as a child," she writes, "seeing a carved ivory ball in some grand palace in Holland. Through the tracery of the outer shell I could see an inner ball, and inside it another, and inside that one still another. The outer shell was necessarily made first but when the tiny ball at the centre was completed, the outer shell came to seem like a final truth" (142). Similarly, for the first of three autobiographical works, Meigs has chosen in her title to create an outer shell, through the tracery of which one sees an inner ball and through that another, and so on.

Meigs' autobiography is offered as a self-portrait by a painter (Lily Briscoe) who is a fictive creation of a novelist (Virginia Woolf) who is, to some extent, creating her own life story. This inter-connectedness of life with art and of art with the lives of artists provides continuous recognition and cross-fertilization. More importantly, Meigs uses this elaborate trope in order to create reflections, alter egos, who become both tools with which to consider the act of self-representation and alternatives in relation to whom she constructs herself.[1] She provides the means, in other words, for us to participate in the assembling of the work of art. But she is doing a number of other things as well.

First, she is an artist, consciously making sense of her experience in terms of painting and writing; this is a natural course for her to take because she believes very strongly that all art is autobiographical. In her responses to painting and literature, as to the writers and painters she knows, she reminds us both that the text creates character and that we must not forget the character behind and beyond the text, the referent, who is, however, an artist and has made a new thing, not a simple reflection. Her choice of her own text, then, is crucial to her own integrity. This point becomes particularly important when Meigs moves from her self-chosen role as Lily Briscoe to the less acceptable role in which she is cast as Dolly Lamb by Mary McCarthy. The artist as generating subject resists becoming anyone else's object. The perceiver chooses how to be perceived. She cannot sit still to be rendered by any artist other than herself. The theft of self and the violation of her central "I am" by such external definition become central issues. (She makes common cause on this point, of course, with much other feminist writing. We may be reminded, for example, of Martha Quest's sympathy with the Jewish woman, Sarah Koenig, whose English family-by-marriage insist on calling her Sally.)

Then, Meigs is a lesbian who has struggled for a lifetime to come to terms with the person she knows herself to be and with the appearance of herself that others will accept. Defining herself in love, therefore, as in art, Meigs resists being altered, diminished, or destroyed by societal pressures, cultural reflections, or the expectations of those closest to her. From her doubly marginal position as a woman and a lesbian, her largest task is to redefine herself so that she as artist and her public around her may recognize the same appearance, to redefine the art that will provide language or medium in which her perception can name and therefore control the ways in which she wishes to be perceived, and possibly to redefine the society that marginalizes her; in this, again, Meigs is writing within the mainstream of North American feminist thinking, valuing the normative impact that art has on life. Finally, to connect art with life and seeming with inner reality, she presents autobiography as a unique and necessary creation from inside the self, effective in determining what is true and, as art, what face or outer shell that truth shall wear. What is true in varying degrees for all autobiography is of particular interest here because Meigs is articulate about the choices she is making; she invites the reader (from the outside peering in) to watch the artist at work in this creation of a mask or a persona that makes integral sense.

The outer shape that is immediately apparent in *Lily Briscoe* is a polite form of memoir. Meigs comes from a distinguished Philadelphia family with a long tradition of privilege and wealth. Her latest work, *The Box Closet*, recreates this family from letters, diaries, photographs, and childhood memories. In this world, memoir is an acceptable form of self-revelation. On the page, Meigs makes just such a first impression as we might well receive were we to meet her; clearly, background and education provide an outer form that conceals an inner turbulence. The gentleness of tone, like a quiet voice, the urbane humor of deprecation, the scope and facility of reference (which letters in *The Box Closet* indicate she shares with other family members) suggest one form of likeness.

In keeping with this first impression, Lily Briscoe uses the techniques of the historian to ascertain objective facts. The reality that she verifies through old letters or with a magnifying glass in poring over old photographs becomes her means to explore less easily identified truths and to illuminate the present. She discovers treasures she had not appreciated before, accepting as integral to her character aspects of family life that she had seemed to reject. She feels that she has lived more fully in letters than in life, but recognizes, too, looking back at an earlier self, "that our most private and delicate feelings cannot be conveyed or guessed at" (92), and that we cannot, therefore, know one another. Indeed she sees her mother's handwriting as chicken wire, a barrier between them, the visible manifestation of how and why they had not "reached out to each other more diligently, more patiently" (71). She also remembers, however, her mother's private closet filled with personal choices and quite distinct from the formality of the public part of the house. Her mother

> had lined the shelves with gold and embossed Japanese wallpaper and had arranged on the shelves a collection of treasures: little tortoise-shell fans and Chinese bottles, cats made of lead glass, ivory and wood carvings, ancient Greek toys and Egyptian scarabs and fragments of statuettes. There, hidden away in the dark behind the painted door, was the fantasy life of my mother, like buried treasure. (55)

Like bound feet that inhibit movement and escape, the closet of such an inner life that cannot manifest itself in outward form is part of Meigs' inheritance.

Formed in the expectation of her mother's public life, Meigs is courteous, reticent, gentle in style. Her autobiography develops through friendships, family, art, dreams, her love of birds, wildflowers, and landscape. Beneath the even tenor of such discourse, however, inside this outer shape, lie the imperatives that alter the whole work. Meigs constructs her autobiographical self as much in strenuous relation to her mother as to Lily Briscoe or Dolly Lamb; the mother–daughter relationship, indeed, provides one of her most fruitful uses of the Lily Briscoe trope. Mary Mason describes the "discovery of female identity" as commonly acknowledging "the real presence and recognition of another consciousness." She finds that "the disclosure of female self is linked to the identification of some 'other'" (210). For the lesbian, this "other" is commonly the heterosexual woman against whose norm the "woman-identified-woman" identifies herself. Charlotte Wolff has described the "emotional incest" that is "the very essence of lesbianism" (72), but it seems more fruitful in this context to recognize mother as also wife and housewife and, in particular, as part of the myth of fertility, posing quite specific problems for the lesbian artist who wants to identify what she is not. "I carried the baggage of that inheritance for a long time," Meigs writes, "though I gradually made decisions ... not to marry, to be an artist, to listen to my own voices" (11).

Learning to accept her sexual nature, to acknowledge it as a part of her whole appearance, becomes accordingly an important part of her autobiography. It involves a continuous tension between the expectation imposed by others and the self that chooses expression. Similarly, learning to be an artist involves, as one might expect, tension between inner aspiration and external realization but tension, too, between the dedication necessary for artistic achievement and personal love or political action. How good does one have to be, Meigs asks, for dedication to be appropriate as distinct from selfish? ("Does every life deserve an autobiography?" she asks. "Does mine?" [11])

What emerges through the external form is an evolution of choices and, through the tension, the courage to recognize and assert those choices as herself for all to see. Others' choices for us, even though made in love, are prisons or cages, damaging and inescapable. The artist, therefore, creates what Canadian painter and autobiographer Emily Carr has called her "yourself shell"; it protects and contains, yet, made from the inside out, it is true to the self inside.

LILY BRISCOE

Narrative, of course, is one of the forms of art and autobiographical narrative is a specific creation not to be seen as a transparency onto any given reality. We cannot, as Kermode reminds us, clean the glass in order to reveal some undistorted truth. "How much more sensible," he suggests, "to study the mode of its partial opacity" (199). The mode of partial opacity also works, however, as a mode of illumination. Meigs introduces her mode at the outset in her title and we should study the effect of Lily Briscoe, Virginia Woolf's artist in *To the Lighthouse*, on Meigs' creation of herself. The relationship extends well beyond the immediately apparent similarities between two women painters and is crucial to our understanding of Meigs' creation of autobiography.

It is important to recognize, for example, that Lily Briscoe is one character among others in a work of fiction. The novel represents a

world of which she is just a part. Similarly, Meigs creates an incre-
mental context of which she is just a part: her world of family, friends,
and fellow artists diminishes the egocentricity of the narrator. Like Lily
Briscoe's, Meigs' role is that of interpreter and recreator of her world.
Lily Briscoe's role and Meigs' relationship with it is further complicated, however, when we remember that Lily Briscoe is, in a sense,
Woolf's autobiographer capturing Woolf's parents as she lovingly
apprehends the presence and the memory of Mr. and Mrs. Ramsay.
Toril Moi suggests that we find here Woolf's crucial concept of
androgyny:

> *To the Lighthouse* illustrates the destructive nature of a meta-
> physical belief in strong, immutably fixed gender identities – as
> represented by Mr and Mrs Ramsay – whereas Lily Briscoe (an
> artist) represents the subject who deconstructs this opposition,
> perceives its pernicious influence and tries as far as is possible in a
> still rigidly patriarchal order to live as her own woman, without
> regard for the crippling definitions of sexual identity to which
> society would have her conform. (13)

One value of the Lily Briscoe trope for Meigs, then, is the discretion
of a representation (at three removes) of ancestral and heterosexual
polarity mediated by the (fertile) daughter/artist. Virginia Woolf's
sister Vanessa Bell was impressed by the likeness to their parents: "as
far as portrait painting goes," she wrote to Woolf, "you seem to me to
be a supreme artist & it is shattering to find oneself face to face with
those two again" (qtd. in Bell II 128).

Shattering, in part, because the passing of time in *To the Lighthouse*
is described as a downpouring of immense darkness. The rendition of
such darkness, however, depends on moments of light, in terms of
which, if only by contrast, the unspeakable and silent dark is repre-
sentable. Mrs. Ramsay thinks in terms of such illuminated moments
alternating with the darkness, like the beam from the lighthouse. She
knows, for example, that her radiant dinner table has become, as she
gives "one last look at it over her shoulder, already the past" (173).
Like Lily Briscoe, who focusses essentially on Mrs. Ramsay, Meigs,
focussing on herself, is conscious of her responsibility to hold that
image, thus creating the permanence of the work of art from the flux of
life and from our changing impressions of it.

From her partial viewpoint, the artist also tries to understand the
complex, multiple, mood-altered viewpoints of those around her. Lily
Briscoe, at the heart of Woolf's novel, sees what other characters also
see. From the center and the periphery simultaneously, she sees a

whole. Her perspective is partial and necessarily colored by her own character and experience, but objective reality, like the removal of the autobiographer from center-stage, is stressed in both books. We have noticed Meigs' use of documentation; this is the *donnée* of her work. More important to the creation of her world is the attention she gives to the perceptions of others not simply in order to understand or to forgive but also so that her characters, like Woolf's, may vouch for the reality of what the painter sees.

The subject of Lily Briscoe's painting, moreover, is not just there for other characters to see; it is as central to their imagination as to hers. Mr. Ramsay, for example, looks up to see his wife and son framed in the window and is "fortified" (56). More important to the context of the whole novel and to the completed painting, Mr. Ramsay in distress actually seeks the figure of his wife reading to the little boy (73). Mr. Bankes looks at Lily's picture and sees Mrs. Ramsay, but he wonders what is meant by a purple shadow, whether this is truly an acceptable way in which to represent the time-honored image of a mother and child. In part, of course, Lily Briscoe is creating herself. Her thirty-three years are there and she must remain true to what she sees regardless of fashions in painting. (Meigs' cover contains a strongly delineated visual self-portrait with her mother's face outlined and faint but inescapable behind her – another unusual adumbration of mother and child.) What Lily is also achieving, however, is the elusiveness of meaning. When Mr. Bankes is annoyed at the dinner table, he feels that Mrs. Ramsay does not matter. Her beauty means nothing. Sitting at the window with her little boy means nothing. Lily's purple shadow, accordingly, is composed of the mattering and the not-mattering of Mrs. Ramsay and of "all this" which she and Mr. Bankes and Mr. and Mrs. Ramsay all love. It contains what Meigs, specifically identifying with Lily Briscoe, has called, like the rhythms of the beam of the lighthouse, "cycles of sight and blindness" (94).

Stasis and flux, the momentary truth or fact and its shifting meaning, can only be combined if the purple shadow represents an aspect of reality that every character in the text can recognize. The novelist provides explanatory context for what become cryptic images in paint. Word and image, for the artist and autobiographer, as for God in the beginning, are one and the same. "If only she could put them together, [Lily] felt, write them out in some sentence, then she would have got at the truth of things" (Woolf 228). Meigs, who has created her mother's life in paint, voices dissatisfaction with her self-portraits and clearly shares Lily Briscoe's desire for the comparative unambiguity of the word. Yet Woolf deplored the railway track of the sentence and wanted to achieve "those splashes" of the painter (Bell II 106) and Lily also recognizes that "words fluttered sideways and struck the object inches too low" (Woolf 274). For the Medusa-head of lesbianism, of course, head-on recognition is ugly and dangerous; Meigs' whole approach enacts Emily Dickinson's suggestion to "tell all the truth/but tell it slant."

The object has less, for novelist, painter, or autobiographer, to do with some incontrovertible fact than with the mode of comprehension and expression. Lily Briscoe's purple shadow, for example, is part of her continuous process of understanding what she knows in terms of shape, color, and image. Similarly, thanks to Andrew's explanation of Mr. Ramsay's work, a scrubbed kitchen table, even, depending on the particular moment, a scrubbed kitchen table lodged in a pear tree, comes to represent Lily's profound respect for Mr. Ramsay's mind. Sections of potatoes describe Mr. Bankes' dedication to science. The specific, even absurd particular provided by subjective comprehension extends, in visual expression, into form and balance; for Mrs. Ramsay, whom she cannot know in full but around whose secret knowledge and wisdom she hovers, Lily creates "the shape of a dome" (Woolf 83). Disturbed by imbalance in her painting, she moves a salt cellar at the dinner table to remind herself to move a tree. Years later, at breakfast, she conjures up the salt cellar, the tree, and the painting which now, in defiance of the passing of time, despite the unlikelihood of success, she will finish.

The image becomes a code, a cryptic and intimate reduction of total experience to its meaning. The painter's effort, then, to recognize what is distinctive about another person or, in Meigs' case, about herself, involves expression of the inner secret in just such terms that are specific and visible and that fit so that others, too, can recognize who or what is meant. Lily Briscoe, for example, knows that Mrs. Ramsay is unreachable. She would understand Mrs. Ramsay's feeling that we are known only by childish "apparitions" (100) when we rise to the surface. Novelist and painter combine in recognition of the wedge-shaped core of darkness into which Mrs. Ramsay shrinks, "something invisible to others," despite the fact that she continues to sit upright and knit. Repeatedly, Meigs explores her characters from new angles, in new relationships, sounding them to different depths, and holds up images of them that serve to represent her recognition of internal life – Marie-Claire Blais as Astarte, for example, or Edmund Wilson's mind moving easily upon silence like Yeats' "long-legged fly upon the stream" (28).

Lily Briscoe imagines a glove; the artist's image needs to belong beyond any doubt to its owner. We see her achieve this perfect match when she recognizes Mr. Ramsay in his boots, which are "his own indisputably" (Woolf 237). Her recognition is so acute that he too accepts it gladly. "It had taken him the best part of his youth," he tells her, "to get boots made as they should be made. He would have her observe (he lifted his right foot and then his left) that she had never seen boots made quite that shape before" (Woolf 238). The fit, of course, grows and evolves with the person, which is how it becomes – in Gerard Manley Hopkins' phrase – "counter, original, spare, strange," indisputably one's own. We may recall those empty shoes at the end of *Jacob's Room* which, in their very ordinariness, describe the absence of Jacob.

The artist looking for the glove or boot that fits another is particularly sensitive to any fit imposed by another upon her and asserts herself vigorously against it. Meigs learns who she is and produces her self-portrait in a constant battle against the limitations others put upon her. Description of herself by another she sees as a shirt of Nessus, painful, destructive, impossible to take off. Lily Briscoe provides the idiom or mode here too. By means of her ability to understand and ascribe meaning to people and to relationships, by virtue, in other words, of her creative role, Lily Briscoe resists as irrelevant the limiting perceptions that others have of her. Mrs. Ramsay, for example, sees "only Lily Briscoe ... and that did not matter" (Woolf 31). One could not take her painting seriously and she would never marry. Yet observing the Ramsays and their houseguests, Lily Briscoe retains years later the clear memory that she had saved herself exultantly from the pressure to marry by knowing what she needed to do in her painting (Woolf 271). She bends like corn under a wind before Mr. Tansley, who says that women cannot write, women cannot paint, and erects herself again by hanging onto her painting (Woolf 134–5). She can laugh and let Mr. Tansley talk all night because she is moving the tree in the morning. In the context of inherited wealth, Meigs identifies with the rich young man who could not give up all he had in order to follow Jesus, thus describing the continuous inadequacy she feels as an artist, her failures of dedication or attainment. Yet it is in terms of her potential for translating her own experience into a new and public form that she too resists the pressures to behave as others think appropriate. Lily Briscoe's exultation, furthermore, is fully justified. Mr. Ramsay, who responds to Minta's glow on her engagement and has referred to "poor Lily Briscoe" as "skimpy" (154), is yet known and created by her both in his person and in the completion of his journey to the lighthouse.

The process of this creation provides a continuous theme through Woolf's novel, connecting the activity of the novelist with that of the fictive painter. This, too, is important to Meigs, whose autobiography records the process of exploration, recognition, understanding, and creation in paint and in words. The self is part of the medium of perception and of creation, which is why Mr. Bankes sees Lily's thirty-three years on the canvas and why both Lily Briscoe and Mary Meigs are afraid to have people look at their painting. "It had been seen," thinks Lily Briscoe. "It had been taken from her" (Woolf 86). She can only say what she means with a brush in her hand, the saying being not a finite accomplishment but a process. Yet the moment between seeing and putting brush to canvas is traumatic because the brush stroke makes shape out of chaos, stability out of eternal passing and flowing, something finite out of the essentially unfinished. Lily Briscoe's final brush stroke represents the ultimate possibility for the artist because it penetrates the obscurity of perception in which the painter struggles to integrate a total picture; it contains Lily's process of seeing and making, Mrs. Ramsay's identification of herself with the last, steady stroke of the lighthouse, the end of Mr. Ramsay's journey, and therefore the end of the book. It demonstrates the complete integration of life, perception, and art that is central to Meigs' process of autobiography.

ARTIST AS AUTOBIOGRAPHER

For Meigs, all art essentially expresses its artist. Lily Briscoe is present in her rendition of a mother and child because she refuses to compromise her perception of what she sees in order to suit the prevailing norms in art. Meigs' love for Marie-Claire Blais is so apparent in a portrait of her as to make Andrée, of the triangle of *The Medusa Head*, fiercely jealous. In the work of Mark Rothko, who wished, Joyce-like, to abstract himself from his painting, Meigs sees "abstractions of [his] inner torment" (38), a form of self-portrait. She believes, indeed

> that the most resolute minimalist is *there* in his work ... that even if one reproduces photographs of soup cans, those cans of soup proclaim not Campbell, but Warhol. The painter or sculptor enters into fluorescent lights, chunks of wood, electrical gadgets, steel girders, by the fact of his having given them new instructions and a new order. (38)

Certainly she would subscribe to the notion that all writing is a form of autobiography. She cites the *Alice* books as forms of subconscious self-analysis that kept Dodgson-Carroll relatively sane. Rilke, she reminds us, objected to analysis on the grounds that it would "derange his poetic universe" (216). Inadvertently when not intentionally, the artist produces a form of self-portrait or autobiography.

For art is spun out of that wedge-shaped core of darkness that is so difficult to identify in another, often so unrecognizable in the self. Recognition of such secret places, furthermore, is potentially dangerous because it penetrates the public mask or apparent role. "Isn't the threat," Meigs asks, "finally, *death* to an essential image of ourselves, to the way we hold our egos together?" (39). In frequent anecdotes about family and friends, Meigs indicates the explosive possibilities inherent in truly recognizing oneself, in acknowledging that secret closet with its treasures of the fantasy life or, in Meigs' own case, acknowledging that she is lesbian. So art, which specifically thrives on this uncensored inner life and translates it into acceptable form, becomes, like dreams, a medium for expression and recognition of the secret self.

It makes sense, then, that Meigs' efforts to come to terms with her own homosexuality, especially within the context of liberation from all the foot-binding expectations with which she grew up, should lead her to identify with characters in fiction and, through them, with their creators. She identifies, for example, with Isabel Archer, but before her marriage to Osmond. Like Charlotte Brontë's Jane Eyre or Shirley, like Jane Austen's Elizabeth Bennett or Emma, indeed, like Lily Briscoe, Isabel Archer has "a sense of her own right" (20). Meigs speculates on Brontë's marrying and on Austen's remaining single. Unmasking heterosexist assumptions, developing and articulating her own unique perspective, Meigs argues anxiously with Edmund Wilson about James' homosexuality. She is distressed by Wilson's denial that Proust was homosexual. Proust, he says, wasn't anything. Such denial, she feels, makes "discussion impossible and conjecture indecent" (27). It forces the morally acceptable correlation of great art with heterosexuality. (Were Emily Dickinson or Virginia Woolf less great as artists because they loved women, she asks?) It serves to protect great reputations for the sensibilities of conventional opinion. It also blinds us to the autobiographical in art.

James' treatment of independent women becomes for Meigs part of his treatment of homosexuality. He mocks the feminist Miss Peabody in *The Bostonians*, for instance, and is ruthless to Olive Chancellor whom he has "pinned on a board, a perfect specimen of a repressed Lesbian" (20). Wilson has written about the governess in *The Turn of the Screw* as a neurotic monster who frightens the boy, Miles, to death. Meigs, however, sees her own mother and governess in James' governess. She recognizes their moral rigidity and righteousness. Theirs is the moral outrage that the homosexual has to face and Miles is one of three Jamesian characters whom Meigs identifies as "not strong enough to bear the image society has of their guilt. Each is suspected of being homosexual, and, in one way or another, James repeatedly killed the homosexual in himself" (58).

The tension and anxiety inherent in Meigs' discussion with Edmund Wilson result, of course, less from her identification of James as evidently homosexual than from what such perception says about her. James was lucky, she feels, to die before his secret was run to earth. It is one thing to translate inner turmoil into art and quite another for it to be identified from the outside.

DOLLY LAMB

Lily Briscoe triumphs through her work over the limited and limiting perceptions that others have of her. Her resistance to such limitations results essentially from her self-assertion, her self-creation, her independence; we should notice Meigs' reminder in her title that this work is Lily Briscoe's self-portrait. Meigs describes how recognition and assertion on her part grow out of such an instinctive resistance to others' perceptions of her. The aunt who wonders why she has not married when she is just an ordinary American girl is like the young man at the party who hesitantly half-speaks his sense of her sexuality. They provide alarm signals according to which the young Meigs, in her bewilderment, must begin to define herself. Edmund Wilson, both courtly and sensitive friend and brutal male minotaur, later asks her whether she is not "really a sort of Lesbian" (14). His "sort-of" identification deeply disturbs her "shadowy world of denial and pretense" (15). It stiffens her pride and opens the whole process of acceptance of herself.

The serious implications of external identification and the need to create oneself are developed in the second part of *Lily Briscoe* which is titled "Dolly Lamb and Lily Briscoe." Quoting from *To the Lighthouse* as preface to this section, Meigs shows Lily Briscoe clasping "some miserable remnant of her vision to her breast, which a thousand forces did their best to pluck from her" (143). For Meigs these forces take the particular form of Mary McCarthy and her characterization in *A Charmed Life* of Meigs as Dolly Lamb. McCarthy, as woman and artist, repeats the creative mother role that opposes Meigs' self-definition; Meigs finds herself misread, like James and Proust, and reacts with a reader-response to her own life.[2] McCarthy's "acceptable" characterization of her as repressed (for which she is at the time partly grateful) becomes part of the resisting and defining process by which Meigs can assert a freed sexuality which she names for herself.

Before McCarthy's book was written, Meigs had "felt this terrible judgement without appeal settling over [her]" (151). She had felt, despite their kindness, as if McCarthy and her husband, Bowden Broadwater, had "slowly, very slowly ... swallowed and reconstituted [her]" (148). Casual details of her life as their neighbor provide constant material for the portrait that she knows is in process. They identify, for example, her type in her choice of a "smoke-grey sleeveless dress of pleated chiffon" and fit their definition over her like a "ghostly skin" that she cannot shake off (150). "How," she asks, "to prove, against the weight of evidence, that you are the person you feel yourself to be?" (151).[3]

Dolly Lamb is Martha Sinnott's friend and neighbor, a single woman with an independent income, and a painter. What Meigs winces at is the portrayal of the repressed virgin, " 'industrious, even in her pleasures, like a sober little girl making mud pies' " (152). Her work, says one character, is sick and cramped with preciosity and mannerisms. If there was anyone else inside her, " 'it was a creature still more daunted and mild and primly scrupulous than the one the world saw' " (150). Her collection of shells becomes a hoarding of her own shit assembled in neat, constipated packages. She is controlled, in her meekness, by everyone with whom she comes in contact. Her money gives her a certain power in the novel but may prevent her from ever becoming a painter. McCarthy's picture of a person almost totally repressed coming at a time in Meigs' life when she was "still resolutely hiding [her] head in the sand like an ostrich" (155), wields significant destructive power. It is "saturated with a kind of burning poison, like the shirt of Nessus" and sticks to the skin of the self; "for although there is an affirmative voice that cries, 'Can't you see that this is my real self?' another self-doubting voice is slyly whispering, 'Could it be true?' " (107). It is, in part, "a germ of truth" that makes external observation so dangerous, to be resisted "with the blind instinct of self-preservation" (121). It is also a matter of the power of definition which may turn semblance into reality, thereby altering the self from the outside in; it is no joke that Gertrude Stein could come to look like Picasso's portrait of her. "Mary seemed to want to quench my faith in myself," Meigs writes. "She activated the dormant seeds of doubt that made me so ready to hate myself and my work. ... I dragged myself about in a state of doubt and self-loathing for a long time" (152–3).

Following Meigs' thesis that all art is autobiographical, however, we can see McCarthy's sword as two-edged. She herself is Martha in relation to Dolly Lamb's "Mary" and is neglecting her higher calling in the busy and complex results of her return with a new husband to an old home territory still housing her former husband, Miles Murphy as Edmund Wilson. Murphy's dominance in Martha's life is irrational and strong. Her pregnancy by him is disastrous. More interesting still, his purchase of her portrait at an exorbitant price that he refuses to pay is surely most precisely that theft of a soul that leaves Meigs feeling indignant and bruised.

Words and paint steal from reality even as they define and create it. The citizens of Wellfleet, including Edmund Wilson, express fear of Marie-Claire Blais because she might put them in her book. Wilson, Meigs feels, had no right to complain for he too had the ruthless eyes of a writer and had "prepared his own friends for a ritual feast and served them up in recognizable form" (111). So Marie-Claire, treated like a witch, feared like a prophet, is slandered or ignored while she, indeed, with her "strange power" (111), sees and hears everything, recording and storing it away for future use. Meigs sees in her the "mighty writer's will that reconstructs the lives of others" (211). These two have recognized the "unchangeable 'me's'" in each other (107), but another writer friend provokes a quarrel "when she, with her writer's zeal, tried, so to speak, to write my life" (212).

The curious dilemma for the creative artist, whether portraying another or the self, is to realize the full potential of the creative act without damage or distortion to the sitter. Meigs' portrait of Marie-Claire is an extension of her love, and illustrations for one of Marie-Claire's books integrate their imaginative lives. The issue is one of taking or giving, which is as subtle and as potentially dangerous in art as in love. "Indeed," says Meigs on the subject of a love that has passed, "it becomes dangerous, the possession of parts of one's self by someone else, and not only have all the pieces to be taken back, but also one has to be careful not to let any escape" (234).

Rothko, the minimalist, preferred Tintoretto's portraits to Rembrandt's because "Tintoretto told the truth about human beings without trespassing on their integrity, and this was the duty of a great portrait painter" (37–8). While resisting Rothko's downscaling of Rembrandt, Meigs describes in numerous ways the importance of respecting the sitter's "I am," which is, after all, the sitter's own most significant creative act.

AUTOBIOGRAPHER AS ARTIST

Just as Marie-Claire guards "the secret of her 'I am'" (109) and Meigs has to wrestle like Jacob with the angel to create a likeness, so she herself has proved elusive to herself; she must track herself down through memories that include joy, anxiety, and regret, through friendships, and through work which is the context for her growth and change both as a person and as an artist.

Meigs finds two beings in herself: "one, who has been free to make choices and shape [her] life; the other, bumbling along, trying this and that" (105). The first is a free spirit that she connects repeatedly with light and with flying, the other is caged in armor, impersonal and rigid. The first enables her to choose and to insist upon those forms of work and love that liberate her. The second, imposed by the sense of duty and the guilty conscience that are inseparable from her class, draws her into roles of social and political responsibility. "The suits of armour in my life," she writes, "served to teach me what I wasn't and what I couldn't do well" (106). Alternatively, Meigs' "pursuit of happiness," or pursuit, which is the same thing, of what is natural to her, enables her repeatedly "to wriggle out of all those suits of armour, just before the nuts and bolts had been tightened for all time. ... I slithered repeatedly out of traps I had voluntarily entered when they began to threaten the indestructible sense I have always had of my 'self' " (106).

Roles imposed by societal expectation are external perspectives on the self. "They make us what we are, even the bad roles, for every choice is both a kind of mask, to which we conform, and something inner, that alters us from the inside-out" (106). What artist and autobiographer are concerned about is this inside-out process, the life behind the face, the integrity that must stand clear of trespass, the invisible self that it is impossible to know (238). A significant aspect of autobiography becomes the rendering visible of that secret identity.

For Meigs, one painful and lifelong issue has been the naming of her homosexuality. It needs to be said in words. The young man's hesitation, Wilson's "sort of," McCarthy's repressed virgin, all containing merely germs of truth, generate Meigs' own expression, which has less to do with sex than with love, with difference than with wholeness, with eccentricity than with artistic integrity. It is the whole person of whom the nameable parts are only parts that she needs to create from the inside out. And for her, as for Lily Briscoe, the mother becomes the absent referent, both desired and feared; in language as in life, the mother's presence contradicts such naming, such fertility in self-procreation.[4]

Her sister, now, years after their mother's death, accepts Meigs' sexuality and says their mother would have too. Even now, however, her "heart begins to thump with the old fear and sickness ... at the very thought of talking" (67). She recognizes other women "consenting to hypocritical silence and coming to believe in the necessity, imposed by their mothers, of lying low and pretending to be invisible" (67). Fleeing hurt and humiliation in love, Meigs at one point seeks just this invisibility. "I spent the month with my mother in Washington," she writes. "I could not tell her the reasons for this surprising and welcome attention to her, but I felt strangely happy with her, as though her ignorance of my life made it invisible, as though a spell had been cast over me that made my New York self cease to exist" (223). This life, however, is what she calls earlier "a dishonest shadowland" (69), and she cites Lewis Carroll's parable about the power of words to change love into fear. In *Through the Looking Glass*, Alice wanders through a wood "where things have no name," her arms lovingly clasped around the neck of a young fawn. Only when they leave the wood is the fawn startled to realize that she is a fawn and should rightly fear a human child. "Like Alice and the Fawn," Meigs writes of herself and her mother, "we could only be friends in a wood 'where things have no names'" (70).

Art, in whatever form, is precisely a matter of naming, however. If Rothko is present in his abstract paintings, if James is present in the homosexual characters whom he repeatedly destroys, if Virginia Woolf is present in Lily Briscoe, how much more present is the artist in the deliberate self-portrait. For Meigs, her stubborn self as she and not as others perceive her to be remains elusive, like the garden in *Alice in Wonderland*, always just out of reach. She is suspended in a moment of what she has called, in a dream, "transparency." "I once heard this word on the edge of sleep," she writes, "and knew that it meant the relationship between trying to understand and the moment of understanding, the open eyes of real attention" (178). She has experienced this in the gap between seeming to understand Yeats in ways that convince others that she should teach and then truly discovering Yeats for herself. The point of recognition, understanding, or realization of vision is a freedom from effort, a moment of grace, which needs to be repeated again and again. It is easy, like Yeats' long-legged fly upon the stream that reduces Wilson to tears, like walking on water with the simplicity of Jesus. Similarly, Meigs describes as "intense attention" (192) that love that is not possessive, not characterized by sexuality, not restrictive of the other's self-definition. "A real flowing of attention into another being," she writes, "is like a transfusion of life" (193). It creates a new thing without damaging the old. She distinguishes very clearly between this kind of creative love which becomes enduring friendship and the possessive, jealous kind that damages and leaves a wake of regret.

Learning to fuse the inner life and its external manifestations, in art as in love, is a process of growth. Meigs describes the movement in her life from copying, as the genteel art of a young lady, to the discovery of color with all its implications for form and space. "Perceiving colour at last," she writes, "was ... an awakening that simultaneously released dreams, like marvellous paintings unable to make the leap into conscious life" (163). Similarly, she has "dreamt marvellous paintings that fade to a confusion of dim colours when [she wakes]" (169). Use of color, for her as for Lily Briscoe, is dogged repeatedly by disappointment in the realization of the vision; but for her, as for Lily Briscoe, it becomes central to how she perceives. (She angers her father with her pleasure in Van Gogh and wears outrageous colors with a keen sense of abandon.)

For Meigs, conscious use of color involves repeated effort and repeated disappointment, like the self-portrait, precisely because it signifies in its connection with the inner life of dreams and self-expression a move away from the making of a copy to the making from the inside of a new thing entirely. The new thing is not the original face but an expression of what that face means, to which other characters in her life-book respond and react. If she holds the portrait up to the mirror, she can see "everything one has done wrong" (255). If she concentrates, however, on "the elements of a portrait of a Lesbian; [her] life with its mixture of shame and pride must be visible in [her] face" (255). The life, in other words, translated from its manifestations onto canvas, as into print, becomes manifest less in seeming than in a new reality which is an art form governed by its own laws. Adherence, indeed, to the original life form will dispel the illusion of profound relationship. Lily Briscoe creates a purple shadow that does not look like a mother and child but is a new and satisfactory definition of Mrs. Ramsay reading to James. And Mary Meigs, in reticent memoir, creates her lifelong struggle to be herself. In personal terms, the evolution takes her from hiding her head in the sand to allowing other people to see her portrait, the form of herself that she has made. As an artist, she has discovered the mode in which her outer appearance becomes a satisfactory rendition of her inner self.

CONCLUSION

Meigs envies the snake which repeatedly sheds its skin and continues to grow. Continuous growth and change in life are stunted by a shirt of Nessus or by any mask or armor that restricts such movement. Life, in a sense, resists and escapes art, refuses to stand still. The necessary movement of life conflicts with the necessary finality of art. So Woolf envied the painter "those splashes" that allow for impressionistic accuracy. Restricted, herself, to language, she created the character of a painter with a work in progress who could then create the Ramsays and their world. It is, then, a fictive painter whose work we cannot see who provides the process or activity by which reality may be apprehended but at a remove from the text on the page which is most fixedly there. Engaging our imagination, in other words, with the printed word about a fictive character engaged in an invisible process of recreation, Woolf asks us each to make Mrs. Ramsay at the window with her child and to recreate the journey to the lighthouse.

Lily Briscoe uses "those splashes" denied to Woolf but she, too, like the novelist, must call her work at some point "finished." It may contain, like a kaleidoscope, many alternatives, many variations, no one fixed picture. But it is also, unlike life, complete. The process may match the evolution of a life and define its character through change. Unlike life, however, the process does at some point become a product. The making of fiction becomes in its own right a fact. It stands still, enduring further change only from the outside in the eyes of its beholders.

Meigs, dealing with emotional turmoil and enlightenment, writes with a perception from the outset that her art form is necessarily fictive. The process of her self-creation is analogous to that of Lily Briscoe, and contrasts with the making of Dolly Lamb, by virtue of being her own creation of herself and not the characterization of her by another. It is what she calls a definition of the self by inscape.

Defining herself from the inside out, Meigs also recognizes other people in their work. She meets and loves both Barbara Deming and Marie-Claire Blais through their writing. In constant discussion of life or of art, she fuses our manner of knowing; she sees writers and painters through their work, and fictive characters or paintings in terms of life. Her sense of art spun from the center of the individual life would be straightforwardly romantic were it not also for the importance to her understanding of integrity in art. This is a different thing from insecurity about her ability to paint or recognition of the gap between vision and attainment. It is different, too, from the sense of personal exposure and nakedness, though she writes about the vulnerability of moulting birds which cannot fly. Rather, it has to do with her belief "that creativity is innate, even in invertebrates, and that the same subconscious forces inspire a seashell to invent its pattern as inspire a painter to paint abstractly, or a member of a primitive tribe to paint his face with geometrical zigzags" (175). Taking issue with what she feels is Freud's limiting focus on sex, Meigs sees dream images not as disguises for our subconscious life but as rich and varied symbols whose meaning we quite consciously repress. "The enormous symbolic vocabulary of dreams does not disguise; it simply gives other forms to the whole of life, forms which can be translated directly or indirectly, for there are the symbols of fear and there is real fear; there are sex symbols and real sex .... What is wonderful about dreams is not that they are tricky and Protean ... but that they are so uncompromising ... dreams never lie" (175–6).

Relating the language of dreams to the language of art and of self-creation in art, Meigs clearly sees both a symbolic or created expression of her life and an original self about whom and for whom that "artifact" is true. This is why she describes not exposure but liberation as a result of autobiography. Her final images are not of vulnerability as she releases her portrait for public view but of freedom and flying. For, unlike the naive autobiographer who hopes to say something about life, the artist knows that self-creation, like love and friendship, is "a long process of simultaneous attention and letting-go" (260). The separation of the finite work of art from the continuously changing self leaves the autobiographer to be assessed not at all in terms of life, though we probably have many and varied responses to the person we feel we have met, but in terms of its own kind, which is autobiography. In this genre, Meigs' contribution is unique; using fiction and art to describe life, she demonstrates what has been for her a continuous process of turning life into art, thereby revealing both the finite outer appearance and the dynamic inner core of an artifact ultimately and inevitably separate from herself and, within its separate mode, true.

NOTES

1. We might compare this process, though it is not the same, with Lillian Hellman's in *Pentimento*; portraits of people significant in her life allow us glimpses of her but only in relationship.
2. See Kennard for a discussion of reading what we are not that enables us to formulate ourselves because it involves full recognition of what is *other*.
3. Christina Rossetti may have felt the same as she sat for her brother's paintings. (Homans discusses unpublished work by Sandra Ludig on Rossetti's angel Gabriel pointing his lily like a paintbrush at the womb of the terrified virgin [310n.].) HD's *Her* reacts in ways Meigs could identify with; when George Lowndes tells her that she is a poem but her poetry is naught, she finds herself a female lover.
4. See Homans for the pre-symbolic, literal, or non-representational language of presence. She focusses on Mrs. Ramsay talking to her son and her daughter in distinctive languages (17–18).

WORKS CITED

Bell, Quentin. *Virginia Woolf: A Biography*. London: Hogarth, 1972.

Hellman, Lillian. *Pentimento*. Boston: Little, Brown, 1973.

Homans, Margaret. *Bearing the Word: Language and Female Experience in Nineteenth-Century Women's Writing*. Chicago: U of Chicago P, 1986.

Kennard, Jean E. "Ourself Behind Ourself: A Theory for Lesbian Readers." *Signs* 9.4 (1984): 647–62.

Kermode, Frank. *The Art of Telling: Essays on Fiction*. Cambridge: Harvard UP, 1972.

Mason, Mary G. "The Other Voice: Autobiographies of Women Writers." *Auto-biography: Essays Theoretical and Critical*. Ed. James Olney. Princeton: Princeton UP, 1980. 207–35.

Meigs, Mary. *The Box Closet*. Vancouver: Talonbooks, 1987.

——. *Lily Briscoe a Self-Portrait: an autobiography by Mary Meigs*. Vancouver: Talonbooks, 1981.

——. *The Medusa Head*. Vancouver: Talonbooks, 1983.

Moi, Toril. *Sexual/Textual Politics: Feminist Literary Theory*. London: Methuen, 1985.

Wolff, Charlotte. *Love Between Women*. New York: Harper, 1972.

Woolf, Virginia. *To the Lighthouse*. London: Hogarth, 1960.

A Signature of Lesbian Autobiography: "Gertrice/Altrude"

LEIGH GILMORE

PREFACE

In the summer of 1932, Gertrude Stein was writing two autobiographies. One, *Stanzas in Meditation*, records the stand-off between Stein and Alice Toklas that developed after Toklas discovered the manuscript of Stein's *Q.E.D.*, a text in which Stein addressed her affair with May Bookstaver. Stein had apparently "failed" to tell Toklas about the affair and Toklas was furious (Dydo 12). The second, *The Autobiography of Alice B. Toklas*, takes the form of a long love letter to Alice, a compensatory gift Gertrude wrote to appease her partner. While it would be possible to read *The Autobiography* within the context of production suggested by these anecdotes, I offer them, instead, as a caution. Although biographical explanation informs our understanding of *The Autobiography* and *Stanzas* by, for instance, exposing the levels of parody and tension at play in seemingly simple statements in both, it may also naturalize Stein's discourse as an "expression" of identity, and may miniaturize her as a member of a spatting couple. More to the point, biographical explanation may foreclose an inspection of Stein's autobiographical experimentalism in *The Autobiography*, her extended inscription of lesbian identity, which, I would argue, departs from the interpretive contexts in which her reputation has been made. Here, I take the contradictory codes of lesbian and autobiographical (self-)representation as the grounds of Stein's experimentation.

The definitional locus of any generic category provides a clue as to what can and cannot be represented through any further analysis or elaboration of the category. In autobiography, that locus is formed by the narrativization of the self and history. In traditional studies of autobiography, both the self and history are overdetermined as "male." From the intractability of Augustine's *Confessions* as a point of generic origin to the formal limits such a precursor sets, traditional studies of autobiography repeat the founding, gendered premise of autobiographical subjectivity and authority. A stable and fixed perspective (Augustine's) conjoins time, space, and identity in a signifier of commanding proportions: the autobiographical *I*. The *I* is then mythologized through the same discourses that confer patrimony and patrilineage upon the proper name.[1]

Even such a brief sketch of traditional autobiography's law of genre will serve to establish the grain against which Gertrude Stein wrote *The Autobiography*. In "The Technology of Gender," Teresa de Lauretis gains considerable theoretical leverage by situating the subject in relation to inter-implicated networks, and by theorizing the contra-dictory and opposing grounds on which (self-)representation must occur: "A subject en-gendered in the experiencing of race and class, as well as sexual, relations; a subject, therefore, not unified but rather multiple, and not so much divided as contradicted" (2). These same contradictions, to a large degree, form the code of autobiographical (self-)representation.[2] In contrast to the "faithful" autobiographer, Stein reads the network of the self-same for its gaps, discontinuities and non-coincidences and rewrites the illusory seamlessness of auto-biography as a contradictory code of (self-)representation through three major displacements: (1) she displaces the function of the auto-biographical *I*, which is to act as the referential anchor for the story of the self, onto the lesbian couple; (2) she relocates the meaning of gendered identity within a contradictory code of lesbian (self-)representation; and, (3) she mobilizes the recognizable constituents of autobiography (such as chronological organization, a "truthful" narrator, and an individuated *I*) against autobiography itself. I will describe the lesbian subject position as a major feature of this code and *The Autobiography* as the location of the code in order to situate the text within a lesbian "economy" of gifts and exchange.

1. CODING THE SIGNATURE: LESBIAN REPRESENTATION AND THE DISCOURSE OF AUTOBIOGRAPHY

> What a history is folded, folded inward and inward again, in the single word I. (Whitman, *An American Primer* 4)

> *J/e* is the symbol of the lived, rending experience which is *m/y* writing, of this cutting in two which throughout literature is the exercise of a language which does not constitute *m/e* as subject. (Wittig, *The Lesbian Body* 7)

In the manuscript of "Lend a Hand," Wendy Steiner found a "doodle" that figured Gertrude Stein's lesbian relationship with Alice Toklas: "Gertrice/Altrude." I want to focus on this marginal note in order to bring out its relation to contemporary feminist interpretations of the lesbian subject position, and to locate that subjectivity within feminist theorizing about autobiography. The commingled names "dragging at the margins" (40) of Stein's manuscript, to use Jill Dolan's phrase, allow a focus on the complicated codes of lesbian semiotics; that is on the historically specific possibilities of making visible or invisible lesbian sexuality. Given the contradictory codes available to Stein for revealing and representing lesbian sexuality, it is not surprising that she both inscribed and satirized these systems. From Krafft-Ebing's sexological discourse on inversion to the salon stylings of Natalie Clifford Barney and others, Stein and Toklas negotiated the space of sexual signification at least in part through their relation to auto- biography. My aim here will be to examine how Stein used auto- biography to inscibe the lesbian couple as the "subject" of *The Autobiography*, so that I may locate her extended autobiographical experimentation within two critical discourses – contemporary feminist and poststructuralist criticism of autobiography – neither of which has yet sufficiently incorporated an analysis of lesbian writing.[3]

Until Stein was taken up by feminist critics, her early work was read as a densely textured kind of metapoetics, a discourse that referred almost entirely to itself. This reading enforces her canonization as a form-smashing modernist. Recently, feminist critics have begun to "bring out" Gertrude Stein – beyond the conventional nod to her "longtime companion, Alice Toklas" – by focussing on the "encoding" of a lesbian autobiography within Stein's asyntactic poetics. In one of the first essays in this phase of criticism, Elizabeth Fifer asserts: "Gertrude Stein's erotic works are demonstrations of disguised auto- biography . . . . Stein invented a witty code that played upon the details of her sexual and domestic self. In such a private autobiographical style she can tell everything – and she does" (472). In "Painted Lace" (1914), "Pink Melon Joy" (1915), and "Lifting Belly" (1917), according to Fifer, Stein creates a coded language and sign system that represents her lesbian relationship with Toklas. By describing this early work as a coherent and definable stage, Fifer offers new insight into Stein's refusal of classical realism and the lyric. Fifer's reading depends on recognizing the contradictory capacity of any sign system – here, specifically, a system that produces a lesbian subject that is not so much suppressed and hence unavailable to the reader except as conjecture, as a lesbian subject that is encoded, and, therefore, not so much repressed and hence unavailable to the writer except as confusion, as consistently occulted. Catharine Stimpson, who has published widely on this topic, offers a similar explanation for Stein's complex name-play and secret language.[4] Through her enactment of a lover's discourse, Stimpson's Stein can write a language of lesbian desire that plays with the names she and Toklas gave themselves and their sexual pleasures. Stimpson thereby links poetic invention with sexual subversiveness.

These feminist readings begin to establish a new spectator/reader for Stein's experimentation, a spectator capable of reading the lesbian in/ as this complex encoding. I would like to extend the insights into Stein's inscription of a lesbian subject position drawn from work on her "secret" autobiographies to a text she titled "autobiography." I will trace the oscillation between the visible and the invisible in Stein's lesbian representation and its relation to critical discourses that compound/elucidate invisibility/visibility. Criticism, here, must also be placed within the shifting network of identity and identification; for one of the ironies of Stein criticism is the extent to which its strategies sometimes obscure the lesbian as they explore Stein's verbal experimentation and vice versa.

For example, in situating Stein within the discourse of autobiography as I wish to do, I depend upon the insights of deconstruction in the following ways: the doodle, "Gertrice/Altrude," reveals Stein's ambivalence about the self as a unified figure. This suggestive marginalia, then, destabilizes the signature on which traditional interpretations of autobiography depend. Phillipe Lejeune's early formulation of a contractual basis of autobiography focussed on the guarantee offered by the signature: the title page was a signed document attesting to the historically truthful representation of the coherent self of an actual person. The autobiographer signed the text with a vow: to tell the truth, the whole truth, and nothing but the truth.[5] In the autobiographical pact, the signature underwrites the coherence of the self suddenly made specular; that is, the writing self and the written self (the *I* who writes *I*) do not properly refer to each other.

Emile Benveniste's essay on the nature of pronouns illuminates Stein's experimentation:

> What then is the reality to which *I* or *you* refers? It is solely a "reality of discourse," and this is a very strange thing. *I* cannot be defined except in terms of "locution," not in terms of objects as a nominal sign is. *I* signifies "the person who is uttering the present instance of the discourse containing *I*." This instance is unique by definition and has validity only in its uniqueness. (218)

Selves proliferate in autobiography and are ambiguously tethered to the overdetermined autobiographical *I*, a linguistic "shifter" that does not properly refer. Many critics of autobiography have sought to insulate autobiography's truth-claim from the radical impossibility of sustaining this claim. The autobiographical code of referentiality, in contrast, deploys the illusion that there is a single *I*, sufficiently distinct from the *I* it narrates to know it as well as to see it from the vantage of experience and still, more problematically, to be that *I*. All of this depends on not looking too closely at the profound shakiness caused by the motion of these *I*'s. They not only redouble their path through the looking-glass of time and space, but press against the constraints of linguistic reference through an overdetermined dependence on the "shifter," *I*.

While Lejeune's autobiographical pact seeks to corral an unruly rhetorical instability, poststructuralist critics have become interested in the internally eroding and re-inventing structures of identity in auto-biography, in the irresistibility and impossibility of autobiography's privileged relation to truth. In "Autobiography as De-facement," Paul de Man has described the way in which a structure of specular substitution of the *I* who writes, the narrated *I* whose experience unfolds within the temporality of the text, and the historical *I* whose past can be verified, obscures autobiography's secret: the super-abundance of *I* – that is, the way in which this figure is overdetermined by the tremendous referential work it must perform – covers up the privative and nostalgic nature of autobiography, and, for de Man, of language itself.[6]

In contrast to de Man, Monique Wittig, in "The Mark of Gender," discusses how gender and personal pronoun use are mutually re-inforcing structures and offers "j/e" in opposition to the false unity of "je." Indeed, Wittig is interested in the feminist politics of naming throughout her fiction and uses "j/e" in *The Lesbian Body* to signify a coupled rather than split female subject, and "elles" as the plural subject of *Les Guérillères*. Just as these words create new possibilities for female definition and representation in the novels, they oppose the univocality of "je" and "ils" and erode their ability to signify unproblematically.[7] Gertrude Stein also subverts the conventions of naming in *The Autobiography* in order to call attention to the problem in it that draws her to the complexity of utterance, to the lesbian couple as an autobiographical subject position.

Given this, we might well expect Stein's experimentation to have informed some of the current poststructuralist exploration of auto-biography. This has not, however, generally been the case. In their introduction to *Life/Lines: Theorizing Women's Autobiography*, editors Bella Brodzki and Celeste Schenck offer *The Autobiography* as

the "ultimate female autobiography – with a difference" (11) for two
reasons: to remark upon Stein's anticipation of and affiliation with
poststructuralism and to question Stein's absence from contemporary
studies of autobiography written by men. Brodzki and Schenck
question how male critics, lured by the postmodernist possibilities of
autobiography, could have missed a star source such as Stein (11).
Stein's fragmentary depiction of the self, her aggressively textual self-
portraiture, and, I would add, her enactment of Foucault's notion of
writing as a game in which the author constantly disappears, make her
an obvious candidate for such studies. The omission of Stein reveals for
Brodzki and Schenck the sexism of the recent boom in autobiography
criticism. "Is it only because Gertrude Stein is a woman," they ask,
"that Michael Sprinker does not use her as a point of reference in 'The
End of Autobiography'?" (11). Also, they suggest that Stein's decision
to tell the story of the self as the story of the other enacts a specifically
female autobiographical mode: "Being *between two covers* with some-
body else ultimately replaces singularity with alterity in a way that is
dramatically female, provides a mode of resisting reification and
essentialism, and most important, allows for more radical experimentation in autobiographical form than recent critics ... have been
willing to attribute to women writers" (11).[8]

In general, I agree with Brodzki and Schenck's insight, but instead
of strictly pursuing the well-placed charge of sexism, I would like
to confront sexism's ideological partner, heterosexism: this means
emboldening Brodzki and Schenck's italicized flirtation – *between two
covers* – in order to argue that the subject position Stein constructs in
The Autobiography that enables this experimentation and revision
is lesbian. The puzzles and pleasures – figurative and literal – of
lesbianism are figured in the autobiographical signature as the inter-
mingling of syllables across a penetrable border. The subject position
represented through this signature destabilizes the unified, solitary
subject whose ability to assure self-identity is the premise of the "autobiographical pact," and recasts the problem of (self-)representation in
the context of a lesbian relationship. In *The Autobiography*, Gertrude
Stein revises the subject position of autobiography by replacing the
solitary *I* bound by the conventions of realist narrative and historical
accountability – the terms of the autobiographical pact – with the
lesbian couple evoked through the signature "Gertrice/Altrude." This
textually marginal note is critical in theorizing the subject of Stein's
autobiography. If we read "Gertrice/Altrude" as the signature, one
that signs a pact which has historically been invisible, outlawed,
closeted, or complexly "out," the poetics of this lesbian autobiography

can be charted through the dispersal and recollection of identity this inscription offers.

"Gertrice/Altrude" flaunts the kind of equivalency drawn between the solitary person and her or his recorded truth. In the terms of the "autobiographical pact" and the legal mythology of the signature it creates, the structure of autobiographical identity is a prolonged naming of the subject. The proper name collects experience, change and continuity, family relations, and social agency in a signifier of commanding proportions; for it signifies not only the person in the present whose birth certificate bears that name, but the very possibility of the subject's temporal and spatial coherence. The name enforces the contractual oath of truth the autobiographer takes, and the reward of such fidelity is a "self" who survives. The guarantee of immortality, or at least remembrance, derives from the truthful solidity and the assertion that "I live, I write, and I bear witness to my self." But Stein represents a lesbian autobiographical identity that history has not written. Thus she does not position herself in relation to confessional or testimonial rhetoric with its assertion of verifiable truth and its authority structure of authenticity. Rather, she plays upon the devices of fiction: Toklas is a character in her own "autobiography"; the "real" writer is a character in Toklas's autobiography. Stein is also a ghost writer, an invisible hand, who capitalizes on the role-playing available within the subject of autobiography.

2. CIRCULATIONS: LESBIAN SUBJECTS AND ECONOMIES OF IDENTITY

... replacing the Lacanian slash with a lesbian bar. (Case, "Toward a Butch–Femme Aesthetic" 57)

To interpret lesbian representation is difficult, given the pervasiveness of what Wittig has called "the straight mind" ("Straight" 107). That is, the multiple networks in which structuralists and poststructuralists agree we exist assume heterosexuality as a premise from which all discourse derives. Wittig makes clear how an analysis such as semiotics derailed its political potential when it confronted the obligatory coding of heterosexuality. For Wittig, a political semiotics would be one that confronts the regularizing and enforcing tendencies of codes and views them as a method of control. Such an emphasis would focus on codes as instruments that train the subject in certain practices – including practices through which one is gendered and heterosexualized – and would expose the incoherence and contradiction within codes as the site of political opposition.[9] The difficulty in this essay, then, is to resist reading the destabilized autobiographical signature primarily through the insights of deconstruction, to resist making more general claims about either lesbian autobiography or all autobiography than one theoretically specific analysis can bear, and, as I will discuss later, to resist analyzing the gift primarily in its aspect of economic exchange. How, then, to direct interpretation toward an explication of how the contradictory interpretive and historical contexts in which this auto-biography may be situated can be used to analyze the contradictory codes of lesbian representation? That is, this argument finds its specificity by engaging a particular lesbian presentation of the other, a particular view of the subject, a particular form of historicization and explanation – all of which depart from the interpretive contexts in which Stein is most familiar.

If we ask: "Whose autobiography is it?" Stein challenges the answers such a question seeks, as well as the assumptions that produce it. Is "Whose autobiography is it?" reducible to or identical with "Whose life is it?" Must that be further reducible to "Who is writing?" Stein's finely-tuned sensitivity to verbal destabilizations found a provocative figure in the autobiographical *I*. By reading and writing linguistic and lesbian experimentation into the autobiographical *I*, Stein exploited its capacity to obscure and reveal particular kinds of difference and non-coincidence as well as the sameness of homo-sexuality (de Lauretis's term for same-sex sexuality). *The Autobiography of Alice B. Toklas*, Stein's auto- and homo-biography, constructs a lesbian subject position in autobiography.

Let us pose a question that will recontextualize Stein's autobio-graphy: What is the discourse of the lesbian couple positioned within an identity-constructing form (autobiography) and what does this inter-pretive reorientation allow? Heterosexuality has been an unwritten context of the autobiographical subject, and as such, women and men representing their identity are bound to each other through structures of negativity. Questions of sexual difference deteriorate to sexual opposition when the program of self-definition becomes "a woman is a woman because she is not a man." By bracketing the negativity of heterosexual self-definition, Stein could explore other possibilities for self-representation.

At first glance, Stein and Toklas seem to have managed a super-ficially "straight," or, more accurately, butch–femme household. They organized their domestic economies according to divisions long en-trenched in heterosexual arrangements: Stein was the reigning genius whose writing was central; Toklas kept the household running. Despite the butch–femme model of Stein and Toklas's relationship, however, their subjectivity should be understood in its lesbian dynamics, rather than as the simple miming of heterosexual domestic relations. The emergent subject position constructed by this practice has a performative force in *The Autobiography* that enables the signifiers of their life together to be read as roles encoded in butch–femme relations rather than as, for example, something grimly essentialist such as the natural expression of their different natures. That is, there is a certain playfulness, a self-construction, involved in adapting these roles.

In "Toward a Butch–Femme Aesthetic," Sue-Ellen Case claims that butch–femme always has been a witty play on the dominant culture's encoding of the couple; thus, it remains so whenever it appears. Butch–femme is a role lesbians inhabit together. Case quotes the old song: "you can't have one without the other" (56). Its performance layers an oppositional agency in behavior. Lesbians can act in certain stylized ways toward each other through a discourse of signs and gestures in which they become knowable as lesbians against tremendous cultural pressure toward invisibility and neutralization. Role-playing, especially as it destabilizes and shifts the possibilities for point of view in Stein's portraiture, underlies her experimentation. While the politics of a butch–femme arrangement, and of a butch–femme interpretation, remain troubling, I suggest we bracket an approbative critique within an historical frame that makes Stein and Toklas's choice visible as a lesbian practice.[10]

Indeed, more complications emerge against the negative take on butch–femme when we historicize its performance, and contextualize Stein and Toklas's relationship within the Left Bank literary milieu of the 1920s. As de Lauretis points out in a discussion of *Nightwood* and *The Well of Loneliness*,

> Gender reversal in the mannish lesbian ... was not merely a claim to male social privilege or a sad pretense to male sexual behavior, but represented what may be called, in Foucault's phrase, "a reverse discourse": an assertion of sexual agency and feelings, but autonomous from men, a reclaiming of erotic drives directed toward women, of a desire for women that is not to be confused with woman identification. ("Indifference" 24)

Gendered sexuality informs our notions of lesbian (self-)representation; yet Stein camps up both gender and heterosexual roles in the wife/husband depiction of Alice and the Genius; she allegorizes their relationship through this depiction and in effect undercuts the referentiality on which this representation of domesticity depends. The reader must be willing to imagine how a lesbian relationship may indicate an alternately gendered view of experience. Butch–femme roles do not flow naturally from sexuality – neither from sexual difference (from men) nor from sexual indifference to men. Neither sense of "difference" explains the lesbian subject of autobiography. If one reads for that kind of familiar definitional pressure – what is a woman as defined against what is a man? – that reading will repeat the conventional heterosexist error of reading everything through its "normative" view.

The narrative practice of inscribing and describing identity as engendered through hetero/sexual difference sustains the non-representation of the lesbian subject. Viewing *The Autobiography* from within gender ideology, one sees the quaintness of Gertrude and Alice, all their witty guests, the fun they must have had. Yet, Stein's lesbian subject compels the codes of heterosexual (self-)representation to detour wildly. Alice's practice of sitting with wives, for example, brings forward the stylization of her relation to Gertrude more than it links Alice with heterosexual women or Gertrude with heterosexual men. As such, it is a parody of heterosexual segregation. If we saw this scene on stage, and thus could read it as a sign, wouldn't we laugh at this "ironized and 'camped-up'" (Case 64) version of party behavior? For just such an emphasis on the semiotic send-ups that Stein presents in *The Autobiography*'s vignettes demonstrates how the gendered practice of "sitting with wives" cannot explain who Alice is, cannot fix her as "woman" in that scene. Contextualizing Alice and Fernande Picasso's chats about hats within Alice's lesbianism certainly underscores gender as performance. In *Gender Trouble*, Judith Butler argues that gender is its own performance: "To what extent do *regulatory practices* of gender formation and division constitute identity, the internal coherence of the subject, indeed, the self-identical status of the person?" (16). And this is precisely the kind of question raised by the problematic attribution of "wifely" attributes to the "femme" lesbian; a question turned back upon itself by a practice that seems to mime the *"regulatory practices* of gender formation and division" – here, for Alice, this means performing the practices through which one is trained to be a wife – without producing a woman who reads herself as a heterosexual.

3. GIFTS, GAZES, AND PORTRAITS

The Autobiography of Alice B. Toklas, as I have mentioned, is complexly coded as a gift circulating within a lesbian "economy." Primarily, the coupled subject deproprietarizes the autobiographical subject and thereby locates the meaning of this gift in the exchange of an *I*. The proprietary claims on identity and narrative (*the* story of *my* life), autobiography's deed and title, are troped here as what one gives rather than what one owns. *The Autobiography* as a gift derives meaning through the two economies in which it is valued and exchanged: the specific economy of a lesbian relationship and the market economy in which it became a bestseller. Stein inscribes a code of lesbian gifts in anti-realist and anti-authoritarian discursive practices and distances herself further from the indebtedness implicit in other theories and practices of gifting. The pressure of realist narrative techniques and nonfiction reporting (autobiography's traditional rhetoric) confronts the subversions and oppositions of Stein's "autobiography" that is not so much interested in "truth" as a record of facts as it is in the lesbian subject of autobiography.

Stein's lesbian subject position interrogates the ideology of auto-biography and the textual apparati through which it is constructed and refuses to authorize a single interpretive economy. She signals the grounds of her experimentation as early as the cover of the text. Gertrude Stein chose as the original frontispiece a photograph by Man Ray. In it, Toklas stands in a doorway, facing the camera, a hand on the doorlatch, ready to enter from the illumined background. In the darkened foreground, pen in hand, sits a writer at her desk. Only the title appears. We must wait until the last paragraph to feel the pleasure of this writer's/lover's gift:

> About six weeks ago Gertrude Stein said, it does not look to me as if you were ever going to write that autobiography. You know what I am going to do. I am going to write it for you. I am going to write it as simply as Defoe did the autobiography of Robinson Crusoe. And she has and this is it. (252)

In a conventional understanding of autobiography, only the title is needed: title and author and photograph would pile a repetition upon a redundancy. In my 1961 Vintage paperback, the reader's initiation into Stein's dislocation of the simple mirroring of identity in representation is foreshortened to the punchline. "Gertrude Stein," in large script, is placed above the title in the way a star's name dominates a movie title on a marquee. The cover photo, by Carl Van Vechten, shows Stein with her hair closely cropped, in profile, her gaze directed away from the viewer. The author and the photo are identical: there is no puzzle, no play. The Man Ray photograph rereads what can and cannot be seen, renders visible the otherwise invisible scene of lesbian domesticity, authorship, and autobiographical representation. The play between shadow and light, background and foreground, title and photograph redirects the focus from the *I* of autobiography to the couple in the frame. The Van Vechten portrait, used as an indexical sign of who/what lies within, denies this. Pursuing the photograph and the possibilities of spectatorship it suggests a bit further, we can note that, when Toklas looks into the camera, her direct gaze may establish a round of lesbian looks. As Marilyn Frye has commented:

> If the lesbian sees the woman, the woman may see the lesbian seeing her. With this, there is a flowering of possibilities. The woman, feeling herself seen, may learn that she *can be* seen; she may also be able to know that a woman can see, that is, can author production ... . The lesbian's seeing undercuts the mechanism by which the production and constant reproduction of hetero-sexuality for women was to be rendered *automatic*. (172, qtd. in de Lauretis, "Indifference" 34)

The photograph Stein chose and the photograph that replaced it are visual representations of the problem of reference Stein seized upon in autobiography. Stein capitalizes on the instability of the *I* when she inhabits it as an other; that is, inhabits the other's *I*. Critics have questioned whether there is not a danger in the usurpation of another's voice, of another's *I*. The resistance has taken two forms. First, some critics object to Stein's "appropriation" of Toklas's voice, and cite her egotism as the text's theme. The persistent attachment of narcissism to lesbian and gay sexuality underlies this objection. In a recent comment, Case has confronted the consistently negative Freudian reading of narcissism, its assumption of the regressive nature of same-sex attrac-tion, and has questioned further:

> What about the seduction of the same? Elsewhere, when I argued for the performance of the butch/femme roles, the masquerade of difference, I neglected to explore how the joke of that, the base that makes the camp masquerade operative is the base of the same. One part of this task would be to untie the notion of the seduction of the same from Freud's idea of narcissism which so dominates that figuration. At the same time, such a lesbian critique would reveal how Freud's notion of narcissism displays his heterosexual anxiety before the seduction of the same. (Case, "Introduction" 13)

Readers who object to the troubling appropriation of Alice's voice evidence a confused and confusing homophobia. This heterosexism, I think, masquerades as feminist concern for female autonomy and glosses over the lesbian dynamic of the exchange. This homophobia involves a double movement in which heterosexualized readers project on to Stein the proprietary traits of the patriarch and attribute to her the act of stealing a woman's voice with the full sense of that theft intact. Even when an explanation of the motive force that would drive such an appropriation is evaded, the negative consequences are still attached to Stein's act. Readers define something in this impersonation as masculine and disturbing, and I would suggest that this "something" is the baggage of Freudian narcissism. Stein's impersonation of Alice does not dissolve the other into a simple mirror of the self; rather, it displaces that conquering consequence in its affirmation of a doubled subject, a relation inscribed against the heterosexist logic of silence/ voice.

The second line of resistance seeks answers to the referentiality Stein purposefully obscures, and tries to judge whose autobiography it "really" is. Again, this is exactly the kind of interpretation that cannot be sustained when we read the autobiography as a gift. Stein dispenses with the traditional narrative we expect, eschewing chronological order for a rearrangement of Toklas's life with Stein's presence as its focal point. Referentiality, or the founding reality upon which a gift's meaning traditionally depends, is re-presented in order to place the couple as the subject that initiates the circulation of itself as gift. Frequently, autobiographies begin with origins: with a place, a family, a birth. *The Autobiography of Alice B. Toklas*'s opening sentence, "I was born in San Francisco, California," is meaningful only as a comment on the weather: "I have in consequence always preferred living in a temperate climate ... " (3). Toklas's "origin" is a *mise en scène*, for it is to be found in a text by Stein. Toklas's life before Stein is displaced from a birthplace to a gloss on a text, Stein's gloss: "In the story of Ada in Geography and Plays Gertrude Stein has given a very good description of me as I was at that time" (4). Here is part of that "very good description": "Trembling was all living, living was all loving, some one was then the other one. Certainly this one was loving this Ada then. And certainly Ada all her living then was happier in living than any one else who ever could, who was, who is, who ever will be living" ("Ada" 16). This representation of Ada's immense and ongoing bliss totalizes the young Alice. Her coming into lesbian *jouissance* marks her origin. Because "Ada" is not quoted in *The Autobiography*, we are pushed toward intertextuality. Toklas's "history" is dispersed across texts. In order to learn about her life, we need not turn to birth registries and newspaper clippings, for the emergence of the lesbian subject of autobiography is told through its appearance as a textual construction. The "real" dates and places of Alice's life reorganize around becoming Stein's lover.

The Autobiography concerns those things which compel Stein: "Identity always worries me and memory and eternity" – the auto-biographer's domain (*Everybody's Autobiography* 115). Stein faces eternity and posterity, and her prospects for achieving fame through her work are bleak. Although she is pursued to write an autobiography, and, indeed, pushed by Alice to pen what became a capital-generating best-seller, the one she might well have produced would not have been to the public's liking. It could have.been something more immersed in "all her unpublished manuscripts, and no hope of publication or serious recognition" (197), and, as such, an apologia for or vindication of her vocation. In short, a traditional autobiography. Yet, the tale we hear within Toklas's anecdotes hints at Stein's great disappointment even as it displaces it: "After all, as she said, we do want to be printed. One writes for oneself and strangers but with no adventurous publishers how can one come in contact with those same strangers" (*Auto-biography* 240). Stein, like Defoe's Robinson Crusoe, writes an autobiography, with its opportunity for self-promotion, in order to disappear. At the end of Defoe's text, Robinson Crusoe's presence is figured as absence, as footprints in the sand. At the end of Stein's text, an invisible hand is left holding the pen. The Crusoe/Friday parallel comments on the isolation Stein experiences. She, too, is only at home in an alien place after leaving the United States to settle in France. She, too, joins a companion who does not speak her language (her asyntactic poetics), but the language lesson here is quite complicated. Stein learns to speak Toklas's language and Toklas learns to translate Stein's: "As a matter of fact her handwriting has always been illegible and I am very often able to read it when she is not" (76). Such a dislocation, or translocation, of the ability to read the script of the other returns the gift in this lesbian "economy." Here Alice is authorized as the primary reader – if not writer – of her own life, and in this version of the puzzle, the autobiography appears more clearly as a writer's/lover's gift. Authority is transferable in this writerly text and functions as a form of gifting, as the reader becomes the writer implied in the autobiography's title.

Moreover, this device distances Stein from what she may not have wanted to write about: the lack of interest in her work. Alice's voice gestures towards "all her unpublished manuscripts," and thereby frames what Stein clearly considered traumatic within a deceptively simple style. Through this technique, Stein could write an auto-biography the public would read. Yet this book must have been composed much in the way of all those others, in the late night and dawn hours of solitude. Therein lives Stein. In the scene that structures both her subjectivity and the writerly authority that scripts this text, Stein's present tense identity is represented as "I am writing." We can read this scene as autobiography's version of the "space-off" shot in order to emphasize how much point of view has been altered by the coupled subject. Teresa de Lauretis explains the space-off shot as:

> the space not visible in the frame but inferable from what the frame makes visible. In classical and commercial cinema, the space-off is, in fact, erased, or, better, recontained and sealed into the image by the cinematic rules of narrativization (first among them, the shot/reverse-shot system). But avant-garde cinema has shown the space-off to exist concurrently and along-side the represented space, has made it visible by remarking its absence in the frame or in the succession of frames, and has shown it to include not only the camera (the point of articulation and perspective from which the image is constructed) but also the spectator (the point where the image is received, re-constructed, and re-produced in/as subjectivity). (*Technologies* 26)

Alice sleeps while Stein writes, thus she cannot narrate this activity in "her" autobiography. Correspondingly, Stein sleeps while Alice practices many of her domestic arts: cooking, sewing, corresponding. This is only one of the portraits (her portrait of Alice? her self-portrait?) whose authorial point of view is difficult to pin down. The coupled subject does not simply open the view to include both Stein and Toklas. It is a space from which to write, and it is also a space that controls perspective, a defining aspect of photography and portraiture.

As in the Man Ray photograph, the representations Stein selects share a playful setting for the "subject," a setting that destabilizes point of view and dethrones the scopophilic gaze of the portraitist. By representing autobiographical subjectivity as a space-off shot, Stein can adjust the frame to focus on the lesbian couple where a solitary figure once posed. Indeed the *Autobiography* is a series of portraits from which Stein escapes – usually by tricking/treating the eye so we look elsewhere. There is the famous portrait by Picasso of the heavy figure sitting solidly, a mixture of browns, greys, and black. There is the loving portrait by Toklas, the "Advertisements for Gertrude Stein," that stake out her place in "the heroic age of cubism" (6) as the sole literary experimenter in the form of portraiture. There is, of course, the third and most complicated portrait of all: the self-portrait that emerges through the voice of Toklas whose truth is "I am writing," a portrait of the *I*. In this representation, Stein has the last word, "I am going to write it," only to disappear: "And she has and this is it" (*Autobiography* 252). We see Stein shifting the portraits in this gallery, positioning herself in relation to them, denying that they represent her. There is another order of portraits that I previously called "semiotic send-ups" with which Stein fills the autobiography – portraits in which she redefines the reputations of the modernists. For example, Stein's ambivalent portrait of Picasso shows him in all his genius and more or less charming pettiness. Matisse exhibits bad form when he follows an invitation to dinner with a query about what will be served. Hemingway is marginalized and mocked. Character emerges in telling vignettes and personality is revealed through gestures. And there is the portrait of Toklas, the ostensible *I* of the autobiography, rendered in Stein's coupled subject and energized by an autobiographical equivalent of the space-off shot.

Alice's Gertrude (or Stein's version of Alice's Gertrude) and Picasso's Gertrude vie for authenticity. During the eighty or ninety sittings for Picasso's portrait, Stein begins composing and perfecting the long sentences of *Three Lives*. Stein's dynamism in this period forms Picasso's "subject" and he discusses Stein's potential in proprietary language: "Yes, he said, everybody says that she does not look like it but that does not make any difference, she will, he said" (12). That Picasso can paint her future, can fix her within his soon-to-be-finished masterpiece, is the source of some anxiety. When he is temporarily defeated by the portrait and paints out the head, we wonder which "tense" of Stein resists representation: "All of a sudden one day Picasso painted out the whole head. I can't see you any longer when I look, he said irritably. And so the picture was left like that" (53). No explanation is given for his inability to see Stein, but something in her refuses his gaze and refuses to be the "other" through which he can express his art:

> Only a few years ago when Gertrude Stein had her hair cut short, she had always up to that time worn it as a crown on top of her head as Picasso has painted it, when she had had her hair cut, a day or so later she happened to come into a room and Picasso was several rooms away. She had a hat on but he caught sight of her through two doorways and approaching her quickly called out, Gertrude, what is it, what is it. What is what, Pablo, she said. Let me see, he said. She let him see. And my portrait, said he sternly. Then his face softening he added, mais, quand même tout y est, all the same it is all there. (57)[11]

Stein resists the finality of the portrait and Picasso's possession of her image. He may render his Gertrude and he may question, "And my portrait, said he sternly." This she allows, but he does not own the self he must strive, if he is faithful to portraiture, to depict. She forces Picasso, in this anecdote, to respond to her own problem with portraiture. The question of his portrait's "objective realism," to which she insisted art must adhere, has become: What is the relation between representation and identity? To underline the dynamics between them, Stein offers this carefully controlling dialogue: "Let me see he said. She let him see ... all the same it is all there." It may be there "all the same," but Stein has escaped as simply its object.

CODA

Autobiography is no mere reflection of a life, translated from lived daily experience in a commonsensical way. Rather, writing itself is a constructive dimension of identity. Within a text, within even the margins of a text, one can write "Gertrice/Altrude" as a puzzle, as a sketch for a self-portrait, and as an autobiographical intertext in order to expose, within the text of autobiography, how "worrisome" identity depends on the possibility of writing the autobiography of (as) the other. For Stein, lesbianism is not an identity with a predictable content, and neither is autobiography. Rather, both become occasions for experimentation. The identity politics of autobiography as seen in the persistence of a belief in its historical reference, the realist manifesto written throughout criticism as versions of the autobiographical pact, are subverted in *The Autobiography of Alice B. Toklas*. So are the identity politics of Stein and Toklas's lesbianism, for this text predates coming-out narratives that constitute the grounds for a literature of lesbian self-identification. Stein's construction of a lesbian autobiographical subject, figured in the signature, "Gertrice/Altrude," resists reinventing a unified, lesbian subject. Rather, for Stein, identity, sexuality and self-representation are irreducible either in identity politics or in autobiography.

Mason, and Brodzki and Schenck, claim that many women adopt strategies that allow them to represent the autobiographical self by representing others. This seems to be the case with Stein, but we must widen our view within this framing device to see the other woman as the lesbian in this picture. Whether she is behind or before the camera or the text, she requires a place in feminist criticism beyond invocation and hasty retreat. Just such a figure, "the other woman," is having a renaissance in feminist criticism, but she is seldom known as the lesbian in and out of the text. More frequently she plays roles in the oedipal drama as mother, sister, daughter or, more problematically, the "racial" other, the postcolonial other, the subaltern woman. The latter positionalities are still based too much on the "self's" non-identification with the "other," and require more work to displace a perspective that dangerously hypostatizes "otherness." To read a lesbian signature requires a different view of otherness, and I invite the reader to sketch her own figure in the margins of this text, to linger at the bar that marks her distance from and proximity to the other woman. Such marginalia would then create a space "not visible in the frame but inferable from what the frame makes visible": a view of autobiography and, possibly, criticism that re-frames the feminist spectator/autobiographer/reader.

NOTES

1. I would like to thank my friends and colleagues who have generously shared insights and arguments on this essay: Marcia Aldrich, Lucinda Cole, Shirley Neuman, Willard Rusch, Richard Swartz and Evan Watkins.
2. Certain categories through which we represent autobiographical subjectivity are opposed or hierarchized for reasons we can historicize; for example, the perils of identifying across class and race have produced the notion of gender as universal. Clearly, its coherence has begun to erode. See especially Riley and Butler.
3. See also Brodzki and Schenck; and Benstock.
4. See Stimpson, "The Mind, the Body, and Gertrude Stein." See also Burke, who, working along the same lines claims: "For ten years, between 1903 and 1913, Gertrude Stein ... converted the predicaments of her personal life into literary material, the better to solve and to exorcise them" (221). Burke takes as her text the textualization of Stein's friendship with the Cone sisters, Etta and Claribel. She sees the dissolution of Stein's friendship with Etta Cone, and Stein's growing dissatisfaction with the friendship's insufficient intimacy, as prelude to her decision to live with Toklas. By combining biographical and literary evidence, Burke breaks the code that mutes the lesbian and the autobiographical in *Q.E.D.* (1903), *Fernhurst* (1904), *Three Lives* (1905–06), and *The Making of Americans* (1906–11). Taking the persona's declaration in *Q.E.D.* – "Why ... it's like a bit of mathematics. Suddenly it does itself and you begin to see" (67) – as an autobiographical statement, Burke sees autobiography, encoded and transmuted though it may be, everywhere.
5. Lejeune has revised his emphasis on the pact in more recent work, though his early formulation marks a critical turn in the study of autobiography.
6. De Man claims that autobiography's key trope is "prosopopeia" (926) – an address to a dead or inanimate thing. In this case, the autobiographer calls to the "self" in the past and confers upon her or him the ability to speak. However, the person the autobiographer was, the events s/he experienced, are not therefore present in any privileged way; they are merely re-presented. The autobiographer can no more bring life to the past than s/he can animate rocks, or waterfalls, or trees, through the trope of prosopopeia.
7. Although Wittig's experimentation usefully contextualizes Stein's interest in pronouns, Wittig's work sketches a different moment in a history of lesbian auto-

biographical representation. A development of this history can be found in de Lauretis, "Sexual Indifference and Lesbian Representation."

8. Brodzki and Schenck are elaborating the initial work of Mary Mason, whose groundbreaking essay on women's autobiography informs feminist criticism of autobiography so widely that her influence deserves constant crediting.

9. I also take this to be very much in line with de Lauretis's analysis of narrative and desire; see especially chapter five of *Alice Doesn't* and the last four chapters of *Technologies of Gender*.

10. See Case for a discussion of Joan Nestle's *Lesbian Herstory Archives*. Also, Case argues that "the butch–femme tradition went into the feminist closet" ("Towards a Butch–Femme Aesthetic" 59) in the 1970s, following a two-pronged feminist attack. The heterosexual feminist movement sought to tame the butch's unfeminized self-presentation and thereby stigmatized the femme's desire for butch lovers. In other words, lesbians were to become more "regular," less threatening to a movement that was increasingly concerned with its mainstream image and decreasingly tolerant of lesbian sexuality. Pursuing the critique from a different angle, lesbian feminists questioned the desirability of roles lifted from heterosexuality. The pressure from these convergent politics succeeded in forcing butch–femme role playing into the bars rather than out in the streets. Case considers the feminist critique of butch–femme thoroughly homophobic. She gives no credence to the argument that it is imitative and even reactionary for lesbians to play out the male–female, husband–wife roles of the dominant culture, or to the argument that the roles carry heterosexist baggage, that they stultify, codify and rigidify lesbianism, and participate in keeping lesbians bound to a heterosexual prison-house of imagery and models. That is, butch–femme roles can offer neither a point of resistance nor a fully fledged lesbian code because they are always already written out of what Fredric Jameson has described as the political unconscious of the dominant culture.

11. Stein's interest in representing the place of the other in her life precedes and extends beyond *The Autobiography*. Her relationship with Leo, her brother, is an example of a failed self/other relationship; for while Leo's star was on the rise, Gertrude's shone dimly. However, when Stein chose to spend her life with Toklas, Leo exited their home at 27, rue de Fleurus. He is reduced in *The Autobiography* to the scantest mention. While this text is ostensibly Alice's autobiography and in it Leo might be understandably viewed as the less significant Stein sibling, it is also the story of Gertrude's life in which the function of the other remains crucial, though the person fulfilling the function can be replaced. So intertwined are Gertrude and Alice's selves and lives that Leo qua "enabling other" figures minimally in their autobiography, without minimizing the significance of the other's role. Leo's response to finding himself reduced to one among many is a classic slander against an autobiographer: "God what a liar she is! ... Practically everything that she says of our activities before 1911 is false both in fact and implication ... " (Qtd. in Neuman 10).

WORKS CITED

Benveniste, Emile. *Problems in General Linguistics*. Coral Gables: U of Miami P, 1971.
Brodzki, Bella and Celeste Schenck, eds. *Life/Lines: Theorizing Women's Auto-biography*. Ithaca: Cornell UP, 1988.
Burke, Carolyn. "Gertrude Stein, the Cone Sisters, and the Puzzle of Female Friend-ship." *Writing and Sexual Difference*. Ed. Elizabeth Abel. Chicago: U of Chicago P, 1981. 221–42.
Butler, Judith. *Gender Trouble: Feminism and the Subversion of Identity*. London: Routledge, 1990.

Case, Sue-Ellen. "Introduction." *Performing Feminisms: Feminist Critical Theory and Theatre*. Ed. Sue-Ellen Case. Baltimore: Johns Hopkins UP, 1990. 1–13.
——. "Towards A Butch–Femme Aesthetic." *Discourse* 11.1 (1988–89): 55–73.
De Lauretis, Teresa. *Alice Doesn't: Feminism, Semiotics, Cinema*. Bloomington: Indiana UP, 1984.
——. "Sexual Indifference and Lesbian Representation." *Performing Feminisms: Feminist Critical Theory and Theatre*. Ed. Sue-Ellen Case. Baltimore: Johns Hopkins UP, 1990. 17–39.
——. *Technologies of Gender*. Bloomington: Indiana UP, 1987.
De Man, Paul. "Autobiography as De-facement." *Modern Language Notes* 94 (1979): 919–30.
Dolan, Jill. " 'Lesbian' Subjectivity in Realism: Dragging at the Margins of Structure and Ideology." *Performing Feminisms: Feminist Critical Theory and Theatre*. Ed. Sue-Ellen Case. Baltimore: Johns Hopkins UP, 1990. 40–53.
Dydo, Ulla E. "*Stanzas in Meditation*: The Other Autobiography." *Chicago Review* 35.2 (1985): 4–20.
Fifer, Elizabeth. "Is Flesh Advisable? The Interior Theatre of Gertrude Stein." *Signs* 4 (1979): 472–83.
Lejeune, Phillipe. *Le Pacte autobiographique*. Paris: Seuil, 1975.
Mason, Mary G. "The Other Voice: Autobiographies of Women Writers." *Autobiography: Essays Theoretical and Critical*. Ed. James Olney. Princeton: Princeton UP, 1980. 207–34.
Neuman, S.C. *Gertrude Stein: Autobiography and the Problem of Narration*. Victoria, B.C.: U of Victoria P, 1979.
Riley, Denise. *"Am I That Name?": Feminism and the Category of "Women" in History*. Minneapolis: U of Minnesota P, 1988.
Stein, Gertrude. "Ada." *Geography and Plays*. Boston: Four Seas, 1922. 14–16.
——. *The Autobiography of Alice B. Toklas*. 1933; New York: Vintage, 1961.
——. *Everybody's Autobiography*. 1937; New York: Cooper Square, 1971.
——. *Fernherst, Q.E.D., and Other Early Writings*. New York: Liveright, 1971.
Steiner, Wendy. *Exact Resemblance To Exact Resemblance: The Literary Portraiture of Gertrude Stein*. New Haven: Yale UP, 1978.
Stimpson, Catharine, "The Mind, the Body, and Gertrude Stein." *Critical Inquiry* 3 (1977): 489–506.
——. "The Somagrams of Gertrude Stein." *The Female Body in Western Culture: Contemporary Perspectives*. Ed. Susan Rubin Suleiman. Cambridge: Harvard UP, 1986. 30–43.
Whitman, Walt. *An American Primer. With Facsimiles of the Original Manuscript*. Ed. Horace Traubel. Boston: Small, Maynard, 1904.
Wittig, Monique. *The Lesbian Body*. Trans. David Le Vay. Boston: Beacon P, 1986.
——. *Les Guérillères*. Trans. David Le Vay. Boston: Beacon P, 1985.
——. "The Mark of Gender." *Poetics of Gender*. Ed. Nancy K. Miller. New York: Columbia UP, 1986. 63–73.
——. "The Straight Mind." *Feminist Issues* 1.1 (1980): 103–11.

Women's Autobiography: The Self at Stake?

T. L. BROUGHTON

If the social contract, far from being that of equal men, is based on an essentially sacrificial relationship of separation and articulation of differences which in this way produces communicable meaning, what is our place in this order of sacrifice and/or language? (Kristeva 199)

Looking back today over my life, I see that its keynote – through all the blunders, and the blind mistakes, and clumsy follies – has been this longing for sacrifice to something felt as greater than the self. It has been so strong and so persistent that I recognise it now as a tendency brought over from a previous life and dominating the present one; and this is shown by the fact that to follow it is not the act of a deliberate and conscious will, forcing self into submission and giving up with pain something the heart desires, but the following it is a joyous springing forward along the easiest path, the "sacrifice" being the supremely attractive thing, not to make which would be to deny the deepest longings of the soul, and to feel oneself polluted and dishonoured. ... For the efforts to serve have not been painful acts of self-denial, but the yielding to an overmastering desire. We do not praise the mother who, impelled by her protecting love, feeds her crying infant and stills its wailings at her breast; rather should we blame her if she turned aside from its weeping to play with some toy. And so with all those whose ears are opened to the wailings of the great orphan Humanity; they are less to be praised for helping than they would be to be blamed if they stood aside. I now know that it is those wailings that have stirred my heart through life, and that I brought with me the ears open to hear them from previous lives of service paid to men. It was those lives that drew from the child the alluring pictures of martyrdom, breathed into the girl the passion of devotion, sent the woman out to face scoff and odium, and drove her finally into the Theosophy that rationalises sacrifice, while opening up possibilities of service beside which all other hopes grow pale. (Besant, *Autobiography* 43–4)

I see this paper on Annie Besant's *An Autobiography* as participating in a debate, or rather a conversation, which has been going on among feminist critics of autobiography for the last ten years. This conversation has turned on the question of gender in autobiography. Is there something which might be called autogynography (to adopt Domna Stanton's coinage [5]) as distinct from male autobiography? And if there is, what might be its (gendered) characteristics?

Autobiography, in its modern, introspective form at least, situates itself at the very juncture of the public world of announcement and the private world of self-analysis and meditation. Early in its short history, feminist criticism of autobiography seemed to founder on this public/ private distinction: a distinction which has determined the shape of much thinking about women for at least two centuries. Initial observations in this field, by such critics as Estelle Jelinek and Suzanne Juhasz, took the form of tentative, and then more confident proposals that women's autobiography in the Western tradition differs from men's in being less linear, less goal-oriented, less public in its concerns. Or, as it is usually put, women's autobiography is (relatively) discontinuous, digressive, fragmentary and concerned with personal relations.[1]

In so far as it interrogates the often unchallenged aesthetics of autobiography, and the literary canon that follows in their wake, this is clearly a helpful suggestion. As an alternative aesthetic, or as a theory of women's autobiography, however, it remains problematic on a number of counts. In the first place, any argument based on similarity of content across a range of women's autobiographies runs the risk, however innocently, of eliding differences between women's lives, of obscuring cultural specificities in the name of an *ad hoc* separate women's "tradition." Suggestions of gender specificity lurch precariously towards assertions of gender *generality*. Secondly, there is the difficulty of application: the seeming impossibility of demonstrating these differences between male and female texts generated within ever-fluctuating discursive worlds, ever-changing possibilities of meaning and value. The exercise invites invidious bids and counterbids: a game in which the feminist critic, for comparative lack of cards, is bound to be worsted. For every female domestic drama, for instance, one could produce half a dozen John Stuart Mills or Thomas Carlyles. Ultimately one plays into the hands of critics who would see gender difference within an economy of opposition, with male characteristics always already the first, dominant term. For the collapsing of form into content to produce an index of gender difference does not necessarily solve, but simply postpones, the vexed question of genre: the question of what we understand by the term "autobiography" in the first place. Digression and fragmentation, for instance, imply a *lack* of linearity and wholeness and it is this implied narrative that we recognize as autobiography (as distinct from "autobiographical writing") in the Western tradition.

Domna Stanton raised the level of the debate in 1984, when she suggested that

> Because of woman's different status in the symbolic order, auto-gynography ... dramatized the fundamental alterity and non-presence of the subject, even as it asserts itself discursively and strives toward an always impossible self-possession. (15)

Though expressed in the kind of abstruse language, and at a level of abstraction, that leaves me feeling, frankly, feverish, this formulation evokes in me a kind of abysmal recognition, as if Stanton were saying nothing *and* everything about women's autobiography.

But what does she mean, exactly? As Paul de Man has demonstrated, what Stanton calls autobiographical "self-possession" and he calls "coming into being" (922) is *always* fictive, *always* impossible, regardless of gender. If there is gender difference in the phallogocentric world of autobiography, then, it must be situated in the "alterity and non-presence" of the feminine subject. But how can "non-presence" be dramatized? And if women as subjects have no place in the symbolic order, how can they be the site of autobiographical discourse at all? Linda Anderson, in a key article in 1986, used the metaphor of the "threshold" to describe, in psychoanalytic terms and with special reference to the *diary* mode, women's relationship to themselves and their written Lives (Monteith 54–7). My anxiety about this approach is that it displaces the "story" from autobiography and replaces it with the "moment of being" a woman. In this sense it acts out the sacrifice of life to gender implicit in the coinage "autogynography."[2] But what of the (apparently) more conventional autobiographies by women? What about the many nineteenth-century women's autobiographies which lean, for their authoriality and authority, on standard narrative forms and on the standard figure of self as convert?

How we answer the question of gender difference in autobiography depends on our critical *and* political positions (the two sometimes in uneasy tension). It depends not just on our understanding of autobiography as gendered "self," gendered "text" or gendered "life," but on our decisions about the historical and ideological meanings of these positions. The question of autogynography hinges on three problematics: the explicit problematic of gender: how are women's autobiographies different from men's?; the deferred problematic of genre: how is women's autobiography different from other kinds of women's writing?; and the hidden or ignored question of history: what conditions enabled the production of this particular conjunction of gender and genre? Only by keeping in mind the fundamental question of *why* we read women's Lives, it seems to me, can we hope to keep these three plates spinning. We read autobiographies for other reasons than we read novels, diaries, letters or edited papers. We read auto-biographies to hear from, learn from, specific historical figures about how they found their own voice, not just as a matter of intratext, but as a product of historical, material forces. In other words, this "finding a voice" is not reducible to the playing out of a particular relationship to language or tradition. It also entails a set of interconnected histories: how the author acquired or came to do without a room of her own; how she came to command an audience rhetorically, ideologically and socio-economically. That the coincidence of the story of finding a voice and the act of using it makes autobiography a privileged site of historical agency for women should not mislead us into conflating the two or subordinating the one to the other. Nor, on the other hand, should the fact that the self-reflexivity of autobiography gives it a modernist appeal distract us from the historiographical and political imperatives which take us to it.

With these questions in mind, I turn to Annie Besant. In Annie Besant's *Autobiography* the question of gender cannot readily be determined at the expense of genre. She is unsqueamishly chrono-logical and factual, bombarding the reader with evidence in the way of extracts from letters, speeches and pamphlets. She neither hides her public role nor evades her private life any more than does a Ruskin or a Mill: she is unrepentant in much of her self-interpretation. She situates herself firmly within the orthodoxy of the nineteenth-century unorthodox, and hence in the mainstream of Victorian autobiography, by accrediting her authority to a series of classically structured (de)conversions.

Several versions of Annie Besant's autobiography exist, dealing with her many religious and political conversions: from Anglicanism, through Freethought and Fabian Socialism, to mystical Theosophy and Indian Nationalism.[3] Among the revisions, modulations and expansions which Besant felt it necessary to produce, in 1893, the fullest and most conventional version, was, predictably, an elaboration of her early religious impressions and spiritual enthusiasms. Less predictable, perhaps, is the form taken by these impressions in Besant's account: the form of a persistent flirtation with the idea of early death.

At issue from the beginning is Besant's engagement with, and ultimate rejection of, what she deems the "religious materialism" of her day:

> I went out into the darkness alone, not because religion was too good for me, but because it was not good enough; it was too meagre, too commonplace, too little exacting, too bound up with earthly interests, too calculating in its accommodations to social conventionalities. The Roman Catholic Church, had it captured me, as it nearly did, would have sent me on some mission of danger and sacrifice and utilised me as a martyr; the Church established by law transformed me into an unbeliever and an antagonist. (13)

To some extent this is simply a classic conversion sequence. The possession of an autobiographical voice is predicated on the eventual arrival and enlightenment of the subject who "went out into the darkness." But the eruption into the text of a "might have been" – competing with the historical narrative – momentarily destabilizes the narrator's authority and alerts us to potential ambivalences. The subjunctive is the locus of loss and desire in autobiography: the obverse of historicity. The theme is taken up again later:

> I read tales of the early Christian martyrs, and passionately regretted I was born so late when no suffering for religion was practicable; I would spend many an hour in day-dreams, in which I stood before Roman judges, before Dominican Inquisitors, was flung to lions, tortured on the rack, burned at the stake: ... But always, with a shock, I was brought back to earth, where there were no heroic deeds to do, no lions to face, no judges to defy, but only some dull duty to be performed. And I used to fret that I was born so late.... (30)

Set this passage alongside Besant's condemnation of the contemporary Established Church, and there emerges an overwhelming sense of self as anomalous: a sense of having been born too late, and into an ethical space that is both too wide (accommodating) and too narrow (meager, calculating).

Besant returns again and again to these youthful "daydreams," connecting them, not only with social, historical and spiritual incongruence, but also, as explicitly as is possible in a Victorian publication, with an awakening (autoerotic) sexuality. It is in part the emotional frigidity of established religion which repels her, and she "brood[s] over the days when girl-martyrs were blessed with visions of the King of

Martyrs, when sweet St. Agnes saw her celestial Bridegroom," losing herself "in these fancies, never happier than when alone" (38). In her chapter on marriage, she quotes eight times from "so-called devotional exercises" to show how, with their imagery of masochistic desire and consummation, they might absorb and direct the erotic life of a sexually ignorant adolescent girl.

As the *Autobiography* progresses, the motif of frustrated self-sacrifice becomes conflated with the thwarting of other ideals – sexual and intellectual – , all converging, significantly, around one particular Easter-time. Besant narrates how, in 1866, at the age of eighteen, she set out to compose a "Harmony" of the Gospel accounts of Christ's last days and death, in order to "facilitate the realisation of" (or rehearse) Christ's suffering and martyrdom. The exercise fails, because

> discrepancies leaped at me from my four columns: the uneasiness grew as the contradictions increased, until I saw with a shock of horror that my "harmony" was a discord, and a doubt of the veracity of the story sprang up like a serpent hissing in my face. (46–7)

This first religious doubt coincides with her first experience of hetero-sexuality. Initially, Besant affects a naive surprise at the coincidence of events, as if, in writing, she had only just noticed it: "strange that at the same time I should meet the man I was to marry, and the doubts which were to break the marriage tie" (44). The lapsarian imagery associated with Besant's spiritual dilemma ("a serpent hissing in my face") is echoed in her account of early marriage: the forcible wrenching of the young woman from carefully cultivated innocence and ignorance is likened to expulsion from the "paradise" of a mother's love. And the word "shock" is used repeatedly to describe the disruption of her daydreams, her religious doubts, her experiences of marriage and heterosexual sex, and her discovery that she is her husband's property.

Though these overlapping discourses have in common the acquisition of certain kinds of knowledge (the attainment of adulthood, the demythologizing of the Scriptures, the acquiring of sexual experience), and thus might be said to constitute an enlightening and empowering "conversion," the effect is rather different. In Christian typology, conviction of sin (or error) leads to personal salvation. As this is played out in male-authored autobiography, exile from paradise is the gesture of deferral which makes the narrative necessary and promises knowledge and wisdom in return. In Besant's version, as we have seen, contemplation of the Crucifixion leads to Eve's expulsion from Eden. The gendered nature of the conversion model begins to emerge. The

constellation of properties – enlightenment, knowledge, authority –
which the convert-autobiographer claims, and which simultaneously
legitimate authorship, have different connotations when applied
to masculinity and femininity. The price of knowledge to Eve is
catastrophe.

Entwined with these narratives of religious, social and sexual frustration is the story of frustrated authorship. The pivotal episode between
Girlhood and Marriage, in which "realisation" of Christ's martyrdom
becomes "realisation" of doubt, exile and fall, is, as we have seen, a
doomed attempt at writing: the composition of a Harmony. This failure
is followed by another: Besant's "Lives of the 'Black Letter' Saints" of
the church calendar does not find a publisher and drops into oblivion.
After the minor success of a few short stories in the *Family Herald*,
Besant's fortunes as author are temporarily frozen. Publishers regard
her new novel as too political, and will only accept from her writing of
"'purely domestic interest'" (69). As a wife, her earnings from writing
are, to her horror, not her own to dispose of. As a mother, her time
becomes absorbed by childcare. With such material and ideological
forces amassed against her, her literary career is "checked" (69).

To the fact that this check, however serious, is only temporary, the
existence of the text bears witness. But the central paradox of the
narrative, I would argue, is that the autobiographical discourse itself is
bought at the price of a highly valued model of self: the fantasy of
feminine self as martyr. The gesture of deferral (the exile topos) which
recurs again and again in the text, will never redeem its promise,
for it promises voluntary renunciation, silence and the knowledge of
death. Indeed, the theosophical discourse framing the story, which
"rationalises sacrifice" by insisting on reincarnation, cheats the reader
of closure to (and beyond) the end of the book.[4]

Because of this, the book's many climactic moments are invariably
bathetic, and it is impossible to isolate one as the decisive transformative "turning point." Besant's contemplated (and rejected)
suicide might be read as the crux between religious despair and
existential freedom, but this would be to read against the grain
of gender. The scene is set symptomatically, with the now familiar
ingredients of psychosexual and religious distress:

> Mr Besant was away, and there had been a fierce quarrel before
> he left. I was outraged, desperate, with no door of escape from a
> life that, losing its hope in God, had not yet learned to live for hope
> for man. No door of escape? The thought came like a flash:
> "There is one!" And before me there swung open, with lure of

peace and of safety, the gateway into silence and security, the gateway of the tomb. (76)

Besant's prose, which in any case inclines to the melodramatic, is at this point self-consciously portentous and "literary":

> I uncorked the bottle, and was raising it to my lips, when, as though the words were spoken softly and clearly, I heard: "O coward, coward, who used to dream of martyrdom, and cannot bear a few short years of pain!" (76)

Along with the bottle of chloroform, thoughts of suicide are defiantly cast aside, and with them the "dream of martyrdom" which has haunted the text. Besant falls "fainting on the floor," a collapse which expresses "surrender" to the conversion process, but also the last gasp of "hysterical" Victorian femininity. It is striking that Besant sounds here like Olive Schreiner at her most souped-up. Dan Jacobson has said of Schreiner's prose that it seems to have an "inner meaning or impulsion quite opposite to that intended" (17). In the same way, Besant's prose works itself up only to cancel itself out. Meanwhile, the mythology of martyrdom cannot survive because, according to its own semiotics, it can never take effect as an autobiographical discourse.

What, then, are the ideological and textual implications of the "fantastic" but foregone romance of self as martyr? To be martyred, as conceived of both inside and outside Roman Catholic theology, is to die for a cause. The meaning of martyrdom lies not so much in the content of the "cause" itself, as in the fact that it has been regarded as worthy of suffering and premature death. The convert may be bound to *bear* witness to a cause or belief through saying or deed. By virtue of being dead, the martyr *is* witness. (The root meaning of martyr is "witness" in the Christian sense.) Historically, the martyrdom ethic appealed to Victorian culture, not just for its defiance of compromise, but for its overvaluation of chastity, youth and innocence at the expense of experience, maturity and knowledge. In obvious ways, it intermeshed with the Victorian cult of feminine moral and physical beauty. A link can also be drawn between the cult of martyrdom and the cultural construction of middle-class female sexuality as passive, indeed as masochistic. Martyrdom, as Marina Warner has pointed out in relation to Joan of Arc, "is the only triumph in an ideological climate where change means deterioration" (263). In the context of nineteenth-century autobiography, change as conversion means anything but deterioration: it is the premise upon which authority is established. In the context of the representation of femininity, however, Warner's claim is clearly relevant. Ideal femininity and change are incompatible.

In short, while the figure of the convert might seem to be non-gendered, most of its narrative manifestations are decidedly masculine: the pilgrim, the *miles christi*, the apostle. Like childhood, ideal Victorian femininity, whose virtues (silence, chastity, restraint, innocence, youth) are for the most part virtues of omission rather than commission, scarcely lends itself to drama: "How much more exciting to struggle with a winged and clawed dragon that you knew meant mischief, than to look after your temper, that you never remembered you ought to keep until you had lost it" (Besant, *Autobiography* 29). The only spiritual model of sainthood upon which Victorian ideal femininity seems to have any real purchase is that of martyr. Its heroism brings with it connotations of passivity, youthfulness, purity, innocence and masochism. It is, moreover, logically incompatible with the autobiographical act: one can speak as convert; one cannot speak as martyr.

Let us return, for a moment, to the question of autogynography. The autobiographical dilemma for women can be posed in a number of ways. Stanton formulates it as a linguistic predicament: for a woman, entry into a symbolic order which designates her as object immediately falsifies her subjectivity. Applicable, arguably, to anyone attempting any kind of writing, this formula might nevertheless have particular relevance when applied to a genre which rests, however unsteadily, on the fiction of Truth to Self. But where might gender come in? If a key component of the "symbolic order" of autobiography is the identification of autobiographer with *convert*, and convert with *authority*, then a gender which is defined in opposition to authority will be excluded from that order. For the Victorian woman, the problem is articulable in ideological terms: the construction of the autobiographer as authoritative, mature, assertive and public is at variance with the construction of femininity as self-effacing, youthful, passive and private.

If, in the symbolic order, women, like martyrs, have meaning ascribed to, or inscribed on them, then to represent the self as feminine subject is as impossible as to represent oneself as having died young. The most that can be done is to represent the self as having failed to die young: having failed to be silenced, extinguished, passive, defined. One facet of Besant's quest for self-possession is her deployment and disposal of her self as martyr. In simultaneously evoking and forsaking this martyr self, she exchanges being for acting; she sacrifices her self as self-sacrificing, passive, and heroically "feminine"; she becomes autobiographer. In ritually entering the symbolic order, which we take here to be the order in which the equation autobiographer = convert = authority obtains, she renounces autogynography.

In highlighting the interest shown by Annie Besant in the romance of martyrdom and early death, it is not my intention to draw crass parallels between femininity and martyrdom, to suggest that femininity *is* martyrdom, or is even *experienced* as martyrdom. What intrigues me are the possibilities for representation that they offer one another.

Avrom Fleishman has suggested that

> autobiographical metaphor may be seen as a supplement that fills the space left by the self, which, in the act of writing, absents itself. The other self written in autobiography may also serve as a supplement to fill many a lack felt in a variety of ways in life – such motivation is legion. (34)

If one tries to apply this formula to women's autobiography, one can see why two complementary autobiographical metaphors might be necessary. For if the self which absents itself in conventional auto-biographical writing (to assert itself in the text) is the self as authority, then the metaphor of the convert takes effect. But if the self which absents itself in any writing is by definition the construction of the self as feminine, then the metaphor of convert alone will not represent it, and the foregone fantasy of martyrdom comes into play. It fills, and *is*, the "lack felt": in Anderson's terms, it is the presence that encircles absence at the threshold of the self. One never remembers one's temper, until it is lost.

What does all this tell us about Annie Besant as a woman auto-biographer? To answer this, we must return to the three interconnected issues of gender, genre and history, bearing in mind that overemphasis on any one component will be misleading. Biographies of Besant, for instance, invariably appeal to a "martyr-complex" as a key to her personality – to her own quirky version of Victorian religiosity – rather than to her self-representation. Rosemary Dinnage in 1986 asserts that Besant wanted to be "a saint, a martyr, and a prophetess" (16). Time after time, biographers draw on this "martyr complex" for its explanatory powers – and Besant's choices in life take some explaining. Even Janet Oppenheim, who is concerned with tracing historical continuities rather than sketching eccentricities, habitually falls back on a literal reading of the *Autobiography* in this respect:

> [Besant] certainly participated, directly and indirectly, in the

major fights of Victorian and Edwardian feminism – for the vote,
for higher education and professional opportunities, and for
equal status under the law – and they satisfied, to some extent,
*aspects of her personality that needed to flout convention and court
martyrdom.* (17 emphasis added)

And again:

Furthermore, as the subject of considerable ridicule in the press,
Theosophy also gratified her preoccupation with martyrdom.
Whether or not Besant realised that she continued a centuries-
old British feminist tradition in adopting the stance of inspired
prophetess when other means of exerting influence seemed
barred, the role was genuinely congenial to her, and she filled it
... with inexhaustible conscientiousness. (18 emphasis added)

The danger of locating Besant here, wedged in a metaphysics of
hysteria stretching tantalizingly from St. Teresa's *Confessions* to Luce
Irigaray's "Mystérique," is that the maneuver does no justice to the
facts of Besant's career. What I have tried to suggest is in fact the
opposite position – that the key to Besant's text is her self-presentation
as *failed* martyr: a double negative which produces self as survivor.
Only this move can retain Besant as prophetess while affirming her as
political and textual strategist.

But the strictly literary reading brings its own problems. What I
have suggested is a useful metaphor which situates the woman autobiographer in a neatly off-beat relation to a phallocentric language or
symbolic order, without having to resort to much extratextual evidence
to establish Besant's subordination or displacement as a woman. I
could substantiate, or at least enhance my argument, by drawing
on examples from the early Victorian period to the 1980s, from
the autobiographies of working- and middle-class women, from the
writings of black as well as white women. I could even posit the self as
failed martyr as a strategy of self-representation characteristic of
women's autobiography cross-culturally and transhistorically, from
Harriet Martineau to Zora Neale Hurston.[5]

But where would that get us? I would have established a tradition of
women self-authors, only to kill them all off in the sweeping gesture of
the poststructuralist. I would have evoked a "feminine condition" vis à
vis language as seemingly timeless, unchallengeable and hegemonic as
the "human condition" of white Western liberal thought, the only
difference being its marginality to an equally changeless masculinity.
Apart from the broadest appeal to a postindustrial ideology of separate

spheres, and to the prescriptive Victorian legacy of idealized femininity as passive and silent, I have not put the case which would determine the autobiography as Annie Besant's rather than anyone else's.

Both readings, then, are problematic. We leave straddled between martyrdom and paranoia a woman who published and debated nationally and internationally for just under sixty years, and who, at the time of her autobiography in 1893, had separated from her clergyman husband and lost custody of her children; had campaigned on Free Thought, Radical, Women's Suffrage, Socialist, Fabian and Theosophical platforms; had been tried and acquitted in 1877 for publishing contraceptive advice; had opposed British policy in Ireland; had been, in 1888, one of the first middle-class women to campaign successfully with the backing of working women, spearheading the Bryant and May strike, and securing benefits such as free school meals for working-class children in her capacity as elected representative on the Tower Hamlets division of the London School Board; had studied science and become a qualified science teacher; had worked alongside some of the best-known intellectuals and activists of her day – Charles Bradlaugh, Edward Aveling, George Bernard Shaw, Edward Carpenter, the Pankhursts, Sydney Webb, William Morris; and had rather mysteriously, it seems to us now, converted finally and irrevocably to Occultism and Theosophy in 1889.

Yet while wishing to recall, and even celebrate, the achievements of the historical Besant as outlined in her book, I am reluctant to cast aside my more "literary" reading. I do not want to abandon my appeal to the romance of the failed martyr as characteristic of Besant's *Autobiography* and of women's autobiography generally, since the generic structure of "classic" Western autobiography, mutating from generation to generation, nevertheless hinges on a discourse of self-as-authority which would, it seems to me, make some kind of reverse discourse necessary to any woman aspiring to generic acceptance *as a woman*. The failed martyr provides one such reverse discourse.

Unfortunately, what the metaphoric reading of autobiography threatens (and I am tempted more and more to call it a "conceited" reading) is the elimination of the life from autobiography: its reduction to autograph. The effect of this elision is to detach the book from the particular material and ideological conditions of its production, and to neutralize it as an expression of specific oppressions or privileges, of contingency, of political resistance, or of struggle for change. So the problem with this kind of analysis is that it flattens out the contours of history, obscuring the crucial issue of why one discourse is adopted over another, and the relations of power this implies. This can only be

retrieved by taking a closer look at history: the complexities of late
Victorian politics and culture as they interlink to form Besant's context.

The 1880s and 1890s witnessed a remarkable new constellation of
gender differences and gender ideologies. The New Woman emerged
as a cultural possibility, and as a cultural obsession. Lucy Bland
has shown that, far from being preoccupied with free love, as is
widely assumed, the New Woman of women's fiction and politics was
primarily concerned with the shortcomings of marriage law, the marital
home, marital sex, male sexual incontinence, the horrors of venereal
disease, and female sexual ignorance (141–64). Feminist debate about
the dismal fate of the respectable (read middle-class) single women of
the 1850s and 1860s, women commonly conceptualized as statistically
"surplus" to the marriage market and therefore in desperate need of
higher education, entry to the professions, and so on, was gradually
giving way to a more critical analysis of marriage itself. Beneficiaries of
reform in education, the opening up of new areas of employment,
and of roles for women in local government and party politics, and
equipped with a lexicon of sexuality derived from the successful
campaign against the Contagious Diseases Acts in the 1870s and 80s,
the New Women were flexing their muscles on the domestic front. The
Woman Question was coming home to roost.

This shift in focus is forcibly registered in Eliza Lynn Linton's famous
attack on the so-called "Wild Women" of the Women's Movement in
1891: "They cannot be on both sides at once. Politics or peace, the
platform or the home, individualism or love ... they must take their
choice which it shall be" (83). Journalists and novelists such as Mona
Caird responded by deconstructing Linton's "two sides." They undermined the very basis of the public/private dichotomy: by questioning the equation of home with peace and love; by elaborating a
sexual politics of the home; and by proposing that greater scope for
individualism in the home might rescue torpid and embittered relationships. Caird's devastating critiques of the contemporary institution of
marriage, published in the mainstream periodicals of the late eighties
and early nineties, read like case histories of Besant's early life.

> "Yes, marriage is often a failure," say the orthodox reproach-
> fully; "it is entered into too early, too thoughtlessly, without (on
> the part of the wife) a knowledge of cooking and the domestic arts,
> without a flawless temper, without absolute immunity from head-
> aches. Society and the institution of marriage are not to blame,
> only the faulty individuals who marry."

> Alas, for much instructed, much badgered, much belaboured individuals! Like the absent, they are always in the wrong. (100)[6]

Here Caird dramatizes, not just the pitfalls awaiting the angel in the house, but also, strikingly, the difficulty of inserting oneself as subject in the discourse of femininity. "Like the absent, they are always in the wrong." Rewriting the script of love, marriage and childcare, Caird, and New Women like her, set about constructing a subject position for the active dissenter from within marriage – what we might now call the "subject of feminism." I think it is important to note, however, that this critique of marriage was not framed within a broader critique of compulsory heterosexuality. The end in view was a reformed, revitalized, egalitarian marriage, based on rights over one's own person, purposed parenthood, and, increasingly, on the spiritualization of sex and the politicization of motherly love. The argument was no longer for personal autonomy and greater opportunities in place of getting a man (though important strands of women-centered feminism persisted), but for the self-development and self-determination of women *as women* in order to regenerate "the race."

At issue were not only competing styles of femininity, but alternative modes of political activism. Self-sacrifice and self-development competed for priority on the feminist agenda. In the early nineties this can be visualized as a debate between generations of feminists. An "Old Worker" in the review *Shafts* pleads with the new, upwardly-mobile activists:

> [With the power of love in your hearts] you will always know what are the times for sacrifice and what for the working towards the development of your own powers. Sacrifice may be a joy, and through it you may learn more and see farther than you could do in any other way. ("Old Worker" 127)

Increasingly, however, where the earlier campaigners had transformed the passive labels of purity and goodness into "active spirituality and passionate social service" (qtd. in Bland 145) the new theorists were re-evaluating maternity (in ideal conditions) as an index of female moral superiority, and as a basis for political intervention. While Mona Caird distrusted the martyrdom ethic as personally stultifying, as giving rise to accusations of hysteria, and as dangerously complicitous with tyranny, as time went on, aspirations to martyrdom were rehabilitated as one extreme of a continuum of activism embracing self-sacrifice, service and celibacy, but analogous to motherhood.

A historically nuanced reading of the *Autobiography* might reasonably ask whether Besant writes as a New Woman in the 1890s sense. In some ways, Besant was too old to identify herself with these changes in femininity and sexual politics. She was already saddled with a failed marriage, and had ignominiously failed to keep her children. Radical in so much else, in the discussion of her own sexuality she adopts a fastidious attitude of compromised celibacy. But the new identification of activism as self-sacrificing motherhood displaced from biology provided Besant with compatible subject positions as both "feminine" and feminist.

Theosophy reinforced this possibility by providing a metaphysics of maternal activism. Its emphasis on self-sacrifice, its high evaluation of the feminine, its grounding in evolutionary theory, made theosophy popular among politically active middle-class Englishwomen well into the twentieth century. Besant articulates this in terms of theosophical cosmology.

> For there is one thing greater even than duty, and that is when all action is done as sacrifice. Now, what does that mean? There would be no world, no you, no I, if there had not been a primary sacrifice by which a fragment of the Divine Thought sheathed itself in matter, limited itself in order that you and I might become self-consciously Divine. (*Spiritual Life* 16)

The fullest case for theosophy's compatibility with feminism, femininity and evolution was to be argued in Charlotte Despard's pamphlet *Theosophy and the Woman's Movement* of 1913. By this time Besant had other fish to fry. Still, the formulations sketched by Despard in the context of the militant suffragism of the pre-war period can be seen as the logical outcome of the discursive negotiations of Besant's *Autobiography* twenty years earlier: feminist political activity is written up as the passivity of the martyr, the natural impulse of the mother, and hence as a necessary, inevitable step in human evolution (which for the theosophists includes spiritual regeneration and spiritual "progress"). Theosophy offered a discourse of feminism which underwrote specific intervention – in this case militant suffragism – while guaranteeing an ever-widening arena of concern.[7]

Whether or not the historical Annie Besant genuinely thought of herself as politically maternal, whether or not she identified herself fully with the (as it now appears) more dubious aspects of theosophy; whether or not, finally, she wanted to be a martyr: these questions may miss the point. What matters, surely, is that all these subject positions were available to her, as writer, as woman, as reformer, as believer. I take my lead here from the excellent work of Alex Owen, who comes to similar conclusions about the even more slippery phenomena of spiritualism in the 1860s and 70s:

> Even as spiritualists reaffirmed the normative feminine ideal, their practice undermined it. Passivity, a vital element in the construction of femininity, became, in spiritualist hands, an invitation to power and subversion. Although it was thought to guarantee weakness and submissiveness in the female sex, passivity was the key concept in a spiritualist understanding of the mechanics of spirit possession. Believers acknowledged it to be an innate element of the female make-up but, as with illness, validated it as a powerful and facilitating quality. Once again, spiritualists reinforced the notion of immutable gender difference but privileged the very attribute used elsewhere to signify female inadequacy. (209)

Like the spiritualists' devotion to passivity, Besant's fantasy of martyrdom is an invitation to power and subversion – within surprisingly elastic limits. How Besant went on to deploy this power in later life is another story, but it is worth remembering that all the discourses I have touched on – feminism, theosophy, social Darwinism, maternal activism – must be seen within the context of a bourgeois and imperialist ideology which, then as now, used self-sacrifice as the moral justification for intervention on a global scale. The next time Annie Besant's voice is heard, it is from India.

I return, with Alex Owen's comments in mind, to the question of women's autobiography. In an important article of 1981, Myra Jehlen suggested that gender was primarily a relationship *to* rather than *in* writing: a function of the "prior choosing and acting" which made writing for women transgressive. She argued that

> the autonomous individuality of a woman's story or poem is framed by engagement, the engagement of its denial of dependence. We might think of the form this necessary denial takes (however it is individually interpreted, whether conciliatory or assertive) as analogous to genre, in being an issue, not of content, but of the structural formulation of the work's relationship to the inherently formally patriarchal language which is the only language we have. (582)

The ambiguous apologia which constitutes Besant's denial of dependence – her insistence upon herself as a failed martyr – is analogous to genre in precisely this way. Superimposed on and in tension with the

"apologia of the convert," which is in effect the genre of mainstream
Victorian autobiography, is the complex structure of assertion and
denial which (in this case) genders genre feminine: the apologia of the
would-be self-sacrifice.

But if gender is analogous to genre, we must not forget that genre
itself varies historically. Autobiography, in fact, bears the double
burden of being both determined by, and itself embodying history.
Located at the particular conjunction of the historically contingent and
the discursively necessary, autobiography's theoretically fragile but
politically tenacious relationship to "real life" makes it especially
ticklish to both humanist and poststructuralist generalizations. I
borrow a timely reminder of this from black feminist criticism:

> A literary tradition, even an autobiographical tradition, consti-
> tutes something more than a running, unmediated account of
> the experience of a particular group. The coherence of such a
> tradition consists as much in unfolding strategies of representa-
> tion as in experience itself. Some would even argue that the
> coherence of a tradition is only to be sought in the strategies of
> representation: the self is a function of discourse – a textual
> construct – not of experience at all. Others, including many
> black feminist critics, would emphasize black women's writing as
> personal testimony to oppression, thus emphasizing experience
> at the expense of text. Neither extreme will do. The coherence of
> black women's autobiographical discourse does incontrovertibly
> derive from black women's experience, although less from
> experience in the narrow empirical sense than from condition –
> the condition or interlocking structures of gender, class, and race.
> But it derives even more from the tension between condition and
> discourse, from the changing ways in which black women writers
> have attempted to *represent a personal experience of condition
> through available discourses* and in interaction with imagined
> readers. (Fox-Genovese 65, emphasis added)

In arguing that Besant's romance of self as failed martyr represents a
gendered, and hence generic relationship to autobiography, I must
recall that the specificity of this relationship derives, in its turn, from
the discourses of identity – of femininity and feminism, of race and class
– available in the 1890s: available, more accurately, to Annie Besant as
a white, middle-class woman choosing to write. The elusive character
of women's autobiography can thus be traced to this three-way transposition: gender takes on the structure of genre; genre adopts the
lineaments of history; and history embodies the conditions of gender.

Hence, in a feminist reading of autobiography, gender, genre and history must dance together.

NOTES

1. See Juhasz. The fullest version of this thesis can be found in Jelinek.
2. Brodzki and Schenck make a similar point about the anthology titled *The Female Autograph* (12–13).
3. See also *Autobiographical Sketches* and *1875–1891: A Fragment of Autobiography*.
4. The *Autobiography* ends:

   > In life, through death, to life, I am but the servant of the great Brotherhood, and those on whose heads but for a moment the touch of the Master has rested in blessing can never again look upon the world save through eyes made luminous with the radiance of the Eternal Peace.
   >   PEACE TO ALL BEINGS (332)

5. See for example, Peers 11; Martineau II 148–9; Hurston 108; and Rosemary Manning's autobiography of a failed suicide, *A Time and a Time: An Autobiography*.
6. Cf. Besant, *Autobiography* 64–5.
7. Three quotations may give a sense of Despard's argument:

   > But what does it mean? Nothing short of this – that the spiritual voices which are going out into the world to-day have found their most ardent response in the heart of woman. Over and over again worldly-wise people have questioned the warrior-women, have asked, "Why do you do these things? Would it not be better to be quiet and wait?" The answer is always the same. "We don't know why. We cannot help ourselves. We must go on until we die and then others will come to take our place, for our cause cannot die." (22)

   > Woman, it should ever be remembered, is an example in herself of what the law of Duty and the deeper law of Sacrifice mean. Giving, often in pain and weariness, sometimes in danger: surrendering, when the imperative summons calls, her life for the life of the coming world, which in her, as in a shrine, lives and moves! doing this generally as a natural thing, imposed upon her by her own mother – Nature – woman, in the natural order of things, comes nearer to the Great Law and its observance than man. (46)

   > Sacrifice? Yes! more gladly than ever before she will render that, but it will be to the race that needs her, that cannot move forward without her help, and so in joyful obedience to law she rises out of the subjection of the curse into the blessed and glorious liberty of the sons of God. (47)

WORKS CITED

Barber, Mary A.S. *Bread-Winning; or the Ledger and the Lute: An Autobiography.* London: William MacIntosh, 1865.
Besant, Annie. *An Autobiography.* Adyar Madras: Theosophical Publishing House, 1939.
——. *Autobiographical Sketches.* London: Freethought Publishing, 1885.
——. *1875–1891: A Fragment of Autobiography.* Adyar Madras: Theosophical Publishing House, 1917.

——. *Spiritual Life for the Man of the World*. Adyar Madras: Theosophical Publishing House, 1914.
Bland, Lucy. "The Married Woman, the 'New Woman' and the Feminist: Sexual Politics of the 1890s." *Equal or Different: Women's Politics 1800–1914*. Ed. Jane Rendall. Oxford: Basil Blackwell, 1987.
Brodzki, Bella and Celeste Schenck, eds. *Life/Lines: Theorizing Women's Autobiography*. Ithaca: Cornell UP, 1988.
Caird, Mona. "A Moral Renaissance." *The Morality of Marriage and Other Essays on the Status & Destiny of Woman*. London: George Redway, 1897.
de Man, Paul. "Autobiography as De-Facement." *Modern Language Notes* 94 (1979): 919–30.
Despard, C. *Theosophy and the Women's Movement*. London: Theosophical Publishing Society, 1913.
Dinnage, Rosemary. *Annie Besant*. Harmondsworth: Penguin, 1986.
Fleishman, Avrom. *Figures of Autobiography: The Language of Self-Writing in Victorian and Modern England*. Berkeley: U of California P, 1983.
Fox-Genovese, Elizabeth. "My Statue, My Self: Autobiographical Writings of Afro-American Women." *The Private Self: Theory and Practice of Women's Autobiographical Writings*. Ed. Shari Benstock. Chapel Hill, N.C.: U of North Carolina P, 1988. 63–89.
Hurston, Zora Neale. *Dust Tracks on a Road*. New York: Arno P/New York Times, 1969.
Jacobson, Dan. Introduction. *The Story of an African Farm*. By Olive Shreiner. Harmondsworth: Penguin, 1987.
Jehlen, Myra. "Archimedes and the Paradox of Feminist Criticism." *Signs* 6 (1981): 575–601.
Jelinek, Estelle. *The Tradition of Women's Autobiography: From Antiquity to the Present*. Boston: Twayne, 1986.
Juhasz, Suzanne. "Towards a Theory of Form in Feminist Autobiography: Kate Millett's *Flying* and *Sita*; Maxine Hong Kingston's *The Woman Warrior*." *Women's Autobiography: Essays in Criticism*. Ed. Estelle Jelinek. Bloomington: Indiana UP, 1980. 221–37.
Kristeva, Julia. "Women's Time." *The Kristeva Reader*. Ed. Toril Moi. Oxford: Basil Blackwell, 1986. 187–213.
Linton, Lynn. "The Wild Women as Politicians." *The Nineteenth Century* 30 (1891): 79–88.
Manning, Rosemary. *A Time and a Time: An Autobiography*. 1971; 2nd rev. ed. London: Marion Boyars, 1986.
Martineau, Harriet. *Autobiography*. 2 vols. London: Virago, 1983.
Monteith, Moira. *Women's Writing: A Challenge to Theory*. Brighton: Harvester, 1986.
"Old Worker." Letter. *Shafts* (24 Dec. 1892): 127.
Oppenheim, Janet. "The Odyssey of Annie Besant." *History Today* 39 (Sept. 1989): 12–18.
Owen, Alex. *The Darkened Room: Women, Power and Spiritualism in Late Nineteenth Century England*. London: Virago, 1989.
Peers, E. Allison ed. *Saint Teresa of Jesus: The Complete Works*. 3 vols. Trans. E. Allison Peers. London: Sheed and Ward, 1963.
Stanton, Domna C. "Autogynography: Is the Subject Different?" *The Female Autograph*. Ed. Domna C. Stanton. Chicago: U of Chicago P, 1987. 3–20.
Warner, Marina. *Joan of Arc: The Image of Female Heroism*. Harmondsworth: Penguin, 1983.

Engendered Autobiographies:
The Diary as a Feminine Form

REBECCA HOGAN

At the beginning of *Reading in Detail: Aesthetics and the Feminine*, Naomi Schor asks, "Is the detail feminine?" (11). In this essay, I want to ask an equally direct question, "Is the diary feminine?". The obvious answer is no, since the names of many justly famous and many less well-known male diarists will instantly spring to mind.[1] On the other hand, if we follow Schor and a number of other feminist critics in defining "femininity" as "a set of culturally defined characteristics" (Moi 182), while "male" and "female" are used to indicate biological differences, it is possible to see how we may describe a writing strategy or literary form as "feminine" or "masculine" regardless of the sex of its practitioner or author. While it would undoubtedly be both illuminating and rewarding to study the presence of the feminine in diaries written by men, my inquiry here will be a more limited one. My purpose in this essay, then, is to combine an exploration of the particular congeniality of diary writing as a preferred form of auto-biography for many women with an examination of what we might call the historical "feminization" of the diary in the last hundred years.

With the aid of Schor's historical study of the "feminization" of the detail, I will return to my initial questions. These two questions are closely linked since the diary is *par excellence* the genre of the detail. Diaries embody the use of detail woven into the whole fabric of what Schor calls

> a larger semantic network, bounded on the one side by the *ornamental*, with its traditional connotations of effeminacy and decadence, and on the other, by the *everyday*, whose "prosiness" is rooted in the domestic sphere of social life presided over by women. (4)

Suzanne Juhasz has characterized the diary as the "classic verbal articulation of dailiness" (224). The importance of both the ornamental and the everyday detail is also stressed by Elizabeth Hampsten in her study of midwestern working women's diaries. She makes an analogy between attention to household arts and to form in writing,

> for it is clear that they lavished upon writing the same care for detail and pleasure in design we see and hear of in dressmaking, embroidery, quilting, darning and mending, baking, preserving, arranging houses, and gardening. All these primarily utilitarian chores women often transformed (and still do) beyond practical use into art, and they did the same with writing. (80–1)

If the detail *is* feminine as Schor suggests, then the diary, which valorizes the detail in both the realms of ornament and everyday, can also be seen as feminine.

Another strand to this inquiry into the "femininity" of the diary exists in the realm of generic definition – "Is the diary autobiography?". A number of current critics of autobiography have suggested that the diary – fragmentary, constructed by associative rather than logical connections, concentrating on the everyday (for which to some extent read "trivial" and "ephemeral"), lacking a sense of the architectonics of shape or plot, non-teleological – is somehow *feminine*; while the autobiography – finished, polished, carefully constructed, providing a shaped image of existence seen from the teleological perspective of the end of a life – is somehow *masculine*.[2] In other words, to borrow the distinction Jane Gallop makes in "Annie LeClerc Writing a Letter, With Vermeer," "Women write letters" – personal, intimate, in relation; men write books – universal, public, in general circulation (143). Substitute diaries for letters and autobiographies for books and she has captured perfectly the relative places and valuations of the two types of life-writing in contemporary criticism.

Even ground-breaking feminist work on autobiography, with its brisk attacks on the male-centered canon, has not always escaped these negative valuations of the diary. In "Toward Conceptualizing Diary," one of the few theoretical examinations of the diary as a "serial narrative form" perfectly designed to capture the multi-layered and contradictory nature of self and reality, Felicity Nussbaum celebrates its resistance to wholeness, unity, and formal closure (128, 132). Surprisingly, on the other hand, in *Interpreting Women's Lives: Feminist Theory and Personal Narratives*, the Personal Narratives Group chooses autobiographies, biographies and life histories over diaries and letters as preferred objects of study because these more unified and shaped narrative texts "illuminate the course of a life over time and allow for its interpretation in its historical and cultural context." They prefer the shaped "life narrative" because it "forces the author to move from accounts of discrete experiences to an account of why and how the life took the shape it did" (4). Though five of the sixteen essays in their collection are studies of diaries, and though their explicit purpose is to celebrate women's life-writing, they implicitly undervalue the form of autobiography that both Margot Culley in *One Day at a Time* and Harriet Blodgett in *Centuries of Female Days* have suggested is most characteristic of and congenial to women, though neither argues that it is a feminine form in an essentialist sense (Culley 3–4; Blodgett 5). Even more strikingly, the Group's objections to diaries reflect the prejudices of more formalist and canonical critics. However, as Harriet Blodgett writes: "the most speculative aesthetic issue raised by feminist criticism ... is not whether the diary is art, but whether the diary is in some literary sense a characteristically female form or one for which women have a temperamental affinity" (5). As can be seen then, there is a close link between the question raised about the gender and the question raised about the genre of the diary.

The problem of discussing the diary as a genre and defining its boundaries lies in its capaciousness as a form.[3] If we consider the diary from the point of view of the writer, we can see its ability to entertain multiple purposes and intentions, often contradictory. If we think about the diary in terms of the reader, we can see that it has a wide range of audiences on a continuum from a confidante for the private self to the wider audience of a published diary. This is a problem similar to the one we face when discussing the novel as a genre; either our generic definition will be trivial and impossibly broad (a long prose fiction), or there will be dozens of "genres" of the novel (romance, *Bildungsroman*, and *Künstlerroman*, to name only a few). Saying that the novel is a genre is like calling poetry a genre. Instead I prefer to see poetry and novel as larger *forms* divided into a number of genres. The diary too is such a form whose genres include historical record (frontier diaries), spiritual search (seventeenth-century religious confessional diaries), search for self (Mary MacClane, Anaïs Nin), "epistolary diary" (Boswell's *London Journal*), pure description (nature or travel diaries). In practice each diary will probably mix two or more genres.

We might also envision a continuum from the private unpublished manuscript diary to one edited, and even to some degree written, for publication. A historical record first motivated by a desire to make a mark of the writer's existence or to leave the trace of the events of a writer's life might very easily move into a process of reflection and self-discovery, and even to thoughts of publication during the writer's life. What these texts have in common is their accumulation of discrete entries (not all diarists write daily), their cyclical, repetitive and cumulative structure, their capturing of a series of "present moments" in the diarist's life, their unfinishedness. As Suzanne Bunkers has said, diaries embody "life as *process*, not *product*" (15).

Let us then pursue the question "Is the diary feminine?" with an eye to some specific formal and generic features of the diary, features of its structure, of its writer's motivation for keeping it, and of its language. The structure will be examined in terms of the diary's privileging of the detail and of the perspective of immersion. Motivation (which varies greatly from diarist to diarist) will be examined on both an historical and intentional continuum from diary as document to diary as "inner sanctum," linking this to the increasing "feminization" of the private, the domestic, and the inner life over the last hundred years. Language will be examined to see how it compares to *l'écriture féminine*, the descriptions and theories of "feminine writing" offered by a number of French critics. My last move will be to try to describe and formulate a tentative "feminine aesthetic of the diary" and suggest how it could be further developed.

In her "feminist archaeology," Schor studies the "rise of the detail" (4), beginning with the neo-classical scorn of the detail and tracing its "ongoing valorization" (3) as it came "to assume its commanding position in the field of representation." She shows that, historically, "the detail is gendered and doubly gendered as feminine" (4). We are of course familiar with the importance of a profusion of concrete details in substantiating the "truth to life" sought by nineteenth-century realistic fiction and representational painting. Indeed "detailism" and Realism become to some extent synonymous terms.[4]

In her study of the detail as feminine, Schor explains that neo-classicism's complaint against the detail was based in the problem of perspective, that is, in the idea that "a profusion of details leads to a loss of perspective" (21). She quotes from Baudelaire's *Le peintre de la vie moderne* to show the neo-classical sense of the danger of the detail (especially of the multiplicity of details): "The more our artist turns an impartial eye on detail, the greater is the state of *anarchy*. Whether he be long-sighted or short-sighted, *all hierarchy and all subordination vanishes*" (21). Concentrating on details, and especially treating all of them "impartially," allowing ourselves to be inundated by the detail of a scene or story will lead to a loss of distance, hierarchy, and subordination. Details threaten orders based on dominance; they get too close; we become immersed.

Here again we see the connection of the "feminine" detail to the "feminine" diary – as Suzanne Juhasz says, "the perspective of the diarist is immersion, not distance" (224). Notice that, for her, immersion in a profusion of details *is* a perspective, not a loss of perspective as it is for neo-classical critics. The neo-classical aesthetic privileges perspective as *distance*. The very immersion feared by this aesthetic is a common generic feature of the diary, and may also help to account for its low status in the canon and among critics of auto-biography. The privileging of the detail in the diary form gives it a structure and perspective which have been culturally and historically seen as feminine.

Along with the structure and perspective of diary form, moti-vations for diary-keeping seem also to show a historical movement toward diary-writing as a primarily feminine activity. Considering the "femininity" of the diary from a historical point of view, Margo Culley explains that diary literature became the province of women writers in the late nineteenth and twentieth centuries because of the "emergence of the self as the subject of the diary" (3). Culley places the modern idea of the diary "as the arena of the 'secret' inner life," as "a record of private thoughts and feelings to be kept hidden from others' eyes," in "roughly ... the last one hundred years" (3). The establishment of "privacy" as one of the generic features of the diary form coincided with the increasing consignment of women and their work to the private domestic realm by industrial civilization. In the course of the nine-teenth century, "those aspects of culture associated with the private became the domain of women" (3). The image of an inner life – the life of personal reflection and emotion – became increasingly bound up with the image of the private sphere (woman's sphere), and women "continued to turn to the diary as one place where they were permitted, indeed encouraged, to indulge full 'self-centeredness' " (4). Almost as if the self retreated from the world, or the public sphere, into the diary, or the private sphere, into "a book of one's own" as Thomas Mallon has called the diary. Here we trace the development of the modern idea of the diary as private, secret, locked – the paradoxical idea of a writing which will remain unread, a sort of "silent" text. If we see "feminine" as a cultural signifier, standing for the historically determined social construction of feminine behavior, psychological characteristics, and the like, then the diary is a feminine form.

The development by French theorists such as Hélène Cixous, Luce Irigaray, and Julia Kristeva of the idea of "*l'écriture féminine*" may provide a promising network of terms for creating a theory of diary-writing. Like the "perspective of immersion," the overwhelmingness of detail feared by the neo-classical critics, *l'écriture féminine* is seen as potentially subversive of the structures, logic, and syntax of masculine language. And the terms used to describe this *écriture féminine* seem to be very close to the terms often used to describe diaries or women's autobiographies. Christiane Makward characterizes this "new feminine writing" with a list of "key words: open, non-linear, unfinished, fluid, exploded, fragmented, polysemic ..." which seem to exemplify perfectly the diary form (96). Discussing the same idea in "Inscribing Femininity: French Theories of the Feminine," Ann Rosalind Jones describes "a set of stylistic and formal tendencies widely recognized in *l'écriture féminine*: double or multiple voices, broken syntax, repetitive or cumulative rather than linear structure, open endings" (88). These terms have also often been used to describe diaries. A diary is a text composed of "fragments" which nevertheless flow continually through the days. The text is by its very nature open-ended, unfinished and incomplete, in some cases ending only with the life of the writer. A diary is both repetitive and cumulative, each entry discrete (and discreet), and each entry an addition to the flow of days.

Like *l'écriture féminine*, then, diary-writing can perhaps be seen as a potentially subversive form of writing because it tends to cross and blur boundaries between things traditionally kept separate. Since the diary records the thoughts and feelings of past selves and present self without necessarily privileging one voice or stage of life over the others, it crosses the boundaries between self and others. Because the diarist both creates and reads the text, the diary crosses or blurs the boundaries between author and reader. Because diarists preserve experiences in writing, trying to record and reflect on life, diary-writing blurs or crosses the boundaries between text and experience, art and life. Diaries are elastic, inclusive texts, which mix chronicle, historical record, reflection, feelings, descriptions of nature, travel, work accomplished, and portraiture of character rather haphazardly together. Like Nancy Chodorow's much-cited description of the female ego as more fluid than that of the male (the famous "permeable ego boundaries" [93]), the diary is a form open to closer relations between world and text, author and text, reader and text. This description of the diary suggests an affirmative answer to the question "Is the diary feminine?", and also suggests that at least as a cultural form or artifact it has *processed* (as opposed to *progressed*) historically into something that the cultural signifier "feminine" describes. Nonetheless I am wary of using that term in a way which would imply some kind of "feminine essence" that erases differences among a large and various body of women's texts – differences of class, race, historical period, intentions and motivations. But what I do see as fruitful in this inquiry into the gender and genre of the diary are the possibilities it offers for new kinds of reading and writing, and for new valuations of recovered as well as of contemporary diaries.

What can be enjoyed in and perhaps developed out of a study of diaries is a revolutionary form of construction put into practice in what I see as a "founding essay" for a new theory of the diary, Rachel Blau DuPlessis's "For the Etruscans; Sexual Difference and Artistic Production – The Debate over a Female Aesthetic." What DuPlessis both discusses and embodies in the thought and style of this essay is the principle of what she calls "radical parataxis" (136).[5] She invents the term to describe the narrative structure of Monique Wittig's *Les Guérillères*, which she describes as "a form of verbal quilt. We hear her lists, her unstressed series, no punctuation even, no pauses, no setting apart, and so everything joined with no subordination, no ranking" (136). In the diary, of course, entries *are* set apart, and there is the punctuation of dates between them, but they are not ranked or subordinated or necessarily linked in any way except in being written by the same diarist. Grammatically, parataxis describes a sentence structure in which related clauses are placed in a series without the use of connecting words (I came, I saw, I conquered) or clauses related only by the coordinating conjunctions. In other words, there is no subordination to suggest that one idea or event is more important than another; the clauses are "equal" in grammatical structure and rhetorical force. But the kind of parataxis DuPlessis uses to describe a new form of writing "based on" the diary or journal operates beyond the grammatical level to become the organizing principle of the text on the level of syntax, relations between diary entries, and content as well.

The way the principle of parataxis works in diary form is not so much on the level of the sentence (though we often find it there too), but on the level of larger diary structure in the relationships existing from entry to entry, from month to month, from year to year. Transitions between entries are usually marked by a new date (often the day and even time of day are given too), but not by any articulated link to the previous entry. Elizabeth Hampsten recognizes the same principle of style and organization in the working women's diaries she studies. For example, describing the diary Grace DeCou kept for over forty years, she writes:

> Sentence parts are short with almost no connectives except *and*; she uses few modifiers, a high proportion of short concrete nouns and pronouns, and verbs of simple action. Nouns and verbs repeatedly refer to time, to weather, money, business, domestic activities. Should anything out of the ordinary occur, that event is fitted as closely as possible into the pattern. (70)

As examples of this paratactic structure, let us look at two entries, one from 1894, the other from 1935.

> July 11, 1894, Wednesday. Jasper came at 5 am to take Mother to Isaac. Their baby is very sick. Isaac came up about noon. The baby died before Mother got there. Isaac went to Sam's for dinner. He wanted me to go down town with him so I called at Sam's for him. Flossie Taylor came after some pieces of Bird and Belle's dresses. Belle and Bird came after their waist, paid me $3.25. I went down town this evening. (qtd. in Hampsten 70)

The report of events flows evenly into the diary, this sickness and death of the baby taking its place horizontally and without special emphasis between mealtimes, errands, chores. An even more striking example comes from the 1935 diary about the illness and death of her husband.

> May 2, 1935, Sunday. Quite nice. T.H. is no better, just as crazy as ever broke a windowpane with rocking chair. Mrs. Fisher, Mrs. Alexander called, Miss Stanzel came to see my new stove. T.H. passed away this evening at 8 PM. (qtd. in Hampsten 70)

As Elizabeth Hampsten puts it, "So much for T.H." (70). For Hampsten, what is interesting about this diary are not the facts of Grace DeCou's life – "hard work, meticulous care over small sums of money, an intricate network of friends, acquaintances, customers, and relatives ... marriage to a disagreeable and violent man" – but "her way of seeing them, so *apparently without selection or perspective*. No one event appears to color or displace another: prices, visits, trips to town – the pattern invariably reasserts itself" (71, emphasis added). As we saw earlier, immersion in the horizontal, non-hierarchical flow of events and details – in other words, radical parataxis – seems to be one of the striking features of the diary as a form.

Grace DeCou's apparent lack of selectivity underscores another important feature of diary-writing, its inclusiveness. This feature is also stressed by a diarist better-known (and more self- and form-conscious) than Grace DeCou: Virginia Woolf. An enthusiastic experimenter with diary as well as fictional form, Woolf often reflected on what one might achieve with this capacious form of writing:

> Moreover, there looms ahead of me the shadow of some kind of form which a diary might attain to. I might in the course of time learn what it is that one can make of this loose, drifting material of

life; finding another use for it than the use I put it to, so much more consciously & scrupulously, in fiction. What sort of diary should I like mine to be? Something loose knit, & yet not slovenly, so elastic that it will embrace any thing, solemn, slight or beautiful that comes into my mind. I should like it to resemble some deep old desk, or capacious hold-all, in which one flings a mass of odds and ends without looking them through. (266)

The method is one of inclusion, not exclusion. Because the diary often treats "small" details at the same length as "big" events, experience flows metonymically into the diary; things are put down one after another as they occur to the memory. Only on later rereading do we see or make discriminations about what was "more" or "less" important, interesting, significant. Diaries are not so much inclusive because they contain *everything* from a given day, as they are inclusive in the sense that they do not privilege "amazing" over "ordinary" events, in terms of scope, space, or selection. So as well as being paratactic on the level of grammar and syntax, diaries are paratactic on the level of full entries and of content too. As Woolf says, "the main requisite ... is not to play the part of censor, but to write as the mood comes or of anything whatever" (266). When she rereads later she is "curious to find how I went for things put in haphazard, & found the significance to lie where I never saw it at the time" (266). Everything goes in equally, horizontally, haphazardly – significance emerges later. For Woolf, "the advantage of the method is that it sweeps up accidentally several stray matters which I should exclude if I hesitated, but which are the diamonds of the dustheap" (234).

As an examination of DeCou and Woolf suggests, and as DuPlessis also sees, things in diaries happen *between* – between entries, between events, between diarist as writer and diarist as reader. Because no particular moment of time, event, reflection, feeling, state of mind, or voice is privileged over any other in the diary, the diarist can create an open, elastic form embodying something DuPlessis calls

> an emotional texture, a structural expression of mutuality. Writers know their text as a form of intimacy, of personal contact, whether conversations with the reader or with the self. Letters, journals, voices are sources for this element, ... expressing the porousness and nonhierarchic stances of intimate conversation in both structure and function. (131)

The relation between diarist and reader (both "real" readers of published or circulated diaries, and the reader constructed by a private text) is "mutual" – equal, friendly, open-ended. This possibility for mutual paratactic relations among genres, entries, and voices in the diary, and for paratactical meetings among self, world, experience, and text at the boundaries of the diary are reminiscent of Nancy Chodorow's description of the porousness, elasticity, and relational structure of the feminine ego.

A paratactic form like the diary can be looked at from at least two perspectives, or the concept of parataxis can be seen to have at least two strands. One is parataxis as a kind of even, horizontal, metonymic flow of events and entries into the diary; this creates the sense of *continuity* required by diary-keeping. The other is parataxis as a series of related items, events and entries without the use of connecting links; this creates the sense of discrete, separate entries also required if what is being written is to be accurately called a diary. We get a very clear sense of this seemingly paradoxical nature of parataxis in the diaries kept by Etty Hillesum, a young Jewish woman living in Amsterdam during the years of the Holocaust. Etty often discusses her thirst for writing as a desire to express "many unconnected thoughts" (102). But at other places, she instead stresses the continuity of diary-writing, a "longing to jot down a few words! With such a strong sense of: here on these pages I am spinning my thread. ... It's not so much the imperfect words on these faint blue lines, as the feeling, time and again, of returning to a place from which one can continue to spin one and the same thread, where one can gradually create a continuum, a continuum which is really one's life" (91–2).

May Sarton, an inveterate diarist, as well as a novelist and poet, gives this description of the thirst for diary-writing and the diary's paratactic form:

> I can't stop doing what I have always done, trying to sort out and shape experience. The journal is a good way to do this at a less intense level than by creating a work of art as highly organized as a poem, for instance, or the sustained effort a novel requires. I find it wonderful to have a receptacle into which to pour vivid momentary insights, and a way of ordering day-to-day experience (as opposed to Maslow's "peak experiences," which would require poetry). (27–8)

"A receptacle into which to pour momentary insights" reminds us of Woolf's description of the diary as a "deep old desk or capacious hold-all," but also sees the diary as a way of sorting and ordering daily experience, reminding us that shaping and selection are a necessary part of diary-writing. The process of selection in diary-writing is different from that exercised in autobiography because the basis for selection may be different every time a diarist writes. Which events to describe or experience to reflect on will be selected according to a different set of rules or impulses on each occasion. It is this kind of process which creates the paratactic nature of the diary.

If Schor's archaeology of the "feminine" detail can be applied equally to writing as to painting, then this broadly defined and applied principle of parataxis operating at the levels of structure, motivation, and language seems to provide the basis for a feminine aesthetic of the diary. The diary's valorization of the detail, its perspective of immersion, its mixing of genres, its principle of inclusiveness, and its expression of intimacy and mutuality all seem to qualify it as a form very congenial to women life/writers. Whether confined to the diary by cultural and personal presuppositions about privacy, propriety, and women's place or set free in it to experiment with language, genre, and self, many women have found in diaries a tangible form for saving their lives.

NOTES

I wish to express my gratitude to the National Endowment for the Humanities for my participation in an NEH Summer Seminar, "Issues in Feminist Literary Criticism: Women's Writing in Theory and Practice," directed by Nancy K. Miller at Barnard in 1987 where the initial drafts of this essay were written. To Nancy K. Miller herself and to all the seminar members, Filishia Camara-Norman, Susan Craig, Shirley Lim, Denise Marshall, Susan Nash, Nancy Paxton, Laura Quinn, Donna Serniak, Julia Watson, Eri Yasuhara, and Gabriele Wickert who provided a feminist community of scholarship and friendship in which writing could flourish, my heartfelt thanks.

1. Samuel Pepys, James Boswell, George Fox, Wilfred Scawen Blunt, Harold Nicholson, Ralph Waldo Emerson, Edmund Wilson, Stephen Spender, André Gide, Amiel, to name just a few.
2. Robert Fothergill grants full autobiographical status only to those diaries which most clearly resemble the "book of a life" told in chronological or some other logical order in a way which looks back over the past to discover patterns, to judge, order and select. Estelle Jelinek, in the first book-length study of women's autobiography, simply says: "Though I occasionally refer to diaries, letters, and journals ... I rarely discuss them because I do not consider them autobiographies" (xii). This seems odd since her main criteria for women's autobiographies are that they are "episodic, fragmented, interrupted and formless, like their [writers'] lives" (19). Domna Stanton's "Autogynography: Is the Subject Different?" gives a good review of current theory and study of women's autobiography. In her excellent book, *A Poetics of Women's Autobiography*, Sidonie Smith explicitly (and disappointingly for this study) confines herself to "formal autobiography" (19), excluding journals, letters, diaries, and oral histories. The two newest edited collections of essays on women's autobiography, Shari Benstock's *The Private Self* and Bella Brodski and Celeste Schenck's *Life/Lines*, both include essays on a broader range of auto-

biographical forms (including poetry); Benstock's essay, "Authorizing the Auto-bio-graphical," offers a suggestive reading of Woolf's diaries as a new (and feminine) form of autobiography.

3.	A distinction is sometimes made between the diary as a form for recording events and the journal as a form for reflection and expression of feelings. Some writers call their "books" diaries and others journals, and almost all mix a record of events with feelings, thoughts, reflections, natural description and the like. Therefore, I use these terms interchangeably.

4.	Schor attributes the neologism "detailism" to G.H. Lewes, but says her own use of the term is not, like his, either pejorative or totally synonymous with realism (4).

5.	From the Greek *para*, beside + *tassein*, to place.

WORKS CITED

Benstock, Shari. "Authorizing the Autobiographical." *The Private Self: Theory and Practice of Women's Autobiographical Writings*. Ed. Shari Benstock. Chapel Hill: U of North Carolina P, 1988. 10–33.

Blodgett, Harriet. *Centuries of Female Days: English Women's Private Diaries*. New Brunswick, NJ: Rutgers UP, 1989.

Brodzki, Bella and Celeste Schenck, eds. *Life/Lines: Theorizing Women's Auto-biography*. Ithaca: Cornell UP, 1988.

Bunkers, Suzanne. "Reading and Interpreting Unpublished Diaries by Nineteenth-Century Women." *a/b: Auto/Biography Studies* 2.2 (Summer 1986): 15–17.

Chodorow, Nancy. *The Reproduction of Mothering: Psychoanalysis and the Sociology of Gender*. Berkeley: U of California P, 1978.

Culley, Margo. *A Day at a Time: The Diary Literature of American Women from 1764 to the Present*. New York: The Feminist Press, 1985.

DuPlessis, Rachel Blau. "For the Etruscans: Sexual Differences and Artistic Pro-duction – The Debate over a Female Aesthetic." *The Future of Difference*. Eisen-stein and Jardine. 128–56.

Eisenstein, Hester and Alice Jardine, eds. *The Future of Difference*. Boston: GK Hall, 1980.

Fothergill, Robert A. *Private Chronicles: A Study of English Diaries*. London: Oxford UP, 1974.

Gallop, Jane. "Annie LeClerc Writing a Letter, With Vermeer." *The Poetics of Gender*. Ed. Nancy K. Miller. New York: Columbia UP, 1986. 137–56.

Hampsten, Elizabeth. *Read This Only to Yourself: The Private Writings of Midwestern Women, 1880–1910*. Bloomington: Indiana UP, 1982.

Hillesum, Etty. *An Interrupted Life: The Diaries of Etty Hillesum 1941–1945*. Trans. Arno Pomerans. Introduced by J. G. Gaarlandt. New York: Pantheon, 1983.

Jelinek, Estelle C. *The Tradition of Women's Autobiography From Antiquity to the Present*. Boston: Twayne, 1986.

Jones, Ann Rosalind. "Inscribing Femininity: French Theories of the Feminine." *Making a Difference: Feminist Literary Criticism*. Eds. Gayle Greene and Coppélia Kahn. London: Methuen, 1985. 80–112.

Juhasz, Suzanne. "Towards a Theory of Form in Feminist Autobiography: Kate Millet's *Flying* and *Sita*; Maxine Hong Kingston's *The Woman Warrior*." *Women's Auto-biography: Essays in Criticism*. Ed. Estelle C. Jelinek. Bloomington: Indiana UP, 1980. 221–37.

Makward, Christiane. "To Be or Not to Be ... A Feminist Speaker." Trans. Marlène Barsoum, Alice Jardine and Hester Eisenstein. *The Future of Difference*. Eds. Hester Eisenstein and Alice Jardine. 95–105.

Mallon, Thomas. *A Book of One's Own: People and Their Diaries*. New York: Ticknor & Fields, 1984.

Moi, Toril. "Men Against Patriarchy." *Gender and Theory: Dialogues on Feminist Criticism*. Ed. Linda Kauffman. Oxford: Basil Blackwell, 1989. 181–8.

Nussbaum, Felicity A. "Toward Conceptualizing Diary." *Studies in Autobiography*. Ed. James Olney. New York: Oxford UP, 1988. 128–40.

Personal Narratives Group, eds. *Interpreting Women's Lives: Feminist Theory and Personal Narratives*. Bloomington: Indiana UP, 1989.

Sarton, May. *House by the Sea*. New York: Norton, 1977.

Schor, Naomi. *Reading in Detail: Aesthetics and the Feminine*. New York: Methuen, 1987.

Smith, Sidonie. *A Poetics of Women's Autobiography: Marginality and the Fictions of Self-Representation*. Bloomington: Indiana UP, 1987.

Stanton, Domna C. "Autogynography: Is the Subject Different?" *The Female Autograph*. Ed. Domna C. Stanton. 1984; rpt. Chicago: U of Chicago P, 1987. 3–20.

Woolf, Virginia. *The Diary of Virginia Woolf. Volume I: 1915–1919*. Ed. Anne Olivier Bell. London: Hogarth, 1977.

Delivery: The Cultural Re-presentation of Childbirth

CYNTHIA HUFF

Academically, autobiography has been a male creation. Riding the tide of New Criticism, critics were quick to establish the literary respectability of the genre-to-be, quick to consider autobiography made in the name of the Father and reflecting the making of the Father. Autobiography became the story of the male self constructed by himself and recreating the metaphors of his life. The more the male self dominated autobiography the better the genre.[1] Even though feminist critics now question the androcentric biases of such a male-centered creation myth, they seem nevertheless uncomfortable with the term autobiography. Much recent feminist criticism has suggested alternative concepts: autogynography, lifelines, personal narratives.[2] At issue in each of these designations is the mythology of creation itself. Can a woman *write* herself? Or has she been so *written on* by patriarchal culture that autobiography *per se* cannot exist for her? Does she conceive of her life differently than men conceive of theirs so that masculine metaphors do not represent her as she would represent herself? Is the very form of her creation different from the linear, unitary thrust of male-defined autobiography, perhaps more reflective of relationship and context? Such questions are particularly pertinent for women's writing which delineates a significant life event rather than the form of a life lived, describes an experience which *only* women can have, and, futhermore, characterizes a cultural phenomenon which metaphorically embodies physical as well as textual creation.

I would argue that for these reasons an examination of women's personal accounts of childbirth helps us chart the terrain of autobiography as an expression of textual and cultural production. The metaphors that affect our responses to childbirth attenuate our analysis of birth itself, thus subverting its autobiographical import and in effect silencing birth as a cultural expression of a woman's life. Part of my purpose here is to talk about how the ways in which women give birth and express their birth experience through the medium of writing reflect the dominant culture's mythology.

I think this approach suggests several meanings of delivery. There is the obvious sense of delivery as in a woman being delivered of a child or herself delivering one. There is the sense as well of delivery as the mode of expression. This can include how a woman has her child, but it may also signify the delivery of her experience of parturition textually. Then there is the cultural sense of delivery as the cluster of signifiers which contribute to our sense of delivery as birth. These include delivery as being set free from bondage, as surrendering or handing over, and as sending forth through releasing or discharging. Such multiple references of delivery contribute to how a mother constructs her autobiography.

But usually a woman finds herself textually and ideologically constrained before she can construct her personal story. Generally speaking, contemporary books about childbirth include the how-to-do-it, the medical, and the historical. Although the how-to-do-it books are ostensibly written with the mother's welfare in mind, the underlying purpose of these is to make the woman's experience fit the outlines of medical procedure by informing her how the medical community views birth. The assumption is that a well-informed woman will be a better patient. The emphasis of medical texts is not on the mother's experience but on how she is acted upon by health professionals as they manage her delivery. Some recent histories of childbirth include partial accounts of women's childbirth experiences but these are not presented as examples of women's writing *per se*; instead they are used to buttress arguments about the changing relationships between women and their birth attendants.[3]

Why hasn't childbirth as one of life's major milestones for the mother as well as the child been highlighted as an autobiographical subject? Or to put it another way, why are most of the childbirth accounts we do have embedded in another text so that their textual delivery becomes subsumed by the whole of which they are merely a part? What does the exclusion of childbirth as a "legitimate" subject for consideration by critics of autobiography tell us about the hegemony and gender bias of academic discourse? How does this exclusion reflect critics' participation in the cultural production of the meaning of birth? I would like to venture some speculations about how the critical assumptions of autobiography interact with metaphorical constructs of delivery by talking about the ways in which women's accounts of childbirth experiences illuminate women's self-presentation of birth textually. The texts I plan to consider come from Victorian women's manuscript diaries and from a series of accounts in letters by American women printed in the *Ladies' Home Journal* in the 1950s.

Both of the British women wrote the birth accounts I've selected only a few years apart, at the height of the Victorian era in England, and the cultural contexts of their lives are similar. Both the wives of rectors, Ophelia Powell composed her birth account in 1849 while Frances Elizabeth Blathwayt penned hers in 1853. Ophelia Powell was a dissenter from a village in the south of England and her biography shows familiar outlines for a middle-class English woman of the last century. Born in 1823 and deceased in 1866, she wrote her diary between the ages of 26 and 41. Moderately educated, she spent most of her life in Colyton, a village near Exeter. Her father was a Unitarian minister as was her husband. The wife of the rector of Langridge, a village near Gloucester, Frances Elizabeth Blathwayt was born in 1830 and kept her diary between 1849 and 1868. Like Ophelia Powell, she was moderately educated, though judging from her diary her class position was higher than Powell's, as she writes of activities typical for the gentry such as badger and fox hunting, day school superintendence, and the tenants' dinner.

Particularly interesting for the student of autobiography is the two women's approach to the question of audience, for their diary practices indicate that Victorian women thought of their volumes as family not personal property. Frances Elizabeth Blathwayt speaks of penning her entries while sitting with members of her extended family, and her comments imply that after the writing session the diaries were circulated among those present. Ophelia Powell considers her audience as not only herself but also "those who look on these lines," for she begins the second volume of her diary by intentionally giving a synopsis of her daily employments, her family's home and composition, and her village and its landmarks. Her sense of possible audience marks her diary as a social document which might very well be read by other childbearing women as well as her family. The latter probability is underscored by the existence of diaries composed by the majority of her extended family.[4]

If Victorian women considered their diaries, and the childbirth accounts embedded within them, as familial and social rather than private documents, as twentieth-century scholars have assumed them to be, then their place within the autobiographical canon would seem more secure, for critics have assumed that autobiographies are meant to be read by someone other than the writing self. What I'd like to suggest here is that a culturally based, and culturally biased, under-standing of public and private has helped keep Victorian women's diaries from being accorded the status of autobiography. As a number of feminist theorists have noted, women's writing has been trivialized simply because it is written by women. Women are assumed *a priori* to write passionate but weak prose about trivial, quotidian subjects which would only interest, at best, other women.[5] It is not a question of whether or not women *have* an audience for their writing, but *who* this audience is, and, if it is made up in part of men, whether the subject matter and the style interest them, since men have been the primary critics. Given such circumstances, women penning their childbirth accounts would seem to be out of the running for any acclaim as autobiographers.

How then do women create themselves textually when they compose their accounts of physical creation? Both Ophelia Powell and Frances Elizabeth Blathwayt follow a format, which is a typical practice among the childbirth accounts I found while researching fifty-eight manuscript diaries of nineteenth-century British women. Powell records the birth of her four children in her diary, a sporadically daily account whose regularity depends on constraints of time and physical health. The entry detailing the birth of her first child in 1857 is typical. Ophelia's description of the delivery follows a format which scrupulously notes when she was taken ill, who attended her confinement, the precise time of the birth and her reactions to it:

> Monday 9 Feeling worse than usual this evening Sent for our good friend Mrs. Batstone who had promised to be with me during my confinement, also for the nurse Mrs. Mitchell and Mr. Gillett who arrived about 12 at night. Oh how thankful I felt when I heard his wheels stop at our door – After 12 hours of extreme pain and suffering, and Mr. Gillett's judicious use of instruments at 25 minutes after four o'clock on Tuesday morning Sept–8–1857 Mr. G announced the birth of a perfect little boy Mr. Gillett remained with us till the middle of the day. (1849)

The formatted nature of Ophelia Powell's description of her son's birth, as well as her inclusion of it in a diary obviously intended to be read by others, may well signify multiple meanings of physical and linguistic delivery. The fear experienced by Ophelia and her reliance on her birth attendants indicate the socio-historical context for her autobiography of birth. She had every reason to be afraid for her life, for the childbearing years were the only time in a Victorian women's life when her health was in more jeopardy than a man's, a fact recognized by the Registrar General in his summary statement for 1870 (Thirty-Third Annual Report x, 121, 123).

Expressions of anxiety and fear also figure in Frances Elizabeth Blathwayt's account. The birth of her first son occurred after forty-eight hours of difficult labor, leaving her an invalid for four months.

When her second confinement in 1853 is much easier than anticipated, she is very happily surprised.

> Monday 26th in the course of two hours or rather less a fine stout boy was shouting lustily on Ellen's [her sister's] knee, she being the only person in the house besides Wynter [her husband] who knew of the event. To my astonishment as well as the other two for I could hardly believe the dreaded time was over. It was sometime before Mama appeared or Mr. Sutton, & I roared at their faces of surprise. We were all too thankful. (n.pag.)

As the "we" of the last sentence implies, the fears surrounding childbirth were experienced by both mother and family, and often the after-effects presented even more cause for distress on the part of both. Childbed fevers accounted for more than twice as many deaths in the latter half of 1837 than did childbirth itself. Mothers often had metria in combination with other diseases, so that the Registrar-General's report lists such causes of death as childbed and rheumatic fever, childbed with measles, and childbed followed by epilepsy (First Annual Report 82–3). Sheila Ryan Johansson argues that consumption was a greater threat to Victorian women than childbirth or its after-effects, but she concedes that giving birth was likely to damage a woman's health. Although there is no statistical evidence to support the causal relation between pregnancy and increased signs of consumption, Victorian doctors believed such a connection existed (Johansson 169–70). Even if a woman was lucky enough to escape the worst perils of childbirth or puerperal fever, her health might well have been damaged enough to subject her to consumption or other diseases.

The perils of physical creation might well bring about long periods of inactivity or even death for Victorian women. Futhermore, Victorian ideology separated people into the categories of well and unwell; a Victorian woman who had to confront the possibility of enforced confinement through the prolonged ill health frequently associated with parturition complications had to deal psychologically with her categorization as an unproductive member in a culture which valued industry. Ironically, even though motherhood constituted the quintessential attainment for a woman in the last century, delivery might imply not activity but passivity.

The ideology which simultaneously derived from, yet contributed to the cultural construction of birth, has corollaries in a Victorian woman's sense of herself as a creative force. If giving birth meant becoming ill, she would think of herself as potentially unfit and useless during parturition and view other forms of creation as destructive powers to be avoided lest they put her well-being in jeopardy. There was certainly cultural support for women's belief in creativity, whether physical or artistic, as enervating and perhaps hysteria-producing.

Charlotte Perkins Gilman's *The Yellow Wallpaper* provides a literary example of the linkage between physical and artistic creativity as strenuous and dangerous activities for women. The unnamed narrator, who presumably suffers from nervous tension occasioned by the cares of childbirth and childrearing, is denied any form of artistic creativity by her doctor/husband, who orders her not to write in her journal because this will unnecessarily tire her. Such a command from a doctor/ husband points to how both the physical bodies and the bodies of writing of women have been inscribed by men ordering them to abstain from, and silence, their creative powers. In fact the gaps and lapses of Victorian women's manuscript diaries, especially the gaps in their journals that occur before, during, and after childbirth, signify both patriarchal silencing and the cultural marginalization that accompanied "being unwell" in Victorian society. The absent text suggests that omissions are fully as important as inclusions in self-writing by women.

Yet other connotations associated with the cultural construction of birth and delivery imply women's passivity and the imperative of male cultural intervention. In her entry of 27 September, Ophelia Powell thanks God for allowing her recovery and refers to being churched. Churching is defined in the *Oxford English Dictionary* as "the public appearance of a woman at church to return thanks after childbirth, especially in accordance with the Anglican ritual." Although the Victorian construction of churching emphasizes God's help in delivering a woman from disease, the roots of churching in purification ceremonies are nonetheless real. A woman who had given birth in the nineteenth century might not explicitly be told she had been defiled and was a target for Satan, but birth still symbolized a religious dread from which God's agents must deliver women. The formulaic nature of purification ceremonies with their rigid emphasis on control of women's bodies through their designation as unclean and in need of purging may well have affected the way Victorian women structured their childbirth accounts. As I pointed out earlier, these accounts follow a specific format, which in itself suggests that childbearing women conceptualize physical and literary creation ritualistically. The outlines of their portraits seem to deviate from those limned by the male autobiographers who are most praised by critics for their ability to construct an individual self. Instead, the formulaic delineations by Victorian women penning their childbirth entries point to a ritual bonding among women, a simultaneous sense of themselves as part of a female group, but one which is nevertheless judged as lesser by the dominant male culture.

But if the cultural constructs of birth and delivery suggest ideological control of women by men during childbirth, they also point to a support system of women, a validation of the Victorian "separate sphere" as a positive cultural space for women to bond psychologically but also as an idea which was actually realized as a physical location. Ophelia Powell's account mentions two female attendants and in her later birth narratives more women, especially family members, are present. Similarly, Frances Elizabeth Blathwayt was attended by her female relatives, for her 1853 account refers to her sister's being present during the birth and her mother's missing it only because it was so rapid. Victorian women were expected to assist other women during childbirth, and their diaries show the concern and anxiety they experienced during others' confinement. Nineteenth-century diarists commonly report rereading their diaries as well as those of other women so that these began to take on the character of a collective autobiography, the recounting of a group experience. The sense of delivery implied here is of women helping others to prepare themselves by offering their textual construction of birth as well as their physical assistance. In her Victorian manuscript diary Mrs. S. M. Miers, the wife of a shipbuilder in Rio de Janeiro, writes of repeatedly assisting friends and relatives through difficult birthing experiences. The exactness of the diary entries, which picture the process of birth and its consequences, would have helped break the silence surrounding the patriarchial taboo on birth as an unfit subject for self-revelation. In particular, critics of autobiography who have insisted that a well-delineated life must capture the writer's public persona have excluded by fiat much of women's writing about childbirth, which, by its very subject matter, is considered too personal to be of interest even though we are all of woman born. The traditional gender-marked metaphor of the masculine self who achieves identity by contesting alone the forces which buffet him is inappropriate for describing childbearing women. As Frances Elizabeth Blathwayt's account shows, women conceptualize themselves relationally rather than individually. Her entry pictures the reactions of others to the birth as equally important with her own, for she comments that "we were all too thankful" that the birth went well.

In 1958 and 1959, over one hundred years after Frances Elizabeth Blathwayt expressed her thanks for a safe delivery, American women were using the pages of a popular magazine, the *Ladies' Home Journal*,

Delivery: The Cultural Re-presentation of Childbirth   115

to voice their birth experiences. Their accounts, written in response to a letter from a registered nurse printed earlier in the *Journal*, indicate changes in the cultural meaning of creation and suggest, as well, the ramifications this has for its autobiographical delivery. Unlike the diary entries of the Victorian women, the letters printed as part of the exposé "Journal Mothers Report on Cruelty in Maternity Wards" generally describe birth as an anonymous, assembly-line experience whose mechanization perpetuates cruelty and dehumanization. In fact, it was just such a characterization of delivery from a registered nurse which prompted what the *Journal* editors call "a flood of letters" (45). In her letter the registered nurse details standard delivery room practice: long hours of being strapped down in the lithotomy position; nurses slowing down births while physicians have dinner, and cutting and suturing without anaesthetic; women left alone during labor since their families are excluded from the delivery room; callousness and indifference of birth attendants; and the assembly-line mentality of hospitals.

The exact ethnic background of the women whose accounts were part of the *Ladies' Home Journal* exposé is impossible to pinpoint, but from the text of the letters we can make some informed observations about this as well as about the writing self who composed them. The letters indicate that these women are probably largely white and middle-class, of somewhat varying religious persuasions, and from different locales in the United States. Their brief yet poignant auto-biographical statements are addressed to an audience delineated as the magazine's readership, an audience which presumably shares the writers' concerns and values and which is likely to have a common ethnic background. The generic character of letters as compositions which the writing self intends to be read, as well as these women's choice of the public forum of a widely circulating magazine as the place where their accounts of childbirth will appear, also underscore the women's intention of composing for a general yet sympathetically selected audience. In the 1950s women lacked the ready-made, con-cerned, familial audience that Victorian women apparently enjoyed, yet their desire to form bonds and to tell their birth stories caused American women to reach out through an anonymous, public medium. Although the idea of delivery as a woman's event, either in its physical management or its textual rendition, seems largely absent from the letters, they show the outraged response of women who have collectively experienced some of the indignities cited in the registered nurse's letter. The sense a reader derives from them is of a collective voice rather than the familial voice expressed by the Victorian diarists.

Apparently, the authors of the anonymous letters had no other outlet for their biographies of birth, which amply suppport the charges of mismanagement and maltreatment cited by the registered nurse. One letter, entitled by the *Journal* "How To Make Childbirth A Nightmare," captures the outrage of many of the other letters:

> I have had three children and three different doctors who delivered my new children in three different hospitals.
> The practice of obstetrics is the most modern and medieval, the kindest to mothers and the cruelest. I know of many instances of cruelty, stupidity and harm done to mothers by obstetricians who are callous or completely indifferent to the welfare of their patients. Women are herded like sheep through an obstetrical assembly line, are drugged and strapped on tables while their babies are forceps-delivered. Obstetricians today are business-men who run baby factories. Modern painkillers and methods are used for the convenience of the doctor, not to spare the mother. There is so much that can be done to make childbirth the easy natural thing it should be, but most of the time the mother is terrified, unhappy, and foiled in every attempt to follow her own wishes about having the baby or breast feeding (most hospitals consider this an unusual quirk on the part of the mother which should be squelched at once). (Schultz, "Report" 45)

The very distancing of delivery, both as an autobiographical expression of this anonymous woman's birth experience and in its inclusion in the medium of a public forum, is symbolized by the letter's signature of "Columbus, Ohio." Even though the particularity of felt pain personalizes the letter, it nonetheless displays the hallmarks of reaching out to other women by making the writer's autobiography a metonym for the suffering of a group. The brief first paragraph only gives us enough information about the writer to convince us that her experience qualifies her as a legitimate spokeswoman for a collective autobiography of birth. It is not her special situation we learn about, but the atrocities visited upon a whole group by a medical establish-ment which controls the literal means of delivery.

The power relations silenced by the suppression of information about the physical relationship of patient and health care provider during childbirth form the bulk of this letter and, as such, help elucidate the cultural meaning of delivery in the United States during the 1950s. Delivery is not, this letter poignantly argues, a spiritual experience for women, although when the writer refers to the naturalness of childbirth the implication is that it could be. Rather, delivery implies the use of force and surrender as male physicians act upon the bodies of prostrate, dehumanized women. Obstetricians deliver in the sense of fulfilling a business contract.

In the 1950s virtually all Americans considered birth a medical event which should only happen in a hospital setting. As histories of the changing attitudes toward childbirth have detailed, the switch from home to hospital occurred in part because of the fear of death which the Victorians associated with childbirth. But with the change in locale, women's agency declined as their ability to control the means of delivery lessened and they lost the power to create their birth experiences. Instead, their physical and textual bodies became worked upon by medical experts whose overriding concern was for efficiency and sanitation, a sterility which effectively silenced women. Not only did physicians consider birth an abnormality, as Joseph B. DeLee's well known comparisons of it to being crushed and falling on a pitch-fork imply, but after World War II hospitals strove to design their operations after those perfected by weapons manufacturers.[6] The conveyer-belt concept was applied to maternity patients, so that, like an automobile, a woman was moved along an assembly-line of health care providers at a certain rate of speed. Doctors thought of themselves as technicians, fixing up unfit bodies which were conveniently supine and draped while they performed their labors. With the mother usually unconscious from drugs, creation seemed the doctors' labor, not hers.

Another *Journal* letter, written by the mother of seven children in five different states who is characterized by her pediatrician as an expert, assumes a collective voice when she casts herself as the spokes-woman for younger women in her warning to doctors:

> If you could listen, these are some of the things that you would hear these women say:
>
> There are still far too many hospitals, far too many doctors and far too many nurses who treat mothers as relatively unimportant cogs in the machinery of the mass production of infants; and who treat the father as a strictly incidental and somewhat comic figure in the well-charted routine of the maternity ward.
>
> For every doctor willing to be with a mother through the last thirty minutes or hour of labor there are too many others who are impatient if called more than fifteen minutes before the mother is ready to deliver; and many who, because of this split-second timing, arrive either too late to deliver the baby, or on time only because nurses have held the baby back with anesthesia or force.
>
> For every nurse who gives a mother real encouragement and

the great gift of human kindness in the sometimes long and lonely hours of the first period of labor (especially with a first baby) there are too many others who specialize in the cold-fish treatment: perfunctory commands to the mother; third-person comments on the slowness (or rapidity) of her progress; and over-her-head hospital gossip with other nurses.

For every hospital which permits a husband to be with his wife through labor and delivery there are many, many others where he is just barely tolerated and kept strictly confined to a fathers' room. (They always let him out in time to pay the bill, though!) Thus the opportunity to share an experience which should be the culmination of all a man and woman have hoped and planned for in an honest-to-goodness marriage is lost.

Far too many doctors, nurses and hospitals seem to assume that just because a woman is about to give birth to a child she becomes a nitwit, an incompetent, reduced to the status of a cow (and not too valuable a cow, at that!). Unless she is a very strong-willed person, she soon has the frightening and frustrating feeling that she has lost her personal identity. (Schultz, "Testify" 59)

The final comment here of "Mrs. L.C.B." sums up the lack of any personal status for women in the 1950s vis-à-vis both literary and physical creation. They could not write traditional autobiographies of their birth experiences because their physical environment denied them agency; the birthing mother of the 1950s lacked the unified self requisite for androcentric autobiography, for "she has lost her personal identity" medically and textually. Like the letter inscribed "Columbus, Ohio," "Mrs. L.C.B." 's biography of birth shows a collective character which captures the metaphoric straitjacket of creation as it was conceived textually and culturally. She describes the mechanization of physical creativity; and her delineation of birthing women as caught in the cogs of a machine contrasts starkly with the presumed agency of the male autobiographer free to create himself as the hero of his own story. In fact, as the spokeswoman for a faceless, nameless group of younger women, we can consider "Mrs. L.C.B." as the only voice those excluded from autobiography might have. The ultimate anonymity of having someone else write your story highlights the extent to which physical and textual silencing are related and shows how the mothers of the 1950s were alienated from the labor of their own creations. These women did not produce traditional autobiography because its generic outlines were not appropriate to their experiences. The body of the autobiographical text of creation had become the province of the physician who had excised the text of the mother by inscribing her body with his story. It is significant that the mothers writing to the *Journal* could only name themselves obliquely in public by initials or place names while the obstetricians were given the full power of identity through complete naming in the signatures to their letters. The ban on women's creativity in the 1950s, especially when they were describing creation itself, extended, it would seem, even to their ability to name themselves. Yet the defensive reactions of the doctors who reply to the accusations levelled against them by these mothers indicate the obstetricians' desire to prevent birthing women from inscribing themselves, and the doctors' wish to have their story back and to control how we conceive of birth physically and textually.

If we compare the *Journal* accounts of birth to Ophelia Powell's, we can see that the way health care providers *deliver* is drastically different. The doctor in Ophelia's account is not a faceless, nameless businessman who works over women in many senses of the phrase, but someone who provides succor through his professional expertise as well as his caring manner. Mr. Gillett remains with Ophelia some eight hours after her son's birth, a telling contrast to the physicians of the 1950s who slow down births to eat. The alleged reasons, of course, for the physicians' interpretation of their role have either a supposed medical or humanitarian basis, for these are the justifications given by those who defend their practices when they write to the *Journal*. The obstetricians defend their meaning of delivery by citing in particular the necessity of a sterile field and the use of restraints to aid both mother and child. Both justifications, in fact, derive from iatrogenic causes, for it is the physician who introduces bacteria and medication which in turn necessitate these medical practices (Haire *passim*).

By the 1950s, it would seem, the cultural construct of delivery implies a lopsided relationship in which men silence women's autobiography of childbirth in multiple ways. At the physical level women are silenced because medical procedure prevents them from choosing the method of birthing their child; at the textual level women turn to the public forum of a national magazine to tell their stories. The inadequacy of such a forum as a means of personal expression is apparent. Although the women who write to the *Journal* are given some voice, they are nevertheless silenced in their very anonymity as their autobiographies become part of a chorus which cries out against a medically-centered definition of delivery: they have "lost their identities" in the sense that critics of autobiography traditionally define the self.

Instead, women's biographies of birth give us accounts which highlight the intricate relationships between the physical, cultural, and textual construction of delivery. Delivery becomes something other than the story of the self *ex nihilo*. Victorian women created formulaic accounts in response to a fear of death and inactivity, as well as a familial and woman-centred support system, while the mothers of the 1950s cast their stories against a cultural designation of themselves as anonymous and of creation as the doctors' story. What both representations of delivery demand is for us to listen to stories of creation on the mothers' terms, not according to the generic hegemony of androbiography.

NOTES

1. Recent critics of women's autobiography have placed their observations in opposition to generic designations which assume the unity of self as it has been conceived by androcentric, Western culture. See Jelinek; Smith; Stanton; Benstock; Brodzki and Schenck.
2. The number of current titles which avoid or call into question the term *autobiography* is instructive and suggests not only the distaste for the connotations surrounding this nomenclature, but the power of re-creation involved in the naming of genre. In *Interpreting Women's Lives*, the Personal Narratives Group designates the life writing they study as "personal narratives" so that these can be considered within their largest contextual framework. Stanton uses "autogynography" to demonstrate women's place within systems of meaning while Brodzki and Schenck in *Life/Lines* employ that terminology to suggest the tension inherent between life and art.
3. Both *Lying-In* and *Brought to Bed* describe the ways in which American birthing practices have changed historically. They detail the social construction of birth but do not deal with autobiographical practices.
4. In the introduction to my bibliography, *British Women's Diaries*, I discuss the self-reflexivity of the diary genre and its application to the question of audience, which is often familial.
5. A number of feminist critics have commented on the marginalization and disparagement of women's writing because it is written by women and perhaps for women and thus differs from men's writing, which serves as the standard. See Mary Ellmann; Spender; Olsen; Russ.
6. *Lying-In* and *Brought To Bed* perceptively detail the intricate relationship between the changing ideologies espoused by health care providers and the concerns of birthing women. *The New Our Bodies, Ourselves* also places childbearing practices within an ideological and historical context which illuminates the importance of the social construction of birth.

WORKS CITED

Benstock, Shari, ed. *The Private Self: Theory and Practice of Women's Autobiographical Writings.* Chapel Hill: U of North Carolina P, 1988.
Blathwayt, Frances Elizabeth. Ms. Diary. Gloucestershire Record Office, Dyrham Park Mss D1799, F249–59.
Boston Women's Health Book Collective. *The New Our Bodies, Ourselves.* New York: Simon & Schuster, 1984.

Brodzki, Bella, and Celeste Schenck, eds. *Life/Lines: Theorizing Women's Auto-bio-graphy*. Ithaca: Cornell UP, 1988.
Ellmann, Mary. *Thinking About Women*. New York: Harcourt Brace & World, 1968.
Great Britain. Registrar General. *First Annual Report of the Registrar-General of Births, Deaths and Marriages in England*. 1939. Her Majesty's Stationery Office, London.
——. *Thirty-Third Annual Report of the Registrar-General of Births, Deaths and Marriages in England*. 1872. Her Majesty's Stationery Office, London.
Haire, Doris. *The Cultural Warping of Childbirth*. Minneapolis: International Child-birth Education Association [1975].
Huff, Cynthia. *British Women's Diaries: A Descriptive Bibliography of Selected Nineteenth-Century Women's Manuscript Diaries*. New York: AMS, 1985.
Jelinek, Estelle C. *The Tradition of Women's Autobiography: From Antiquity to the Present*. Boston: Twayne, 1986.
Johansson, Sheila Ryan. "Sex and Death in Victorian England: An Examination of Age- and Sex-specific Death Rates, 1840–1910." *A Widening Sphere*. Ed. Martha Vicinus. Bloomington: Indiana UP, 1977. 163–81.
Leavitt, Judith Walzer. *Brought to Bed: Child-Bearing in America, 1750–1950*. New York: Oxford UP, 1986.
Miers, Mrs. S.M. Diary MS. M795 EHC 27. 1850–60. Edward Hall Collection, Wigan Record Office.
Olsen, Tillie. *Silences*. New York: Delacorte, 1978.
Personal Narratives Group, ed. *Interpreting Women's Lives: Feminist Theory and Personal Narratives*. Bloomington: Indiana UP, 1989.
Powell, Ophelia Catherine. Diary MS 13–15. 1849. G.E. Evans Bequest, National Library of Wales.
Russ, Joanna. *How to Suppress Women's Writing*. Austin: U of Texas P, 1983.
Schultz, Gladys Denny. "Journal Mothers Report on Cruelty in Maternity Wards." *Ladies' Home Journal* (May 1958): 44–5, 152+.
——. "Journal Mothers Testify to Cruelty in Maternity Wards." *Ladies' Home Journal* (December 1958): 58–9, 135+.
Smith, Sidonie. *A Poetics of Women's Autobiography: Marginality and the Fictions of Self-Representation*. Bloomington: Indiana UP, 1987.
Spender, Dale. *Man Made Language*. London: Routledge & Kegan Paul, 1982.
Stanton, Domna C., ed. *The Female Autograph: Theory and Practice of Autobiography from the Tenth to the Twentieth Century*. 1984; rpt. U of Chicago P, 1987.
Wertz, Richard W. and Dorothy C. Wertz. *Lying-In: A History of Childbirth in America*. Expanded ed.; New Haven: Yale UP, 1989.

Figuration and Disfigurement: Herculine Barbin and the Autobiography of the Body

ROGER J. PORTER

> Isn't the final goal of writing to articulate the body? ... The word must comfort the body ... reconnect the book with the body. (Chantal Chawaf)

Throughout the history of autobiography writers have emphasized their beliefs and thoughts far more than their physical natures. Even Rousseau, whose candor about his corporeal existence radically undermined existing standards of autobiographical decorum, subordinated descriptions of bodily function to his predominant concern – his relation to society. On those relatively rare occasions when the body comes to the fore, it is generally to provide a metaphor, or to raise issues that are largely concerned with consciousness, or because illness has temporarily disabled the subject.

The reluctance of autobiographers to focus thematically and psychologically on the body may be due less to propriety than to an assumption that the physical being is neither sufficiently distinctive nor interesting. It may also stem from a fear that an emphatic concern for the corporeal inhibits any significant self-analysis, as the body armors the soul. But there are important exceptions, however few, and I want to preface this account of Herculine Barbin's *Memoirs of a Nineteenth-Century French Hermaphrodite* with a brief look at two of those exceptions. We shall find in each work an emphasis on the body as the locus for investigations into the psyche. Each writer sets forth the figure of the body and its disfigurements as indices to anguish and openings to speech. And each is preoccupied with dual sexuality – the meaning of intertwined gender identifications, whether as anatomy or metaphor. In these texts the body dominates the life and becomes obsession.

Edward Dahlberg's *Because I Was Flesh* is devoted to as intense a preoccupation with the glories and the sorrows of the body as any autobiography I know. Early in the work Dahlberg announces that "whatever I imagine I know is taken from my mother's body, and this is the memoir of her body" (4). The book is as much biography of his mother, a lady barber in Kansas City during the first several decades of this century, *and of her body*, as it is autobiography, but Dahlberg's text is also an account of his search for his father and of his gradual realization that his mother's body is "sepulchred" in him (88). The dominant self-image that emerges is of himself as a "sack of woe" (2) to be filled by the elusive father, who, in the book's dominant pun, is seedy Saul, a "baleful seminal drop of a depraved rotting forefather [who] lived solely to discharge his sperm" (44). What fills the emptiness that haunts the book's melancholy narrator is the presence of other bodies, the generations which inhabit his corpus and generate his sorrow. Only when he acknowledges without shame the similarity of his flesh and theirs, does he feel whole, and gain his subject: the pleasures and sufferings of his physical being.

The book is obsessed with physical sensation, especially with bodily decay. As Dahlberg asserts, the book is "the song of the fungus" (75), a veritable "lazar house of literature" (141). The preoccupation with physical corruption and sexual nausea affirms his humanity – the "flesh" of the title. He cannot surrender the preoccupation with disintegration; nausea brings a form of delight; he clings to the vilest memory of rot, shame and sexual degradation because they remind us of our ordinariness. To deny or transcend our base nature is a violation, placing us above even the gods who, much as we, are in constant agony of the flesh. "The Kosmos is the seminal cornucopia, and the Kabbalists speak of the massive genitals of Jahweh" (105). All wisdom for Dahlberg comes from the body; our physical afflictions both torment our existence and provide the ground for our creativity.

Dahlberg's project in his autobiography is to give textual birth to his mother; in this verbal act he becomes the double of the grand inseminator, Saul the father. Dahlberg's preoccupation with the body – with his own and with his mother Lizzie's – dramatizes the anguish of the progenitor even as he joyfully writes the mother's image into renewed existence. His identification is with both the unknown father Saul *and* with his mother, the "*mater dolorosa* of rags" (4). Dahlberg is both willful writer and victim of the lustful corruption which begot him, and in the autobiography he expresses through his body both male power and female passivity. He demonstrates the inevitable duality of the autobiographical genre, where the writer is at once begettor and begotten, the active creator of a self and the self brought into being. Dahlberg's autobiography is the result of a generative impulse: the past or the "self composed" is inseminated by the present of the "self composing." The ambiguity of the "I" results from this bifurcation – his work is, we might say, hermaphroditic at the core.

The dominant figure of the book is the body as verbally incontinent – it must always speak its needs. In both the life and in the text, the body will not be silenced. The book is a vast outpouring of speech about the corpus – words from antiquity, from the Kabbala, from both Testaments, from the horde of literature remembered and fabricated, from friends, family, and prophets of the word. "As soon as the Word was made flesh, man was unable to be quiet, or work, or think, until he had dropped his seed" (105). The book is full of long, careening speeches, a piling up of vituperation and scorn and lamentation, as if words alone will repair the tears in the world. The body must gain a voice – and the voice is a cry. It is both a cry of carnal lust (he hears his mother's sexual moans throughout his childhood) and a cry of despair. He will never "forget my own crying flesh" (75); it is as if the wounds of his spirit cry out eternally. The absolute necessity of speaking out is not merely a desire for confession; it is a primal effort to assuage the pain, as if by identifying his woe with that of all creatures Dahlberg can find the community of sufferers to erase his solitude.

In the first volume of his on-going autobiography, *Manhood* (*L'Age d'homme*), Michel Leiris indulges in a litany of physical defects, limitations and grief. Loathing his image in the mirror, he sees thin, hairy hands, with distinct veins; inflamed eyelids; a bald head. He lists such habitual gestures as the tendency to gnaw his thumbs and scratch his anal region. He gives us in excruciating detail an account of a horrifying tonsillectomy and an infection and inflammation of the penis. His impotence, his aging, his self-lacerations with scissors, his dreams of losing his powers of speech, his anticipated cancer, his penchant for self-torment (he has worn a piece of barbed wire as a badge of shame), and especially his feeling of abjection and his fear of life, all testify to an obsession with physical discomfort (what he calls "corrosion"), self-victimization, and the recollection or dread of wounds. His fantasies combine the inflicting of pain upon others (wounding a woman as if he were a bull goring his opponent) with suffering himself the piercing of the deadly horn. It is often difficult to tell if his accounts of pain given and received are the recollected past or fantasies of future masochistic joy.

Susan Sontag has written that Leiris seeks not to understand himself but to appal us by exposing himself, laying himself open to pain. By expressing profound self-loathing he courts his own punishment, and makes us confront what is obscene and repulsive. If Leiris' fundamental impulse is suicidal – attacking the body and attacking himself in the body of the text – he declares that act to be an aggressive blending of male and female, as each reaches out to become the other in death:

> Examining the circumstances in which Cleopatra, Queen of
> Egypt, ended her life, I am struck by the contact of these two
> elements: on the one hand the murderous serpent, the male
> symbol par excellence – on the other the figs beneath which it
> was concealed, the common image of the female organ I
> cannot help noting with what exactitude this meeting of symbols
> corresponds to what for me is the profound meaning of suicide: to
> become at the same time *oneself and the other*, male and female,
> subject and object, killed and killer – the only possibility of
> communion with oneself. (93)

Joan of Arc, a childhood heroine, is for Leiris "the hermaphrodite
progeny" (29) of the Virgin Mary and Vercingetorix, so designated
because she is both chaste and murderous, combining in her person the
two archetypal women whose images dominate the book: Lucrece who
turns coldly against herself and Judith who turns fiercely upon her lover
and victimizer, Holofernes. Leiris' focus on the body is not merely a
morbid obsession with his own disfigurement, but an ironic assertion
of sexual duality. He becomes his own imaginary hermaphrodite,
actively aggressive and passively self-denying. His emphasis on both
wounded men and wounded women, when they combine into a kind
of integrally massacred self, represents a fantasy of self-generated
sexuality immune from a fixed gender identity.

He asserts a willingness to expose everything; autobiography for
Leiris is an open wound; self-exposure is the sole courageous act
available to him, and if he cannot act in life, in the text of his life he will
take his chances:

> to say everything and say it without 'doctoring,' without leaving
> anything to the imagination and as though obeying a necessity –
> such was the risk I accepted and the law I had fixed for myself ....
> It was therefore necessary that this method I had imposed upon
> myself – dictated by the desire to see into myself as clearly as
> possible – function simultaneously and effectively as a rule of
> composition. (162–3)

Leiris will see *into* himself, that is, through the wound. Leiris is
a speaking mouth from that wound – and weeping or laughing
he produces a confession of the orifice. He flirts with the idea of
androgyny, though only as a metaphor. But there is no mere figuration
about the androgynous status of my central text, for here the
hermaphrodite is no longer a fiction.

The question that poststructuralist critics inevitably ask – "Who speaks here?" – is profoundly relevant for the reader of Herculine Barbin's *Memoirs*. Written four years before his death at 29 and five years after Barbin – assumed by his parents to be a girl and so reared – was declared medically and legally to be male (and renamed Abel Barbin), the *Memoirs* dramatize the central problem of autobiography itself: that of identity. If a crisis of identity stands at the heart of most autobiographical texts, what issue could be more fundamental than the identity of gender? Who speaks here, Herculine Barbin as woman or Herculin Barbin as man?

Adélaïde Herculine Barbin, born in 1838 in Saint-Jean-d'Angély, attended a convent school and later became a school mistress. At 20, after having been discovered in bed with a woman friend, she was examined by a local doctor, and following consultations with her Bishop, was designated a man by both the physician and a local magistrate. Leaving the school in anguish and with hints of a scandal behind her, Herculine, now renamed Abel, went to Paris where he lived alone in a wretched garret, worked for the French railroad, led an isolated life, wrote the memoir at 25, and finally committed suicide in 1868 at age 29. The *Memoirs* were discovered by Foucault during his research on sexuality; they were published in 1978, and included in the same volume were detailed medical reports alleging Barbin's true hermaphroditic nature, as well as a lurid short story based on the case, entitled "A Scandal at the Convent," written a quarter-century after Barbin's death by a German psychiatrist, Oscar Panizza.

We might postulate that Barbin could not truly gain a voice until he had been declared a male; prior to that moment, she is Lacan's infamous gap or silence. Social conventions of female silence suggest that Barbin would not readily turn to serious written self-analysis. When "she" becomes a "he," Barbin gains the power and cultural authority to write the inappropriate gender. If Barbin does not achieve representation until he is a man, it is a great irony, since he really wishes to remain a woman. Toril Moi has said about Gilbert and Gubar reading nineteenth-century women writers that "they apparently believe that there *is* such a thing as a 'distinctive female power,' but that this power, or voice, would have to take a rather roundabout route to express itself through or against the oppressive effects of the dominant patriarchal modes of reading" (59). Related to this issue is that of the conditions provoking self-consciousness: in the paradise that was the convent school where she was raised, and the school where she taught several years before her gender was questioned, she seems to have avoided the self-consciousness necessary for the reflective act of bringing the self into writing. Identity-formation, what Herbert Spiegelberg, according to Paul John Eakin, terms the crucial "I-am-me experience" of childhood (218), seems not to have occurred until Barbin suffered an expulsion from the bliss of an extended and largely innocent childhood and adolescence. Her life at that time, as Foucault suggests in the introduction to his edition, was essentially genderless, an androgynous sexuality before declarations had to be made. It is an almost mythic time, devoid of the social constraints that sexual identity imposes upon our behaviors and sense of self, and of the tormented self-reflexivity that dominated her life after the gender change.

As the text unfolds, we sense that the imposed exile from a sheltered world of girlish delight was the precipitating event which moved Barbin to self-knowledge and to speech. She cannot articulate her experience in her childhood; she can only do that in the narrative. When Barbin's self is fragmented and torn asunder, or, less dramatically, inscribed by others, he attempts to reclaim identity through writing. But ironically, gaining representation is ultimately an act of self-denial. What autobiography normally seeks to overcome – anonymity – in this case is brought into being, for the text announces again and again how the enforced acquisition of maleness is really an emptying out of self, a terrifying absence. For Barbin, writing turns out to be *de-composition*. Barbin may have acquired a penis but he has lost a sense of self. The assignment of a new gender identity seems to have replaced what in traditional autobiography is the epiphanic moment of self-recognition. Having been defined and designated by society (by priest, doctor and judge), and having been victimized into signification by an external agent, Barbin eschews self-exploration largely because he engages in a course of self-denial. Barbin is condemned by others to repudiate the female aspects of himself, and inclined by instinct to deny the male aspects of himself. What might be misogyny in a male becomes self-hatred, masochism, and eventually suicide. He cannot gain his (or is it *her*?) body back through writing – he can only speak out his sorrow, while cherishing the anonymity that precludes the necessity of choosing a definitive gender identity.

But how to speak? One of the most arresting aspects of the first two-thirds of the book is its tone of a sentimental, romantic novel of the period. Many of Barbin's descriptions of her fellow students, especially of their blooming bodies, or her own now-shy, now-bold, advances to them, or her adventures in their beds, and the scene of parting from Sara (who was a kind of lover of hers): all could have been the typical fare of Emma Bovary's early reading. In speaking of her adolescence Barbin mixes lyrical tenderness, effusive adoration, clichéed sentiment, melodrama, and rank hyperbole:

Holy and noble woman! My memory of you has sustained me in the difficult hours of my life!! It has appeared to me in the midst of my frenzies like a celestial vision to which I have owed strength, consolation!! (28)

In the movement I made, her chignon became unfastened, and her hair, tumbling down, flowed all over my shoulders and part of my face. I pressed my burning lips to it! (50)

What a destiny was mine, O my God! And what judgments shall be passed upon my life by those who follow me step by step in this incredible journey, which no other living creature before me has taken! (35)

I submitted to my destiny, I fulfilled – courageously, I believe – the painful duties of my situation. Many people will laugh. I pardon them, and I hope they shall never know the nameless sorrows that have overwhelmed me!!! (85)

That tone comes partly from early joy, partly from a sense of gradual victimization, but generally it emerges from his intuition that her early life could have been novelized. Twice he tells us of her reading in Ovid's *Metamorphoses*, as if her life imitates myth. Borrowing a typical topos of nineteenth-century fiction, he depicts a storm as "an omen of the dark and menacing future" (14). He narrates numerous acts of confession, as if in her life, as much as in the *Memoirs*, she were preoccupied with voyeuristic, judging or forgiving readers. In fact she authorizes and entitles herself only when she turns to confession, converting the confused life into a narratable story. She continually dramatizes herself: she is an Achilles out of place, a passionate lover with no proper mate, a monster, a shameful and repugnant creature, a slave to devotion in a courtly love scenario.

Seeing her life as novelistic suggests that Barbin is not really in possession of it. The book's narrative terms, as well as the events in the life itself, are imposed from outside. The *Memoirs* often allege a panic that things are out of control. She speaks of the "inevitable catastrophe" (53) and of "an unexampled fatality" (51); she wonders if she "were not the plaything of an impossible dream" (79), and occasionally she imagines scenarios of authoritarian figures employing abusive power against her, and fears being tyrannized over or victimized by men. Barbin is constantly defined by others, or by cultural norms for which she is not responsible.

Of course the body is the major defining system, for it has shackled her in cruel fashion to an identity, or rather to a confused complex of identities, that others force upon her. Like Foucault, Hélène Cixous tends to regard the hermaphrodite as a " 'fantasy of unity' " or a "myth of totality" (Suleiman 16), but it seems to me that once Barbin is made (self-)conscious about her condition, far from feeling whole, she feels fragmented into duality and vulnerable to a destiny not of her making, unable to achieve any coherent identity outside what she is given by others.

In a curiously prefiguring episode she is drawn to another young girl in the convent normal school, who is sickly and doomed to an early death. Barbin dwells on a body that always seems inappropriate to her: a "sickly pallor," a "certain hardness" in her features (26), her body hair are all felt as marks of her status as stranger and pariah. She will not swim with her fellow students, for fear of offending "those who called me ... their sister" (39). At times Barbin comes close to speaking of the problem: "a gross mistake had assigned me a place in the world that should not have been mine" (54), but he pulls back from directly confronting the issue. Immediately after this passage he invokes the dreaded "confessor" (55), who, when he learns about Herculine's activities with Sara, is filled with horror. It is here the book takes on the form of both Augustine's and Rousseau's *Confessions*, the one full of shame of sin, the other justifying and absolving a self that resists being constructed by society's shams. There are times when Barbin, a dis-inherited creature asking forgiveness, throws himself like Augustine at the mercy of God; and there are times when he stands defiantly against custom and convention, indifferent as Rousseau to the social strictures which have turned his life into agony. But Barbin seems less at home with the act of confessing than do her two predecessors. Unlike Augustine, he has no secure place from within which to look back with equanimity or confidence. From Barbin's precarious perspective the reader becomes the most dangerous auditor of all; as a result there are things he simply will not tell us.

One of the fascinating aspects of the book is its author's evasions about the body and the secrets it contains. Barbin cannot speak directly about the medical issues: "reality is crushing me" (104). "Reality" can be found only in the "Dossier" that Foucault publishes with Barbin's text, a file containing the doctors' reports at the time of the gender reassignment and again at the time of the autopsy. It is in the "Dossier," not in the *Memoirs*, that we find the particulars about genital morphology, and the "Dossier" reveals what Barbin cannot. When a doctor first examines her, Barbin feels exposed, probed, prodded; when, late in the book, he expresses his fear of death, it is not extinction that disturbs him, but the humiliation and exposure in a life already exhausted with degradation:

> ... a few doctors will make a little stir around my corpse; they will shatter all the extinct mechanisms of its impulses, will draw new information from it, will analyze all the mysterious sufferings that were heaped up on a single human being. O princes of science, enlightened chemists ... analyze then, if that is possible, all the sorrows that have burned, devoured this heart down to its last fibers; all the scalding tears that have drowned it, squeezed it dry in their savage grasp! (103)

One of the puzzles of the *Memoirs* is that we are never sure if Sara thinks of Barbin as male or female. Is their relation an adolescent sisterly dalliance, or a heterosexual affair? Barbin will not tell us, for he needs to keep that issue a secret. He must harbor the enigma, for he maintains dignity only if she retains some of her own identity *as embodied mystery*.

Barbin prefers not to reveal too much, and is generally fascinated with illusions and buried truths. She lives in a sea of mystifications. When the dénouement finally arrives, there are indirections, deceptions, theatrical evasions: Sara, her mother and Barbin all play roles and dissemble with professional aplomb. Barbin speaks of her secret self as "a terrible mystery" (74), as if the androgyny were a cult for initiates. Leslie Fiedler notes that "the Hermaphrodite challenges the boundaries not just between male and female, but illusion and reality" (179). Barbin's narrative continually draws a veil between autobiographer and reader, though the gesture encourages us to peer – we are turned into voyeurs, but discern little about what Herculine really felt at the time.

What we peer into is not the mystery of the anatomy – there is little enough of that, and besides, we have more detail than we could imagine in the "Dossier"; rather we peer into the mystery of the degree of awareness and knowledge on the part of the leading participants. The textual style is one of euphemisms; Foucault calls it "elegant, affected, and allusive" (xii). We never learn from Barbin what she looked like. Of course all autobiography is essentially a dialectic of what cannot be said and of the impulse to narrate stories; of the *interdit* (what can only be shown *between* speech) and the outspoken; of fictions and the impulse toward truth. But Barbin's text demonstrates not just these commonplace autobiographical tropes, but in addition a confusion of the will: should she seek being or oblivion? On the one hand she desires to rescue herself, to gain an identity in the face of everyone's impulse to obliterate her. (She fears that even her beloved Sara will quickly forget her. Barbin must write herself into being, and the cultural authority of being male empowers her discourse.) On the other hand, what is written leads inevitably to non-being. In its inability to assert an active self that can make a mark in the world, in its enormous evasions, and in its declarations of emptiness, the book is an act of oblivion.

The reticence about the body stems from Herculine's fear that she has been reduced to mere body, forced to see herself as an anatomical problem, not as a complex self. For the hermaphrodite, especially, the body is a maze of secrets, a labyrinth of indirection. In the *Memoirs*, instead of a graphic depiction of the ambiguous body we have a duality of styles corresponding to the shift in genders. As the narration moves to what the civil court termed the "rectification" (87), the romantic mode gives way and the tone becomes bitterly denunciatory, vindictive, mocking, contemptuous, though still with elements of wistful nostalgia, languorous fantasy, and self-dramatizing posturing. Desire itself shifts, from one bent on sisterly community to one bent on eliciting our compassion for her anguish.

"Anatomy is textuality," declares Elaine Showalter (17). If, as Gilbert and Gubar have asserted, isolated women writers in the nineteenth century tended to alienate themselves into silence, experiencing their own gender as an obstacle or inadequacy, can we regard Barbin in these terms? If I may elide French and Anglo-American feminist theory momentarily, I would argue that Luce Irigaray's claim that women speak with "doubleness, contiguity and fluidity of women's sexual morphology and the multi-centered libidinal energy that arises from them" (qtd. by Jones 86) applies even more so to the hermaphroditic voicings of Barbin's text. Does Barbin then speak for this multiplicity, or for a transcendence of binary thought and feeling? Is Barbin a precursor of Jean Genet, the paradigmatic bisexual writer whom Cixous lauds in *Souffles*? Barbin's predicament makes a mockery of Cixous' now-famous imperatives in "The Laugh of the Medusa." Removed from her essential femaleness, condemned by his new situation to obliterate all consciousness of his femaleness, how could Barbin cut through cultural barriers by writing with and through the body? Here is Cixous:

> By writing her self, woman will return to the body which has been more than confiscated from her, which has been turned into the uncanny stranger on display – the ailing or dead figure, which so often turns out to be the nasty companion, the cause and location

of inhibitions. Censor the body and you censor breath and speech at the same time.

Write your self. Your body must be heard. Only then will the immense resources of the unconscious spring forth... .

To write. An act which will not only "realize" the decensored relation of woman to her sexuality, to her womanly being, giving her access to her native strength; *it will give her back her goods, her pleasures, her organs, her immense bodily territories which have been kept under seal...* . (250 emphasis added)

Those "bodily territories" have been denied Barbin, and he cannot get them back again in the writing; nor does his writing compensate for the loss. Or perhaps we should say that transgressing boundaries is not an act of freedom but encapsulation in monstrosity. The book ends with a long section of denunciation, in which he attacks both men and women – which is to say him- and herself! – , men for their "false oaths" and "hideous copulations," women for their "faithless[ness]" (99). The voice of over-protesting is strong, for even as Barbin unleashes his jeremiad against the degradation and "slime" of love (100), we recall her longings for romance – "I was born to love ... . I had a passionate heart" (27).

The last section veers between desire and the transcendence of desire; between an urge for a dematerialized, almost ethereal existence unmoored from the savage reality of earthly concerns, and a wish to observe and criticize folly, as if people were merely "actor[s] in the comedy." "Looking down from the height of my proud independence, I establish myself as a judge" (106). Becoming a judge of slime-covered men is a desperate attempt to reverse her victimization at the hands of the priest-confessors she has come to loathe – perhaps a trope for an even deeper fear, namely that she will be shamed by the horrified criticism of intolerant readers. But every cool, caustic analysis of the human comedy is undercut by a cry to God for pity and relief from suffering. Then again he cultivates that suffering as a mark of his superiority to the ordinary run of humankind: "I am sorry for you, for you have not suffered. You have lacked the noble, the great heart, the generous soul, that are needed in order to suffer" (100). Finally, Barbin desperately attempts to make of his "immaterial, virginal nature" (100) a cause for celebration, not for remorse and anguish, as if it were an elected, defiantly willed division between himself and others which he can possess freely.

No doubt we are fascinated by the hermaphrodite because it represents the incorporation of the other who is buried in ourselves, and because it embodies the person who has double knowledge. Like Tiresias, the hermaphrodite knows what it is to be both woman and man, and the immense power that accrues from this possession represents our fantasy of knowing all sides of human relations. Perhaps the bisexual comes close to this achievement. But Barbin, like hermaphrodites inevitably, is trapped in his anatomy, double but finally nowhere. That body imprisons him inside its constraints, even as it mocks him with the illusion of *un*-constraint. It is all a matter of perspective: from outside, the figure seems powerful; from within, utterly impotent. For Barbin the problem is not merely a cruel physicality, but the burden of excess knowledge:

> I, who am called a man, have been granted the intimate, deep understanding of all the facets, all the secrets, of a woman's character. I can read her heart like an open book. I could count every beat of it. In a word, I have the secret of her strength and the measure of her weakness, and so I would make a detestable husband for that reason. I also feel that all my joys would be poisoned in marriage and that I would cruelly abuse, perhaps, the immense advantage that would be mine, an advantage that would turn against me. (107)

Barbin wishes to be a woman again, or at least someone of indeterminate sex. As a man he knows too much of women, and that advantage would work against him in marriage, for he would terrify the woman with his knowledge, would become doubly powerful, not harmoniously congruent. Our fantasy is his felt torment.

It is with Barbin's continual uneasiness with his state that we end the *Memoirs*, appropriately perhaps because only feelings of disjunction and *dépaysement* could give birth to this text, the representation of a self in exile from the self. But Barbin is uneasy with his uneasiness: he needs something more definitive, and the only solution seems to be death. Death is the sole healing of the fragmentation of identity that marks this many-named life: at different times he nominates him-and-herself Herculine, Herculin, Adélaïde, Alexina, Camille, Abel. Death is the only permanence for the hermaphroditic ego, that eternally divided consciousness.

Towards the end Barbin depicts himself walking in Père-Lachaise cemetery: "Devotion to the dead has been born in me" (109). Graves and tombstones keep secrets best of all, and Barbin's ultimate attraction to death is that he will finally be free from the accusations and suspicions of others, which may really be his own projected guilt. This preoccupation symmetrically rounds the text, which had begun with the suspicion that "I am beyond any doubt approaching the hour of my death" (3), though the suicide was not to occur until four years after the *Memoirs* were started. But that death is prefigured in the *Memoirs* themselves, which are the painful rendering of what had already been killed in Barbin. Her identity had been lost, and the book becomes his own attack on the body after he has "introjected society's hostility to her deviance" (Higonnet 76). Barrett Mandel has an optimistic reading of autobiography as an art form that immobilizes death: "As self-affirmation, autobiography 'discovers' death in all that is not itself." And, "One writes not only to affirm, but also to stave off non-being ... turn[ing] life into art ... fix[ing] it in a changeless form" (181). But I think this characterization of autobiography will not work for Barbin, for the *Memoirs* are a suicide note. And yet Barbin manages to discover a voice, however self-lacerating, however perplexed in his own self-abnegation. There is no triumph inside the writing, but the *fact* of the writing – even an autobiography of abjection – may stand as a mournful testament to Barbin's lonely vigil of herself.

Let me turn finally to a brief theoretical speculation. This is a work which attempts to break the norms of conventional autobiography, where so frequently a chronologically linear text and a unified tone assert a conception of character constituted by wholeness and integrity, even when a conversion marks a turning and a new direction in the life, deferring meaning and an identity which ultimately crystallize with greater distinctiveness. If Barbin invokes an old life and a new life, as in conversion autobiography generally, he mocks these terms implicitly, for the new life and self is a devastating subversion of the old. Instead of a gain in epistemological certainty that brings self-knowledge – another trait of conversion narratives – , there is bewilderment and uncertainty. The conventional awakening to one's truest essence never takes place in Barbin, and the text, like the author's baffled identity, expresses a warping of coherence. Foucault says in his Introduction: "what she evokes in her past is the happy limbo of a non-identity" (xiii).

Barbin's *Memoirs* function as an unconscious parody of the crisis-and-conversion form. Barbin almost sounds like Augustine – "O my God, what a fate was mine! But you willed it, no doubt" (87); but whereas conversion autobiographies are usually exemplary, urging that we follow the path expressed in the text because we are capable of imitating the life of the autobiographer, Barbin's work presents him as a unique, unnatural creature, unable to be imitated because so monstrous. The "conversion" is a cruel joke, and Barbin knows we cannot join him. It is the very severance from tradition and conventional form that marks Barbin's life and text. Unlike Rousseau

troping on Augustine, or De Quincey on Rousseau, there is no tradition
for Barbin to follow, no ready-to-hand structures that could emplot his
life, let alone give him a coherent identity.

As the coherent and self-comprehensible part of the life – the so-to-
speak "pre-conversion" part – comes to an end, and the life crumbles into
confusion, the narration begins to collapse into vituperation, invective
and despair, all coherence falling away. There is no true self because
there is finally no clear gender. Denied the feminine aspects of himself,
Barbin is conflicted and tormented, almost incoherent because he
repudiates not a female "other" but a female "self." And the text, that
wholeness which is supposed to repair bodily fragmentation, turns out to
be another kind of de-composition.

What results is something very different from Jan Morris' autobiography *Conundrum*. Morris, whose gender-journey reversed Barbin's
and was decisively willed, characterizes her life as "thirty-five years as a
male ... ten in-between, and the rest of my life as me. I liked the shape of
it." Her writing is an attempt at "liberated self-expression," for "a
troubled soul achieving serenity" (146). By contrast with Barbin's ironic
discourse, Morris' story of bodily transformation is nothing less than
androgynous pastoral, the corpus cured.

WORKS CITED

Barbin, Herculine. *Herculine Barbin: Being the Recently Discovered Memoirs of a
    Nineteenth-Century French Hermaphrodite*. Ed. Michel Foucault. Trans. Richard
    McDougall. New York: Pantheon, 1980.
Chawaf, Chantal. "Linguistic Flesh." Trans. Yvonne Rochette-Ozzello. *New French
    Feminisms: An Anthology*. Ed. Elaine Marks and Isabelle de Courtivron. New York:
    Schocken, 1981. 177–8.
Cixous, Hélène. "The Laugh of the Medusa." Trans. Keith Cohen and Paula Cohen. *New
    French Feminisms: An Anthology*. Ed. Elaine Marks and Isabelle de Courtivron. New
    York: Schocken, 1980. 245–64.
Dahlberg, Edward. *Because I Was Flesh: The Autobiography of Edward Dahlberg*. New
    York: New Directions, 1959.
Eakin, Paul John. *Fictions in Autobiography: Studies in the Art of Self-Invention*. Princeton:
    Princeton UP, 1985.
Fiedler, Leslie. *Freaks: Myths and Images of the Secret Self*. New York: Simon and Schuster,
    1978.
Higonnet, Margaret. "Speaking Silences: Women's Suicide." *The Female Body in Western
    Culture*. Ed. Susan Rubin Suleiman. Cambridge: Harvard UP, 1986. 68–83.
Jones, Ann Rosalind. "Inscribing Femininity: French Theories of the Feminine." *Making a
    Difference: Feminist Literary Criticism*. Ed. Gayle Greene and Coppélia Kahn. London:
    Methuen, 1985. 80–112.
Leiris, Michel. *Manhood: A Journey from Childhood into the Fierce Order of Virility*.
    Trans. Richard Howard. New York: North Point P, 1963.
Mandel, Barrett John. "'Basting the Image with a Certain Liquor': Death in Auto-
    biography." *Soundings* 57 (1974): 175–88.

Moi, Toril. *Sexual/Textual Politics: Feminist Literary Theory*. London: Methuen, 1985.
Morris, Jan. *Conundrum*. London: Faber and Faber, 1974.
Showalter, Elaine. "Feminist Criticism in the Wilderness." *Writing and Sexual Difference*. Ed. Elizabeth Abel. Chicago: U of Chicago P, 1982. 9–35.
Sontag, Susan. "Michel Leiris' *Manhood*." *Against Interpretation and Other Essays*. New York: Farrar, Straus & Giroux, 1964. 61–8.
Suleiman, Susan Rubin. "(Re)Writing the Body: The Politics and Poetics of Female Eroticism." *The Body in Western Culture*. Ed. Susan Rubin Suleiman. Cambridge: Harvard UP, 1986. 7–29.

Autobiography, Bodies, Manhood

SHIRLEY NEUMAN

And so at last we come down to it, the body – that small hot engine at the centre of all these records and recollections. (Malouf 53)

1. AUTOBIOGRAPHY, OR, LIFE (DIS)EMBODIED

Despite David Malouf's getting "down" to the fact that the lives represented in autobiographies are *embodied*, he gives only a few brief pages to his own body. Nonetheless, in this his *12 Edmonstone Street* does more than most autobiographies, which almost completely efface the bodies in which the lives they describe were lived. We can cite many reasons for this, chief among them a Platonic tradition which opposes the mental/ spiritual to the corporeal and then identifies "self" with the spiritual. The same opposition informs the elevation of soul over body in Christian theology and operates powerfully in confession which, in its careful eliciting of precise details of the desires of the flesh, particularly in its early practice, aimed at mastery of that same flesh. Autobiography, Georges Gusdorf showed us some time ago, grew out of confession and it inherited both the legislation toward the incorporeal codified in confession and the increasing reserve in the questions asked, particularly about sex, counselled in confessors' manuals from the late seventeenth century on (Foucault 18–19). By the eighteenth century, Foucault notes, the practice of confession had been transformed and extended to relationships such as those between child and parent, student and teacher, patient and doctor, and much of its use aimed at the regulation of sexuality (63). The ultimate goal of these confessional practices remained, however, the transcendence, through regulation, of the corporeal: witness Descartes' definition of "man" as "a thing or substance whose whole essence or nature is only to think, and which, to exist, has no need of space nor of any material thing or body" (25). The body, defined as "natural," functioned as the binary opposite and as a metaphor by which the spiritual was understood; it remained necessary to this understanding at the same time that it had, necessarily, to be transcended in philosophy and effaced in representation. Freud's work would seem to constitute a definitive break in this binarism of body and mind insofar as it theorizes a libido-driven consciousness and elaborates a somatic symptomology of psychic disturbances. In fact, much in its analytic procedures is continuous with confession and its diversification into post-Enlightenment pedagogical and medical practices. Like these earlier practices, Freud's is preoccupied above all with the *sexed* body, and, like theirs, his aims at constructing an interiorized experience of the self and somatic manifestations of that experience consonant with public, cultural values. The hysteric's symptoms analyzed away, the body as signifier once again cedes to the life of the mind.

Confession, whether practised in the church or by means of one of its avatars in childrearing, tutoring, or medical consultation, remains an intimate and *private* discourse, one of the aims of which, as Foucault has shown, is to manage the body, to make it conform with *public* and *cultural* values. In the traditions of life-writing, therefore, bodies, in all their aches and illnesses, as sites of unease, and, more modestly and fleetingly, in their beauties or their desires, are far more apt to make an appearance in the private genre of the diary than in the avowedly public and cultural genre of the autobiography. Redirected into autobiography and its criticism, not the practice but the goal of confession determines the narrative which, like others in western "high" cultures, establishes access to public discourse about the self as synonymous with spiritual quest and defines the "self" or "identity" as synonymous with continuity and coherence of consciousness rather than of the physical body. That western cultures assume an analogy between mind, masculinity, and culture, and between body, femininity, and "nature," only reinforces the disembodiment of the self characteristic of most autobiographies.

In what follows I will look at two anomalous moments in which a masculine body ruptures and exceeds the discursive effacement of the corporeal which is characteristic of autobiography. I will do so neither from the long-held assumption that anatomy determines and defines sexuality and gender nor from the more recent distinction between biological sex and social gender. Rather, I hold, as Bryan Turner, who follows Foucault, puts it, that our bodies are both material and "the effects of cultural, historical activity" (49) – codified by adornment, exercise, surgery, gestures, pleasures, performances, diet, labors, punishments, idealizations, etc. These mediated bodies are in themselves representations of social values. They are *"always already cultural"* (Grosz, "Notes" 7), socially constructed and codified from before birth. Their codification or "inscription," to use Grosz' metaphor, is "directed towards the acquisition of appropriate cultural attitudes, beliefs and values," that is, toward the production of a body's "interiority." Rather than standing opposed to mind, then, the body becomes a medium, or an "*interface* between 'privatised' experience and signifying culture" ("Notes" 10). One of the main effects of this process in western cultures is that sexed bodies whose biological and material characteristics and capacities and whose psychosexual experiences and drives exist on a broad continuum have been socially coded into the categories of male and female and this polarization of heterosexual difference has been at the expense of many possible positions along the continuum.[1] Finally, and again along with recent feminist theorists of the body, in what follows I conceive of bodies as not only produced or constructed by social power but *also* as potentially resistant to that power and productive of other ideologies and other social powers. The question for the reader of that rare autobiography which represents the body becomes, then, one of the extent to which that representation reiterates and reinforces the social codes constructing bodies or the extent to which it reconfigures them.

The *Memoirs* of the nineteenth-century French hermaphrodite, Herculine Barbin, and Michel Leiris' *L'Age d'homme* (*Manhood*) – my two autobiographical "moments" – both foreground the masculine body by representing its penis metonymically. However reductive this seems, it is not, I would suggest, the equivalent of the fragmentation of female bodies which, historically, has characterized much erotic representation of women, nor does it anticipate Lacan by asking the Phallus as transcendental signifier to stand up for a more-or-less (in)effective penis. This direct, if obvious, metonymy for masculine bodies, used in autobiography, does constitute an explicit subversion of the social relegation of penises to folktales, locker room talk, jokes, pornography, sex manuals, soldiers' songs, colloquial idiom, profanity, and the intimacy of the therapist's office, a relegation concomitant with a minimalization of the penis in "high" culture, particularly in the classical traditions of the visual arts. The motivation to that subversion, the autobiographers' understanding of the social construction of their "masculine" bodies, the extent and kinds of agency which the written representation of their masculine bodies produce for Barbin and Leiris and the implications for our understanding of gender of that agency are my subject in the remainder of this essay.

2. LAW, THE HERMAPHRODITE, AND THE GENDER OF STYLE

Adélaïde Herculine Barbin, called Alexina, was born in France in 1838 and grew up about equally, if incompletely, endowed with male and female sexual morphology. Registered at birth as a girl, she was educated in a convent and at a normal school, and, nineteen but "completely ignorant of the facts of life" (Barbin 33), went on to teach in a girls' boarding school. There she fell in love with, and made love to, the daughter of the school's proprietess, with whom she lived, to all appearances, on sisterly terms. Alerted to her anomalous situation by the surprised remarks of a doctor whom she consulted about abdominal pains, she sought the advice of a bishop who referred her to a Dr. Chesnet. He, after examining her, counselled her to apply to the courts to "rectify" her "civil," that is, her gender, status (Barbin 78). On the basis of his recommendation, the courts ruled her a man. Moved by "disgust," "shame," and a "vast desire for the unknown" which "made [him] egotistic" (80–1), Abel, as he now became legally, or Herculine as the literature usually refers to him, or Camille as he names the narrator of his *Memoirs*, broke with her lover, went to Paris where he worked in railroad administration and, in 1868, asphyxiated himself by means of the fumes from a charcoal stove.[2] The following year, Dr. E. Goujon published his report of the autopsy he performed on the body, and Professor Auguste Tardieu edited and published in the medical literature in 1872 and 1874 the *Memoirs* of Herculine Barbin, written between the time Barbin assumed a masculine identity and his death.

Two aspects of this instance of hermaphroditism and of Barbin's description of it in the *Memoirs* can tell us something about the ways in which various discourses shaped understanding of the sexed body at this particular historical juncture. One is to be found in the religious, medical and legal decisions and discourses about her gender, that is, her "civic" status, as well as in Alexina's own reaction to having made love to a woman: all these constructed Barbin's hermaphroditic body as masculine. The second is to be found in the rhetoric of the *Memoirs*.

The medical reports of both Dr. Chesnet's examination of Alexina and of Dr. Goujon's autopsy of Abel continuously assert and simultaneously deny her/his hermaphroditic and female sexual morphology, assimilating both to the morphology of the male body. Dr. Goujon's autopsy report characterizes Abel as "one of the most typical cases of *masculine* hermaphroditism" but then goes on in the next sentence to note that "it is difficult ... to discover a more extreme mixture of the two sexes, as concerns everything relating to the external genital organs" (129, my emphasis). It details a narrow vagina two and one-half inches long and a "penis" which, flaccid, is two inches long and one inch in diameter. Although the autopsy report concludes that this "was a large clitoris rather than a penis" (131), it nonetheless consistently calls it a penis. Both reports note that Barbin's "penis" is imperforate, making it homologous to her vagina which is closed at its nether end. Neither manual examination nor autopsy reveal a uterus. What Dr. Chesnet first describes as labia majora, he later concludes is "only the two halves of a scrotum that remained divided" (126). Both doctors note sperm ducts descending on either side of the vagina; the autopsy report indicates that the "seminal fluid . . . did not contain spermatozoa" (143). The vaginal mucous membrane Dr. Goujon found "very congested" (135) and full of ducts indicating that it produced the fluids characteristic of sexual arousal in a woman. The urethra is definitely feminine. Secondary sexual characteristics are absent or, minimally present, tend to the "masculine": there is no breast development nor is there hair on the chest, and the beard is sparse, although hair is abundant on the buttocks and thighs.

Barbin lived out this hermaphroditism at a historical juncture when two contradictory paradigms defining masculinity, femininity and the relation between them were culturally current.[3] The *psychology* of masculinity, femininity and heterosexuality, since the seventeenth century, had increasingly been defined in terms of the *differences* between the sexes. Moreover, nineteenth-century culture represented sexuality as a specific "problem" which needed to be "faced" by means of the investigative and theorizing capabilities of the medical profession (Heath 16). The "problem" was largely the political and social one of control of female sexuality, and its "solution" depended largely on medical confirmation that conception could take place without orgasm, allowing for the idealized gendering of women as "different" from men in being both "maternal" and "passionless."

At the same time, however, the medical discourse of sexual morphology was still formulated, as it had been from the time of Aristotle and Galen and through the Renaissance, in terms of the *similarities* between the sexes. For the long tradition growing out of Greek medicine, generative organs and "substances" were homologous and "incontrovertible elements in the economy of a single-sex body" which was then socially gendered into a higher, male and a lower, female form (Laqueur, *Sex* 42). Moreover, by the mid-nineteenth century the discoveries of embryogeny had confirmed that the penis and the clitoris develop out of what begins as an undifferentiated embryonic structure, as do the testicles and the ovaries, and the labia and the scrotum (Laqueur, *Sex* 10, 169). Indeed, the precision brought to sexual morphology by nineteenth-century medical discoveries meant that "true sex" – as Dr. Goujon would have it – was decided on more rigorously and narrowly anatomical grounds than ever before. With reference to Barbin, for example, Professor Tardieu insisted that sex "is a pure question of fact that can and ought to be resolved by the anatomical and physiological examination of the person in question" (cited in Laqueur, *Sex* 136, 278–9 n.41). Morphology and not experience decided the question of sex, as the case of Herculine Barbin so graphically demonstrates; in Thomas Laqueur's succinct formulation, "The autopsy, not the interview, was the moment of truth" (*Sex* 188). The simultaneous development and entrenchment of a psychology of gender *difference*, however, exerted enormous pressure on the interpretation of anatomical evidence and virtually precluded an understanding of the sexed body that would have allowed for a place somewhere between the heterosexual poles of male and female: the object of the examination was to decide which was the "true sex," not to decide where, on a continuum, the individual experienced his or her body and sexuality. This tension between a same-sex model and a different-sex model for the human body remained an unresolved part of the medical and legal discourses which exercised such a decisive role in Alexina's life. Only when Freud, ignoring the considerable medical evidence pointing to the paucity of nerve endings susceptible to erotic stimulation in the vagina as compared to the clitoris, relocated mature female sexual pleasure from the clitoris to the vagina did a complete shift in sexual definition from the establishment of similarities to the establishment of differences between the sexes *seem* to have taken place.[4] Freud displaces morphological evidence in order to theorize a different female body stamped by the imprimateur of his new psychological "science." What he theorizes is a female body whose mature sexuality is ineluctably in the service of reproduction, a body purged of the temptations to self-pleasuring or homoeroticism that had always lurked within the "one sex/flesh" model.

Alexina was diagnosed a man, then, at an historical juncture when the medical discourse of men and women as sexually homologous, if socially different, had partially but not entirely given way to both a medical and a social discourse of sexual difference. That her sexuality and her body were constructed and represented in religious, medical and legal discourses in terms of the *confusion* of this (rather prolonged) historical moment is nowhere so evident as in the two medical reports, the details of which imply a place on a sexual continuum between male and female which both doctors' conclusions emphatically deny. Dr. Chesnet, in the report which became the basis of the legal decision, after listing the anatomical details I have cited above, sums up:

> What shall we conclude from the above facts? Is Alexina a woman? She has a vulva, labia majora, and a feminine urethra, independent of a sort of imperforate penis, which might be a monstrously developed clitoris. She has a vagina. True, it is very short, very narrow; but after all, what is it if it is not a vagina? These are completely feminine attributes. Yes, but Alexina has never

menstruated; the whole outer part of her body is that of a man, and my explorations did not enable me to find a womb. Her tastes, her inclinations draw her toward women. At night she has voluptuous sensations that are followed by a discharge of sperm; her linen is stained and starched with it. Finally, to sum up the matter, ovoid bodies and spermatic cords are found by touch in a divided scrotum. *These are the real proofs of sex.* We can now conclude and say: Alexina is a man, hermaphroditic, no doubt, but with an obvious predominance of masculine sexual characteristics. (127–8 emphasis mine)

And on the basis of his autopsy, Dr. Goujon suggests that the

formation of the external genital organs of this individual permitted him, *although he was manifestly a man*, to play either the masculine or the feminine role in coitus, without distinction; but he was sterile in both cases. He could play the role of the man in this act by virtue of an imperforate penis that was capable of erection . . . . As we shall see later when it is described, this organ was a large clitoris rather than a penis . . . . As he tells us in his memoirs, it was possible for the erection to be accompanied by an ejaculation and voluptuous sensations. (131–2, my emphasis)

There are two sticking points for Goujon, both of which he finesses. The first is Alexina's female urethra, which leads the doctor into a discussion of the uses of the male urinary canal as an "analogue of the vaginovulvar canal of the female": "As a matter of fact, it is above all the propulsor of the semen. It only *lends itself* to the excretion of urine." Men, this argument runs, have "no urethral canal, strictly speaking"; instead they have a seminal canal. Only women have a urethra (142, his emphasis). Alexina, therefore, is not, in a "strict" sense, missing a male urethra. Instead, because she has not one, but two, ejaculatory canals, albeit uncharacteristically displaced from the penis to the sides of the vagina, she is clearly male: "Procreation is the natural goal of marriage, and Alexina possessed the organs that are characteristic of his sex and whose functions he exercised" (143). But this raises the second sticking point: the absence of spermatazoa. Goujon sets that difficulty aside with the observation that "this state of affairs might well have been only temporary . . . and at another time one might well have noted the presence of spermatozoa in his seminal fluid" (144).

The confused nomenclature of these accounts, the sleights of hand by which ambiguous sexual morphology is assimilated to the masculine, the heterosexual assumption that because Alexina is attracted to women she is male: all make plain that there is no more provision in these medical

readings of morphological evidence for a continuum of sexuality between
"male" and "female" than there is in the era's psychology of heterosexual
difference. Instead, two assumptions underlie the reading of the evidence
which ensure that the subject's "true sex" can be discovered and that, in
cases of ambiguity, that sex will be "male."

The first assumption is not stated but is clearly operative in the priority
given to "masculine" over "feminine" morphology when it comes time to
draw conclusions. Despite Chesnet's observation that "this little member
. . . because of its dimensions is as far removed from the clitoris as it is
from the penis" (126); despite Goujon's conclusion that the penis was in
fact a clitoris; despite the fact that French medical literature of the
nineteenth century held that the clitoris was the locus of female sexual
pleasure and the vagina only a comparatively uninteresting passage of
ingress and egress for reproductive purposes;[5] despite the fact that
Alexina/Abel is able "to play either the masculine or the feminine role in
coitus, without distinction"; and despite the fact that s/he is sterile in
either role, the "penis" becomes the dominant signifier of sexuality.
Masculinity is the "norm" against which sexuality and gender are defined,
and the clerical, medical and legal practitioners can, quite simply, only
see a penis. In this, their interpretation is entirely consistent with the
history of medical discourse about the sexed body; they read the evidence
before them in terms of "the classical one-sex model" (Laqueur, *Amor*
104) which shaped medical discourse from the Greeks to Freud, a model
which sustained "only one canonical body and that body was male"
(Laqueur, *Sex* 63). Combined with the still-lingering Aristotelian (and
Renaissance) conviction that all forms tended toward the more perfect,
this model ensured that medical science could see the ambiguously sexed
hermaphroditic body only as tending toward and needing to be assimilated into the canonical male body.

The second assumption determining the physicians' conviction that
Alexina is a "man" is stated by Goujon. "Procreation is the natural goal
of marriage" (i.e., sex), he begins his concluding remarks which will be
about Alexina's capacity to ejaculate. Here, "evidence" so imprecise as
to be retrospectively undecidable, is used as a determinant of masculinity. It is worth noting that Barbin's *Memoirs* do not, as we saw
Goujon suggesting earlier, tell us that he ejaculates. At their most
precise, they tell us that she is "dominated . . . completely" by "an
incredible sensation," also described as "nervous trembling" (32). The
detail of ejaculation Goujon actually takes from Dr. Chesnet's report
that "At night she has voluptuous sensations that are followed by a
discharge of sperm; her linen is stained and starched with it." We have, of
course, no way of knowing what Alexina told Dr. Chesnet about these

nocturnal emissions; however, given either the terms of their description by Dr. Chesnet (voluptuousness, an emission staining and starching her underwear), or the terms in which she describes her orgasms in the *Memoirs*, there is no *a priori* or *necessary* reason to read the "incredible sensation" as male orgasm or the emission as spermatic. (Orgasm during sleep, sometimes as a consequence of dreams, remains a subject passed over in silence by medical discourse about female sexuality.) Once again, the medical profession can only see a penis and its products. Not to do so, in this case, would be to acknowledge that Alexina's hermaphroditism might include something of an impassioned woman, one outside male heterosexual control and one capable of orgasmic dreams and of "tribadism."

Alexina's experience of "real passion" (48) for Sara, at least as "Abel" recounts it in the *Memoirs*, falls into the same pattern. She approaches Sara as a woman to another woman, but, having made her her "lover" (52), she conceptualizes the situation in terms of illicit heterosexuality, terming her "my *mistress*!!!" (54), and fearing she has impregnated her. Given the euphemistic style of the narrative, as well as Alexina's own avowal that she was still ignorant of the facts of life at the time that she moved from normal school to Sara's boarding school, one perhaps cannot take this heterosexual language or her fears too literally. Neither Alexina's knowledge nor Abel's literary conventions and language equip her/him to describe with precision the physical aspects of the relationship. What is clear is that, once the dalliance had passed beyond the sisterly, Alexina thinks of it heterosexually. To make love to a woman is to be a man, for her as for the medical profession.

For both Alexina and her doctors, all rests then on the penis and its reproductive function, even if organ and function are separated as in the case of Barbin's genitals. Hence the particular unease caused Dr. Goujon by the fact that there are no spermatozoa in the vesicles of the deceased Barbin and his need to hypothesize their possible presence at other times. To firmly ensure not only the canonicity but the unassailable priority and perfection of the male body in this heterosexual narrative of hermaphroditism (to ensure in effect that, as Dr. Goujon asserts, "hermaphroditism does not exist in man" [139]), the cause of that unease must be rationalized away. Goujon, constrained by the facts of the autopsy, can only hypothesize other, more reproductively virile, moments for Barbin. But one Oscar Panizza, psychiatrist turned soft-porn writer, took the license of fiction to insure that all was right with the world when he used Barbin's case history as the basis of his "Alexina Besnard" in "A Scandal at the Convent." His directive epigraph cites the reproductive mandate from *Genesis* I:27–28: "male and female created he them. . . . and God said unto them, Be fruitful, and multiply" (155). And his conclusion quotes a report of the doctor's examination of his protagonist which relies for most of its details on the actual medical reports about Barbin but from which he also makes significant departures. These increase the "masculinity" of Alexina's secondary sexual characteristics, render the vagina so tight as to make penetration impossibly painful, suppress all suggestions of a clitoris in favor of "a succulent body, perforated at the tip, which proves to be a well-defined *membrum virile*" (198). The perforation, he makes plain, is the opening of the urethra which, for this fictional Alexina, performs both its usual functions: "he had, in the course of the examination, . . . an involuntary emission of semen, which proved under the microscope to contain normal, mobile spermatozoa" (199). Lest any doubt remain about the virile capacities of the "male hermaphrodite," Panizza's final paragraph tells us that Alexina's lover "found it necessary to leave [the convent] after about six months, for the home of an aunt in a distant part of the country" where, we are to conclude, she had Alexina's child in more privacy than the convent permitted (199). One of the ideological mandates of this fiction, then, is to resolve, in favor of maleness and more conclusively than the medical reports could, the crisis of reference and representation produced by Barbin's ambiguously sexed body.

On the evidence of the church, the law, medicine and of fiction, Alexina is a man and a changed codification of her sexed body is simultaneous with this decision. He gives up her job as schoolmistress, adopts masculine dress, takes up a masculine job, and, in the last words of the *Memoirs*, determines on spiritual quest out of his "thirst for the unknown, which is so natural to man" (115).

The effects of this gendering of the body are nowhere so evident in Barbin's memoirs as in her/his style. Throughout, the style adopts the gendered rhetoric of the romantic novels of the period, which frequently interpret sexuality in terms of obstacle-ridden love and characterize women in terms of excesses of sensibility, in an overwrought and euphemistic rhetoric of which Barbin imitates (Butler 98–9; Porter 127–8). Describing her experience as a woman, Barbin tells us about her anxieties about her physical appearance (26–7), about her physical shame, about her feelings for her mother, her protector, her girlfriends, her lover, her employer. A reticence sometimes obscures her self-representation as when she describes her refusal to take part in a bathing party with her schoolmates, but she is retrospectively clear that this reticence reflects her own innocence at the time of what restrained her and that she was motivated by (appropriately "feminine") modesty (39). But her language also marks her emotional connectedness to others and it is, above all, intimate as to her feelings.

This style changes decisively at the juncture in the manuscript at which Herculine, now a "man," departs for Paris, when these details and this intimacy fall away and a pained rhetoric of Olympian spiritual superiority and Promethean defiance begins to dominate. We do not know precisely what adjustments of attitude and manner Alexina makes to become Abel. We do see him become more summary, and more alienated, aloof, and judgmental than was the Alexina who engaged her emotions and others directly. Of others, he concludes, "There is an abyss between them and myself, a barrier that cannot be crossed . . . I defy them all" (102). Most particularly, Abel/Herculine no longer speaks of his body. Instead he sets the "degraded women," "hideous copulations," "faithless" wives and "filthy sores" of those "enchained here below by the thousand bonds of . . . gross, material senses" against his own participation in "the nature of the angels" and his spirit's "plunge into that limpid Ocean of the infinite, where . . . my soul drinks deep" (99). Any conclusion about the gendered construction of the self or about its embodiment in life or in autobiography that we might wish to draw from this rhetoric must be tempered by a recognition of the fact that someone redefined as masculine at twenty-two is hardly gender-representative and by a recognition of the real alienation Herculine experiences as an object of curiosity and newly burdened with specific medical knowledge, as well as with a sense of moral opprobrium with regard to her lover. His rhetoric is shaped by suffering, self-pity, isolation, shame, regret and a compensatory arrogance at least as much as by his considerable awareness of the ways in which gender, and even the sexed body, are socially constructed.

Moreover we do not know that this repression of the "material senses" for a rhetoric of the spirit plunging into the "limpid Ocean of the infinite" – lying perhaps across the boundary of suicide – is entirely Barbin's doing for we have for his life as a man only the incomplete and edited version of the manuscript presented in the medical literature by Auguste Tardieu. His editing, as Michel Foucault describes it, "neglected the recollections of Alexina's final years – everything that in his opinion consisted only of laments, recriminations, and incoherencies" (119). Which is to say: Tardieu excised precisely that content and rhetoric which, in the misogynist traditions of literature and medicine, have been associated with women's writing and women. Moreover, Barbin writes his memoirs from the knowledge and the perspective of his "masculinity"; the extent to which his depictions of his life as a girl and his life as a man are the result of a gendered perspective assumed along with the legal status of manhood is impossible to determine. We do not know, therefore, whether Barbin's disembodiment within his own memoirs once he is reaches the point in the narrative of being *legally* identified as masculine is an effect of his own narrative, and what motivated it if it is, or whether it is an effect of Tardieu's editing of it to conform with the discourse of the medico-legal venue in which he published it. But whichever is the case, both the medical reports and the edited version of Barbin's life as a man enact a reading of hermaphroditism which strongly suggests that the masculine body is constructed *as always already seen*. The edited *Memoirs* also suggest that because what is always already seen becomes the "canonical body," it *need not be represented for it is what the reader knows is there*. The reader himself is indisputably masculine: Herculine addresses "Men!" in their relations to women (99). We *see* Alexina's body because she is painfully aware that its thin gracelessness, its "sickly pallor," its "hardness" of feature, and its hairiness "all struck the eye" (26–7) as deviating from the norm of female beauty as object of the gaze. Once that body is medically and judicially defined as male, has been made to conform, however ambiguously or inadequately, to *the* sexual body, Barbin, or Tardieu, can assume rather than display it in the *Memoirs*. Masculinity, as rhetoric, consists precisely in this disembodiment. Alexina may have gained a voice by assuming masculinity, as Roger Porter has suggested in the previous essay in this volume, but she has lost her body to discourse and to death. Alexina Barbin's suicide is but the logical extension of the understanding of gender that church, state, law, medicine and literature have effected on and by means of her body.

3. IN THE SHADOW OF THE BULL'S HORN

In *L'Age d'homme*, the hermaphrodite again figures briefly when Michel Leiris imagines Joan of Arc as the "hermaphroditic progeny" of the Holy Virgin and Vercingetorix,

> a warrior virgin sharing the attributes of both of them and whom I am tempted, briefly, to regard as prefiguring, by her double quality of chastity and murderousness, those two images of bloody women that rise in my mind today: Lucrece the cold and Judith the sword-handler. (60)[6]

Leiris' metaphor of the hermaphrodite, however, is not enlisted in the service of either reproduction or masculinity. He is explicit about his "disgust for pregnant women, fear of childbirth, and frank repugnance toward newborn babies"; "it would be impossible for me to make love if ... I thought of it as anything other than sterile," he avows (28). Here the hermaphrodite takes part in what had been an intensifying shift in discourse about the sexed body and the relations of sex, during the seventy years between Barbin's death and Leiris' writing of *L'Age d'homme*, from an emphasis on reproduction and reproductive "alliances" to an emphasis on sexuality (Foucault 106ff). And here the emblematic figures which, taken together, constitute the hermaphrodite, are both female; the hermaphrodite signifies the unconscious forces propelling the sexual life, and not a reproductive or juridicial puzzle.

Born in 1901 to the Parisian middle class (where Alexina was the child of a provincial upper house servant), Leiris had been actively affiliated from 1924 to 1930 with the Surrealists, among whom were the most sophisticated lay theorizers of psychoanalysis in France (Roudinesco II 19–49). He broke with them by 1930, during a period (1929–30) when he himself was undergoing an analytic "cure" with Dr. Adrien Borel to whom he was introduced by another patient, Georges Bataille. Interrupting the treatment in 1930, he began *L'Age d'homme* in 1930–31 as an alternative therapy, first writing the sections on Judith, Lucrece and Holophernes "as an autobiographical piece touching on eroticism" for a series Bataille planned but never published (Gobeil 51). 1931–33 he spent on an ethnographic mission in Dakar, a trip that resulted in his taking up a career as an ethnographer at the Musée de l'Homme in Paris. The filters through which his lifework in autobiography – *L'Age d'homme* and the four volumes of *La Règle du jeu* – would be read by most critics as either "para-Freudian" or "auto-ethnographic" were now in place.[7] On his return from Dakar, Leiris resumed work on the autobiography, completing it in 1935. He added six brief paragraphs by way of a postscript for its 1939 publication; after the war he expanded that postscript into the much discussed essay "De la littérature considérée comme une tauromachie," included as a preface in the 1946 and all subsequent editions.

Readers have frequently remarked *L'Age d'homme* as unusual among autobiographies in that it opens with a chapter about the physical body of the man sitting at his desk writing. Like Dante in the tradition of spiritual autobiography, Michel Leiris has just achieved "la moitié de la vie" (25); he is 34. He is also of middle height, thin and unmuscular, with a narrow nape, a prominent forehead, thin hairy hands, narrow shoulders, and so on. He finds himself "humiliatingly ugly" (26). He bites his nails, bends his head to one side, hides his eyes with his hands when he has to make a decision and scratches his anus when he is alone "etc." (26). Sexually, he is not "abnormal" but "simply a rather cold man" who holds himself "quasi-impotent" (27–8). Two of these characteristics are not without esoteric associations with "masculine" emblems; astrologers, he reminds us, find in necks like his "a typical characteristic ... of those born under the sign of Taurus" and in his "broad forehead a connection ... with the sign of the Ram" (25). But as Philippe Lejeune has remarked, it is astrologers, not the narrator, who advance this virile identification (17); indeed the narrator shows marked scepticism in phrases such as "*if* one believes in astrologers" and "*according* to what astrologers say" (25, my emphasis). The overwhelming effect is of a body which falls far short of any ideal of masculinity; the very fact of its description's beginning the autobiography challenges such an ideal. In what follows, this unmasculine body is soon figured as a castrated body. Describing his childhood and youth in "The Head of Holophernes," for example, Leiris presents himself as "entirely dominated by ... childhood terrors" (103), virtually all of which are encompassed within the theme of "hommes blessés" or "wounded men" (104). I will cite only two of many such incidents. At 12, shortly after having learned from a comrade the details of sexual intercourse (134–5), he is hurled during a game against a nail protruding from a brick wall and opens a large and bloody gash in his temple. His first thought is for his disfigurement – "How will I be able to make love?" (132). The transposition of a facial wound into this fear suggests that the child experiences the gash as "feminizing," by emasculating, him, a suggestion reinforced three sentences further on when he recollects that his trousers "must have been" bloodstained. But the incident also leaves him with "a deep, private joy at being someone who has seen death up close" (134) for the wound proves only millimetres short of being fatal. Even earlier Leiris' penis had become locus and sign for the conjunction of desire and death figured in this and other incidents which he understands as castrations. As a child of six, he suffers from an enflamed penis which he conflates with his first erections: "I believe that in the beginning an erection made me afraid because I took it for another attack of the illness .... It took no more for coitus to seem to me like ... an eminently dangerous act" (106–7). One of the consequences of this apprehension is a long list of women, not "terrifying" (144) in themselves but endowed with terror by Michel, leading to an equally long list of occasions on which he is impotent either through an excess of feeling or drunkenness, and also to occasional real and imagined sexual violence. In "The Loves of Holophernes," he tells us that his impotence has a further "material" cause in a "a little malaise in one testicle" (190), which he links explicitly to the gash in his forehead and which produces, again, the question, "How will I be able to make love?", as well as "a constant discomfort which plunges me still deeper into my feeling of weakness and cowardice" (192).

Within this visible construction of masculinity, then, a wounded body becomes the sign of cowardice and is not only unmasculine, but feminine, as Leiris makes plain in "Lucrece," in another series of associations beginning with a childhood incident in which he accidentally shoots a dart into the eye of a promiscuous servant. He identifies his fear that he might have put out the woman's eye with a later game, played at age ten or eleven, in which he, blindfolded and finger extended, is led toward his sister to put out her eye, an illusion created by having her cry out at the moment his finger is pushed into an eggcup full of moist breadcrumbs. Leiris connects the two incidents and projects the wound onto female sexuality in a gloss on the game: "The significance of the 'eye put out' is very deep for me. Today I often tend to regard the female sexual organ as something dirty, or as a wound, no less attractive for that, but dangerous in itself, like everything bloody, mucous, and contaminated" (81; *Manhood* 46). The identification of cowardice with the wounded "feminine" body and at least partial impotence, which signals Leiris' inability to produce his own body in the terms of masculinity, leads to literal, if not whole-hearted, attempts at self-castration, as when, having failed to persuade "a little black American dancer" to his ends, he disturbs a friend at 5 a.m. "to ask him for his razor with the intention, more or less feigned, of castrating" himself (197).

Seeking deliverance from these fantasized and actual gestures in "a psychological cure" (197), Leiris projects his anxieties about masculinity by means of a series of analogies with art and ritual: the first of these is with the operatic roles sung by his Aunt Lise, the second with Lucas Cranach's painting *Lucrece and Judith*, the third with the bullfight understood as sacred ritual, and the fourth with Géricault's *The Raft of the Medusa*. Carmen, Electra, Dalila, Tosca, Salomé: Leiris always gives a secondary place to the deaths of most of these heroines if he notes them at all. For him, the most intensely theatrical moment of these operas comes when Dalila cuts off Samson's hair, when Tosca stabs Scarpia. For him, Carmen is a "sanguinary goddess" to whom the matador offers the slaughtered bull at the risk of his own evisceration (92). In a notably gendered reading of operatic plots, Leiris' identification is entirely with the male roles, and with the ideals of chivalric and heroic masculinity which they emplot. "Even now," he insists,

> it is impossible for me to love a woman without wondering ... what drama I would be capable of throwing myself into for her, ... what crushing of bones or tearing of flesh ... a question I always answer with such a precise sense of my terror of physical suffering that I am never able to extricate myself except crushed by shame, feeling my entire being rotten with this incurable cowardice. (51)

Leiris' own anxiety about masculinity did not begin with women at all but with childhood illnesses, accidents, humiliations and medical interventions. Nonetheless, because he experiences opera's injunctions to heroism and virility as strong, and his own flesh in relation to those injunctions as weak, he projects his anxiety about masculinity onto the heroine who, as she has been emplotted, demands his castration and responds to her as more murdering than murdered. Indeed, "Tragiques," the chapter which describes young Michel seeing life as an opera, is framed by representations of Medusa. It opens with a citation from Goethe's *Faust* in which Mephistopheles identifies a simulacrum of Marguerite as in fact the head of Medusa which, he is careful to remind Faust, Perseus cut off (43). Its recollections of opera come to a close with, in rapid succession: Hoffman's muse Stella, "changing shapes like the Medusa in whom each man believes he sees the woman he loves"; a return to the image of Medusa in "Goethe's *Faust*, the Faust I first knew in the stage version of Gounod's librettists" (50–2); and an association of Medusa with Anne Boleyn. The diva's roles, with the injunctions to heroism and virility they embody, become Woman as Medusa, reducing the male hero to an impotence that is, paradoxically, stone-hard and rigid. But whether Medusa beheaded is figured as murdered queen, opera heroine or monster slain by Perseus, these "allegories" also figure her as Leirisian anti-hero in that her capacity to petrify those who look on her is, finally, cut off.[8]

In a second set of equally multivalent analogies, two figures allegorically represent Leiris' attraction to and anxieties about female sexuality as the object of masculine dominance: Judith and Lucrece, as they are painted by Lucas Cranach. *Lucrece and Judith* is usually read as a paired image of self-sacrificing heroines; art historians sometimes note in its Judith an iconographic inversion of Benvenuto Cellini's *Perseus*, in which the hero holds up the head of the slain Medusa. Leiris, however, re-reads these images so as to downplay their representation of heroinism and patriotism and to emphasize a narrative of sexual aggression.

As the story is usually told, Judith, inspired by God, uses her beauty to gain entry to Holophernes' tent and table where, once he is drunk, she is able to kill him, saving the Hebrews from his conquering army which, leaderless, retreats. Leiris himself quotes this version of the narrative from *Nouveau Larousse Illustré* (86), thus the more strongly marking his departure from it. In his reconstruction of Cranach's pictorial narrative, he imagines Judith as an "image of a punishment feared and desired at the same time" (202). In her right hand: a sword "naked as herself" with which she has just decapitated Holophernes. In her left hand: the head, held "like a phallic bud that she could have cut off simply by closing her lower lips at the moment when Holophernes' floodgates opened, or that, an ogress in full passion, she might have detached from the large member of the drunken (and perhaps vomiting) man by a sudden bite" (143). That is, in Leiris' figuration of Judith as fatally wounding Holophernes at the moment of ejaculation, the head becomes conflated with the "large" virile member cut off by the *vagina dentata* of the "ogress in full passion." Under that emblem, Leiris subsumes the operatic heroines who exercised such a fearful, seductive hold over his youthful imagination, while under the emblem of "the Head of Holophernes" he collects the memories and images of his own wounded male body. This double attribution in order to account for the experience of ejaculation points to an aspect of some masculinities which Paul Smith has recently elucidated with reference to men's lived experience of their male bodies which "both carry and lose; ... accumulate and spend" (101). Leiris' psychic projection speaks, as Smith puts it, "to a masculinity for which the hysterical desire for somatic loss, the death of the body in an efflux of bodily substance, is a paramount element in its constitutive reality" (107).

Lucrece, however, is not wounding, but wounded, first by another, then by herself. Raped by her brother-in-law, who had told her that if she resisted he would kill her and spread the rumor that he did so because she betrayed her husband, the next day she tells her story to her husband and father, then fatally stabs herself before them. Cranach portrays her at the moment the dagger makes its first contact with her flesh. Leiris represents the picture this way:

> Lucrece, pressing to the center of her white chest, between two marvellously hard and round breasts ... the pointed blade of a dagger at the end of which already pearls, as the most intimate gift stands at the tip of the male organ, several drops of blood, and preparing herself to annul the effect of the rape to which she submitted, by a parallel gesture; a gesture which will soon plunge into a warm sheath of flesh, the weapon inserted to the hilt for a bloody death, like the inexorable virility of the rapist when she was forcefully entered through the orifice already gaping between her thighs, soft pink wound which a few moments later gave back the libation in great gulps, just the way the wound – deeper, more damaging too, but perhaps even more intoxicating – made by the dagger will let gush out, from the very heart of Lucrece fainting or dying, a sea of blood. (143)

The erotic charge of Leiris' re-imagining and the propulsion to death/ orgasm effected by the rush of its style are inescapable; the direction in which its desire flows, if clear, is more contradictory. The subject of the painting and Leiris' use of her as self-allegory suggest that the process of identification should be with the hand and the consciousness holding the knife. But Lucrece also remains the eroticized object of a masculine gaze – her perfect breasts and "soft pink wound" duly noted – and the object of masculine aggression: Leiris' erotic identification is clearly with the dagger as a stand-in for the rapist as well as with Lucrece dying.

What makes *Lucrece and Judith* so powerfully emblematic in Leiris' construction of his anxieties about masculinity is, then, a common element of aggression and victimization which he reads into the representation of the two figures. Judith, he insists, is the more appealing figure, but Judith and Lucrece come to the same thing for him, for, "if, dreaming of Judith, I can conquer only Lucrece, I take from this such a sensation of weakness that I am humiliated" and must substitute pity for "holy terror" by means of "a sort of moral rending that I seek to introduce into the heart of daily life, trying to change it, little by little ... into a 'raft of the Medusa' on which a handful of starved people lament and devour one another" (152). The "intoxicating upset" that he derives from this process "comes especially from the *remorse* attached to it because it is I who have behaved in a cowardly way .... By a circuitous route, this pleasurable remorse leads me back to terror ... : a superstitious fear of punishment" (152–3), of becoming the head of Holophernes.

By now it should be abundantly clear that whether he casts a woman as Judith or as Lucrece, whether he imagines himself encountering Medusa or adrift on *The Raft of the Medusa*, anxiety motivates Leiris' relation to social constructions of masculinity and of masculine sexuality. But the image of Lucrece, while it involves aggression in his identification with the dagger/penis, also involves self-directed aggression just as does the identification with Holophernes beheaded. Here questions of the relationship of Leiris' problems with and resistance to masculinity expand from questions of sexuality to questions of the relationship of self and world, and questions of the masculine values of literature.

Love, Leiris posits, is "the only possibility of a coincidence between subject and object," and, therefore, "the only means of acceding to the sacred" (176; *Manhood* 120). Ideally he would play all parts in the "little death" of ejaculation. In the conjunction of death and desire which determines the erotic for Leiris, suicide becomes the ideal third term by which to effect the (ejaculatory) collapse between two poles. "I cannot help noting," Leiris remarks of Cleopatra's suicide by means of a symbolically "male" asp hidden amid symbolically "female" figs,

> with what exactitude this meeting of symbols responds to what for me is the profound meaning of suicide: to become at the same time *oneself and the other*, male and female, subject and object, killed

and killer – the only possibility of communion with oneself. (141; *Manhood* 93)

Or, we might say, suicide enables the renunciation of masculinity at the same moment that one takes up the male hero's task of subduing Medusa.

Were this all, we as readers would be confronting an instance of male masochism by which a man fantasizes himself within the cultural constructions of gender as "a 'feminine' yet heterosexual male subject" (57), as Kaja Silverman so concisely puts it. But Leiris carries the wager against and within masculinity even further with yet a third analogy which stipulates the arena of this death-in-love as analogous to the bullfight. "Just as the *matador* or 'killer' gives the measure of his worth when he finds himself face to face with the bull . . . so in sexual commerce, enclosed face to face with his partner whom he must dominate, a man discovers himself in the presence of a reality" (70), he asserts. By the end of *L'Age d'homme* he has expanded the symbol of the bullfight to incorporate the analogy with Judith and Lucrece and to extend it to a paradigm for his "intellectual impotence" before the world. "I remain a prisoner of this alternative," he concludes:

> the world, real object, which dominates and devours me (like Judith) in suffering and fear, or else the world, pure fantasm, which dissolves between my hands, that I destroy (like Lucrece stabbing herself) without ever having succeeded in possessing it. Perhaps it is especially a question for me of escaping this dilemma by finding a way in which the world and I – object and subject – can stand face to face before one another, on an equal footing, as the matador stands before the bull. (201–2)

One might well read such a passage as the logical outcome of Leiris' earlier involvement with Surrealism and Freudianism in both of which sex and death had been intimately linked. *La Révolution Surréaliste* (1924–29) had included an "enquête" into suicide in its first issue and into love in its last, and the Surrealists had increasingly turned to Charcot's hysterics and to contemporary women anarchists and murderers for "evidence" of the heroism of murder in a corrupt society (Roudinesco II 30–7). Freud's *Beyond the Pleasure Principle*, in which he theorized the death instinct, had been translated into French in 1927 and his *Civilization and its Discontents*, with its hypothesis of a psychic tug-of-war between the forces of Eros and Thanatos, in 1934, when Leiris was resuming work on *L'Age d'homme*. Moreover, a pronounced cultism around the bullfight, and the thematization of the minotaur and of a tauromachia were very much a part of certain Parisian literary and artistic circles from the 1920s through the 1960s. Leiris had introduced the metaphor of the bull into his 1927 *Grande fuite de neige* and his ethnographic mission to Dakar had led to an article on bull-sacrifice which he published in *Minotaure* (1933). Bulls were a recurrent metaphor in the work of his friend and colleague Georges Bataille and another friend, Picasso, had used the minotaur in his *Vollard Suite 1930–37* to image animal nature struggling to free itself from the constraints of human intellect. Moreover, in 1937, between completing *L'Age d'homme* and drafting the first paragraphs of what later became the more elaborated analogy of "De la littérature con-sidérée comme une tauromachie," Leiris had written *Albanico para los toros* as well as two essays, "Tauromachie" and "Miroir de la Tauro-machie," to accompany drawings by André Masson. In short, given the pervasiveness of minotaur/corrida imagery at the time and given his own other writings, one might well conclude that his conjoining of love and death, boudoir and bullring in his autobiography is hardly surprising, or even very original.

Nonetheless, when we recall the resistance to and anxiety about masculinity inherent in Leiris' refusal to idealize his male body, in his identification with Holophernes imagined as beheaded/castrated in the act of love, in his fear of and desire for castration – in short the many signs of what, in terms of masculinity, amounts to feminization – to move the act of love into the bullring is an astounding gesture. It reinserts him into one of the most ferociously and exclusively virile of all closed worlds. To make his erotic dilemma – to be castrated/killed or to castrate/kill himself – paradigmatic of his relation to the "world" symbolized as bullfight is to play out that dilemma not in relation to women but in relation to what Eve Sedgwick calls "homosocial desire" or "the affective or social force, the glue ... that shapes" "the *structure* of men's relations with other men" (2). To do this in an autobiography in which one has consistently represented oneself as failing to meet any ideal of masculinity suggests a highly compensatory strategy before the fear of humiliation, particularly humiliation before other men. How, we can ask, does Leiris' analogy of the male world of the bullring minimize the fear of maximum loss of masculinity which his autobiography so exhaustively documents?

The autobiography explains the "more-than-human beauty" of the bullfight as resting, first of all, "on the fact that between the killer and his bull (the animal enrobed by the cape which lures him, the man enrobed by the bull which circles around him) there is union at the same time as combat" (71), that is, collapse of self and other, subject and object by means of the art of the cape. The second essential is "the murder of an animal according to precise rules" and the third "the danger of death for the man who kills it" (73). By introducing style and order into the killing and increasing its risk, the rules ensure that the slaughter becomes sacred ritual with a prescribed aesthetic and a moral import (19–20); at the same time, skillfully used they enable the matador to face down the dangers of humiliation or death. The pleasurable terror of the bullfight lives in the (Lucrece-like) vulnerability of flesh to the death-dealing horn, its "sacred" end in the moment when virility and art triumph over the flesh's weakness. For, in the final, post-slaughter dénouement of this ritual, the dead bull in all its fleshliness is of no more moment; the matador's victorious gestures and the crowd's response speak to a virility constituted by the transcendence of flesh and mortality.

In the postscript-become-preface, "De la littérature considérée comme une tauromachie," Leiris extends this analogy from lovemaking to literature, theorizing autobiography as an encounter with "the shadow of the bull's horn" (11). Confession commits Leiris, first of all, to the danger inherent in self-exposure, for it is predicated on the revelation of the most intimate facts (12).[9] But while risky, it is also an *act*: an act with regard to himself for it will, as do all autobiographies, modify its writer; an act with regard to his other work for it will expose the "realities" behind the poetry and fiction; an act with regard to others who will regard him differently as a consequence of it (14–15). To save himself from the withdrawal of sympathy threatened by his confessed ugliness, cowardice, impotence, fantasies, aggression against women, extramarital relations and general inability to live up to the ideals of masculinity, he permits himself only the resources and strategies of literary style and symbol (13). Should he fail to keep our sympathy, the horn of the risk he has run (Judith-like) will leave him dead to masculinity and to autobiography.

In this equivalence between the writer and the matador, to act by writing is to reinsert oneself within a masculine code which values action over contemplation, even as one engages in self-contemplation.[10] Through action, the matador kills the bull. Through autobiography Leiris recuperates for immortality and virility the petrification inflicted for gazing on the Medusa; he retrieves his "life in one solid block (an object that I could touch as if to insure myself against death, even though, paradoxically, I was claiming to risk everything)" (20). Most particularly, the act of writing places him in relation to other men. It does so by virtue of an absence because, when the confrontation with "reality" shifts from bedroom to bullring, women cease to figure in the social or psychic construction of masculinity. Indeed, Peter Schwenger has argued that the chief function of the allegory of the writer as matador in the work of writers such as Mishima, Hemingway and Leiris, is to close the "gap" of "the female in himself" that threatens the masculine self (137) – that gash in the head that first prompts Leiris to ask "How will I be able to make love?". The act of writing places Leiris more positively in relation to other men through the self-imposed rule that he can save himself only by art. But neither the danger of the content nor the rules of the form can be academic. "The horn is present" only "where the author assumes the direct risk either of a confession or of a subversive work ... which presents a conception of life 'engaging' its partisan – or its victim" (22; *Manhood* 163). Substituting Theseus for the matador in the metaphoric chain, he qualifies as " 'authentic' " only the work in which "one cannot see ... any other rule of composition than the Ariadne's thread the author followed throughout the explanation he was making (by successive approaches or at point-blank range) to himself" (22; *Manhood* 163).

   Authentic. Engagement. In the brief concluding paragraph which recalls the balcony above war-rent Le Havre on which he positioned himself at the beginning of the preface, Leiris will use these words again as he speculates that had he been closer to "that authentic horn of war," more "materially engaged," he might be less "obsessed" by the need to make literature a risky act (23). Nonetheless, he concludes his prefatory essay, there remains "an essential engagement one has the right to demand from the writer ... to ... tip the scales ... toward the liberation of *all* men, without which none can achieve his own" (23–4; *Manhood* 164). Leiris freely admits that this is an *a postiori* definition of what he was about (21–2). The rhetoric of *engagement*, which he signals by his quotation marks, depends on Jean-Paul Sartre's writings during the war and was not in place when he completed *L'Age d'homme* in 1935. However, his representation of his earlier aims in the rhetoric of political ethics does point to the context for the production of his fourth analogy for anxiety about his masculine body and manhood: Théodor Géricault's *The Raft of the Medusa*.

   Substituting metaphors for Judith and Lucrece, Leiris had concluded that "a woman, for me, is always more or less Medusa or the Raft of the Medusa. I mean by this that, if her gaze does not freeze my blood, then everything must happen as if we made up for it by tearing one another to pieces" (149). The gloss points less to Géricault's actual representation than to the circumstances of the loss of the ship *Medusa*, their social and political ramifications, and the aesthetic subversion and risk of Géricault's painting. A government frigate carrying soldiers and sailors to Senegal, the *Medusa* had run aground off West Africa on 2 July 1816 after her captain, a returned emigré nobleman who owed his appointment to political patronage rather than naval experience, had separated from the rest of the convoy.[11] When it broke up on 5 July, the ship's officers and captain "commandeered" the lifeboats, insufficient to the 400 people on board, while the 150 unaccommodated passengers and soldiers crowded a makeshift raft which the lifeboats were to tow ashore. In order to hasten their own safety, those in the boats cut the ropes to the overloaded raft, leaving it to drift. Over the next days, the soldiers and sailors on it mutineed, and the survivors cannibalized the dead and murdered the weakest among their number in order to stretch their meagre supplies. On 17 July, the fifteen survivors sighted the *Argus*, but failed to get its attention and "lost all hope." Two hours later the *Argus* returned and rescued them. Géricault's painting does not depict the survivors "tearing one another apart" (although many contemporary representations did), but rather the moment of their greatest hope and despair when they tried and failed to catch the attention of the *Argus* (Eitner 7–9). It is this moment that Leiris invokes when he titles his final chapter "The Raft of the Medusa," using the metaphor to describe "that hideous impotence – as much genital as intellectual – from which I still suffer today" (197; *Manhood* 138) and which led him into analysis.

Like the bullring, the raft of the *Medusa* was exclusively male (the one woman passenger had drowned). Unlike the bullring, it is an arena in which first the captain and officers, then the survivors abandoned virile responsibility, in which "civilized" values gave way to a brute instinct for physical survival. By codes both military and masculine, the story of the *Medusa* is scandalous in its cowardice and abjection. It quickly became a political scandal as well when the Ministry of the Navy tried to cover up the actions of the captain. The public received the survivors' accounts as evidence of a crime in which political patronage had preferred incompetent noblemen over Napoleonic War veterans left on half-pay. For many, "the catastrophe of the *Medusa* summed up the plight of France under the Bourbons" (Eitner 10). The shipwreck and Géricault's painting have frequently been invoked ever since in support of political causes, sometimes by figures as prominent as Jules Michelet (Eitner 56).

Informing the political ramifications of the loss of the *Medusa* and Géricault's painting, then, are questions of war and the nation-state raised by the French Revolution, the Napoleonic Wars and the restoration of the Bourbons. Much the same genre of questions informs the iconography of the Medusa (the Gorgon, and not the ship) as "*politically apotropaic*" (Hertz 51 n.9). Having cut off Medusa's head, we should recall, Perseus gave it to Athena/Minerva who placed it on her warrior's shield, where its eye had the same petrifying power on the enemy it had had in life. Hence representations of Minerva's shield to speak to the State's capacities for self-defense in a considerable number of paintings (Hertz 51–2 n.9). So too, as Neil Hertz has demonstrated, revolution, which forced society to look on that which most terrified it, had been imaged in eighteenth- and nineteenth-century political reflections, il-

lustrations, and visual and literary art as a Gorgon, either petrifying
onlookers by exposing herself or, more frequently, usurping the role of
Perseus and cutting off heads.

Leiris thematizes his "chimerical fear of punishment," including the
punishment of "social disgrace" (198; *Manhood* 138) by means of a series
of symbols associated with nationhood, self-defense, and war: Judith,
defending her tribe against an invading army; Lucretia, raped while her
husband is at war and vindicating not only her, but his and, through him,
his city's honor by her suicide; Medusa, whose apotropaic powers defend
against enemies and who symbolized the terrors of revolution; the
Medusa, whose loss raised the scandal of the rights of the nation's
warriors ceded to incompetent courtiers. He attributes his fear at least
partly to "a civilization which kills the criminals it produces and solves by
destruction or war pure and simple problems such as overproduction and
unemployment" (198). As the *Medusa* incident came to represent corruption in a nation and its leaders, so World War I raised painful questions
about the values actually being defended at such heroic cost and about the
competence of national leaders. Particularly acute in France, on the soil
of which so many battles humiliating to the nation's pride had been
fought, this questioning produced – and nowhere more so than among the
Surrealists – a nihilist disavowal of the national and "masculine" values of
the time as entrepreneurial and politically corrupt. For Leiris, then, *The
Raft of the Medusa* symbolizes "the void in which I move. . . . I have come
to understand that nothing will save me except a certain fervour, but that
this world definitely has nothing FOR WHICH I AM CAPABLE OF DYING"
(201).

In a world in which the most incontrovertible proof of masculinity as it
has been sociopolitically constructed – to die for a cause, ideally military
and national – is unavailable because no cause is perceived as worth dying
for, "castration" thematizes the cultural erosion of the "masculine."
Leiris' assertion that only punishment "makes the game worth the
candle" occurs as an elaboration of his confession that "Generally
speaking, sadism, masochism . . . constitute . . . for me . . . only a way of
attaining a more intense reality" (197–8). Deleuze's reading of masochism as an attempt to abolish the father from the symbolic order is
germane here. "What is beaten, humiliated and ridiculed" in the masochist, he hypothesizes, "is the image and the likeness of the father, and
the possibility of the father's aggressive return. . . . The masochist thus
liberates himself in preparation for a rebirth in which the father will have
no part" (58). Masochism, then, resists the sociocultural injunction to
masculinity – in Leiris' context a masculinity already called into question
by the "fathers" producing contemporary political and social events. In

actual social circumstances, of course, a great "gap" lies between the Symbolic Father and embodied men and fathers. The first symbolizes the psychic interiorization and codification which the culture demands in the name of masculinity and to which the second prove more or less inadequate. Masculinity as typically constructed in western cultures, and social and political circumstances, and as evidenced in individual manifestations of psychosexual development, ensures that a man will be in an incompletely masculine, that is, feminized relation to the Symbolic Father.

L'Age d'homme, as Leiris completed it in 1935, left its potential readers with this nexus of the erotic and the political, with seemingly no escape for its narrator from the failure of masculinity. In the six brief paragraphs, written "on the eve of the 'phony war'" (11; *Manhood* 154) and inserted as an "Afterword" in the first edition, Leiris confirms his disillusion with the political "edifice of facility" (9); he identifies manhood with the test of war, "candidly avowing that his true 'manhood' remains to be written when he will have endured, in one form or another, the same bitter trial that his elders faced" (9–10); and he suggests that the "aesthetic" nature of literature might be "amended" by "introducing even the shadow of the bull's horn into the literary work" (11). By the end of World War II, when the manhood of all those in occupied France, insofar as masculinity was constructed in terms of military and national honor, was under siege, the need to construct masculinity, personally and collectively, in alternative terms had become more pressing for Leiris. It gave rise to the expansion of the nexus of eroticism and politics to include writing and the writer as the new masculine avatar in the ironic, but also serious, "De la littérature considérée comme une tauromachie."

Géricault's *Raft of the Medusa* is again apropos. Subversive of contemporary painting in several ways, it had taken a subject (shipwreck) that, by convention, demanded a genre painting and had treated it on a scale deemed more suitable for historical subjects monumentalizing the Empire. However, the *Medusa* incident called into question national pride and represented its survivors from the back, a composition read by critics as inviting viewers to participate in "a tragedy without a hero, a scene of physical suffering without redemption" (Eitner 6). *The Raft of the Medusa*, then, not only offers Leiris the example of anti-heroic art, a symbol for a state of mind of "suffering without redemption," and a connection of that state of mind with a larger context of political and social corruption, but it also offers a powerful example of the assumption of agency in the face of dominant artistic codes by means of acts of subversion and "amendment."

IV. AUTOBIOGRAPHY, AGENCY, DISEMBODIMENT

For it is the question of agency that emerges most strikingly from the artistic manifesto "De la littérature considérée comme une tauromachie" with which Leiris prefaced the post-war edition of *L'Age d'homme* and that introduces the third term of writing into the nexus of the erotic and the political. Where the medical profession was determined to make a man out of Alexina Barbin, and so reduced her to its construction of the morphology of the penis, Leiris makes "castration" the emblem of a social condition. Barbin can represent the social inscription of her body but cannot re-write it even against the body's loss: there is no agency in her act of writing. And the agency s/he assumes in suicide remains personal and limited, though following theorists of masculinity such as Peter Schwenger, who argues that "Only death closes the gap and consummates manhood" (153), it could be read as Barbin's first and final successful embodiment of manhood. Leiris cannot achieve the death he desires and fears, a failure which, in the retrospective notes to the 1946 edition, he no longer reads as "castration" but as a more generalized "fear of commiting myself, of taking up responsibilities – whence my tendency, counterbalanced by an inverse desire, to flee as formidable any virile determination" (211). His afterword-turned-preface transfers agency to writing itself. By making the act of writing and not what writing represents the scene of virility, he takes the step unavailable to Barbin of using his "unmasculine" body to resist and reconfigure the social construction of masculinity.

Leiris thus re-takes masculinity for himself and for writing, though it is a masculinity with a difference, one which lets him have his experience of physical and intellectual impotence and his masculinity too, one which proffers his most unmasculine body and his contemplative activity as the lure by which he intends to vanquish the masculine world. "I imagined the bull's horn," he tells us. "I could not resign myself to being only a man of letters" (12). In a double gesture, he attempts to undo his impotence by reiterating it in autobiography, by cherishing it in representation while renouncing it by writing. This act of public tale-telling under the sign of the bull's horn, with its attendant risks to be overcome by strategy, is a way of claiming his incapacity for masculinity and his fear of being incapacitated by it while at the same time taking on the code of masculinity in its most dangerous aspect, its willingness to court literal and symbolic death. If he succeeds, he claims the glory of the matador: he has exposed himself to "the shadow of the bull's horn" in the form of ruthless dismissal as a man all the while he is enacting masculinity in the skill of his literary strategy. If he fails, impotence and death: literature that is only feminine gesture – "the vain graces of the ballerina" (10). In either case, what stands in for the penis petrified by Medusa's gaze is the virtually indestructible and excessively destructive bull's horn. Yet, at this point, we have a sense of *déjà vu* and, with it, of the real limitations of Leiris' agency-through-autobiography, for, like the forms in Plato's allegory of the cave, the horn remains but a shadow. The autobiographer's lived experience of his body, so powerfully and counter-discursively represented in *Manhood*, once subsumed to the metaphor of writing as bullfight in the preface, disappears, yet again, into the metaphysics of the disembodied "voice" of masculine autobiography.

NOTES

1. Cf. Wendy Hollway (in Henriques *et al*) and Teresa de Lauretis' discussion of her argument (15–17); also Weeks; Laqueur; Butler (8); and Grosz ("Inscriptions" 72–3).
2. In my use of masculine and feminine pronouns for Alexina, I follow her/his own practice in the French text. See the translator's note (xiv).
3. I am indebted to the work of Foucault, Laqueur, Weeks, and Heath for what follows on the history of the discursive construction of sex and gender.
4. Freud, however, could not have posited vaginal sexuality as a basis of female sexual difference without nineteenth-century medicine's discovery of the embryonic homology of clitoris and penis. Early medical science held that the vagina, not the clitoris, was the inverted homologue of the penis. It held, therefore, that men's and women's sexual morphology was the same, rather than different, precisely because, like Freud, it located female sexual pleasure in the vagina. (See Laqueur, *Making Sex*, for a detailed account of these changing representations of female sexual morphology in relation to the male. And see his "Amor Veneris" for a discussion of the clitoris as the most frequently new found, and lost again, land of female sexuality.)
5. Laqueur, *Amor* 99–100 summarizes some of this literature.
6. Mehlman 82–3, and 94 reads the "figures of Judith and Lucrece [as] collapsing into a single figure, in an identical context of hermaphroditism ... [in] the suicide of Cleopatra" later in the book.
7. Germaine Brée and André Clavel read Leiris as using ethnographic practice in his autobiography. Boyer, Schou and Pontalis are among those who, to a greater or lesser extent, read Leiris in psychoanalytic terms; Mehlman provides a detailed Lacanian reading; and Lejeune elaborates a reading of Leiris as a "para-freudienne" (146). French critics in particular tend to read Leiris as moving from the thematization of sexuality in *L'Age d'homme* to that of language in *La Règle du jeu* (see especially Butor 266; Pontalis 319; and Lejeune 147ff and chapter 5)
8. Cf. Freud, "Medusa's Head." While this essay was not available to Leiris in the 1930s, the contradictory significations of losing potency by being turned to stone were not lost on him. Mehlman elaborates the analogy between Freud's and Leiris' imagery of the Medusa in more rigorously psychoanalytic terms (80–2) where Lejeune reads the image of Medusa in the passages on opera as an occasion for "reflection on the illusions of the staging of autobiography" (69–72).
9. In the autobiography itself, in the context of the "depressing influence" on his development of his Catholic education, Leiris speaks of the "imperious attraction" for him of " 'confession' " by virtue of "its humiliating aspect, combined with all that is

scandalous and exhibitionistic about it," claiming to find "a delight as intense as it is severe" in feeling like a "'damed soul' eternally pursued by his punishment" (202–3; *Manhood* 142). The effects of Catholicism in Leiris' construction and representation of the male body and of masculinity needs another study; it might well begin with Foucault's observation that the confessional, its procedures secularized and disseminated into science, is the foundation of all discourse about sex in western cultures (58–65).

10. Cf. Schwenger 110.
11. My information about the personal and political circumstances surrounding the painting and reception of *The Raft of the Medusa* is drawn from Eitner, who in turn relies to a considerable extent on a standard work, Charles Clément's *Géricault, étude biographique et critique* (3rd enlarged edn; Paris, 1879). I am substantively indebted, and grateful, to Len Findlay for bringing to my attention some of the ramifications of Géricault's painting for Leiris' autobiography and for pointing me to Eitner's work.

WORKS CITED

Barbin, Herculine. *Herculine Barbin: Being the Recently Discovered Memoirs of a Nineteenth-Century French Hermaphrodite*. Intro. Michel Foucault. Trans. Richard McDougall. New York: Pantheon Books, 1980. [*Herculine Barbin dite Alexina B.* Paris: Gallimard, 1978.]

Boyer, Alain-Michel. *Michel Leiris*. Paris: Psychotèque Editions Universitaires, 1974.

Brée, Germaine. "Michel Leiris: Mazemaker." *Autobiography: Essays Theoretical and Critical*. Ed. James Olney. Princeton: Princeton UP, 1980. 194–206.

Butler, Judith. *Gender Trouble: Feminism and the Subversion of Identity*. New York and London: Routledge, 1990.

Butor, Michel. "Une autobiographie dialectique." *Répertoire*. Paris: Minuit, 1960. 262–70.

Chesnet, Dr. "The question of identity; the malformation of the external genital organs; hypospadias; an error about sex." In Barbin, above. 124–8.

Clavel, André. *Michel Leiris*. Paris: Henri Veyrier, 1984.

de Lauretis, Teresa. "The Technology of Gender." *Technologies of Gender: Essays on Theory, Film, and Fiction*. Bloomington: Indiana UP, 1987. 1–30.

Deleuze, Gilles. *Sacher-Masoch: An Interpretation*. Trans. Jean McNeil. London: Faber and Faber, 1971.

Descartes, René. *Discourse on Method and Meditations*. Trans. Laurence J. Lafleur. Indianapolis: Bobbs-Merrill, 1960.

Eitner, Lorenz. *Géricault's Raft of the Medusa*. London: Phaidon, 1972.

Foucault, Michel. *The History of Sexuality. Volume One: An Introduction*. Trans. Robert Hurley. New York: Vintage, 1980. [*La volonté de savoir*. Paris: Gallimard, 1976.]

Freud, Sigmund. "Medusa's Head." *The Standard Edition of the Complete Psychological Works of Sigmund Freud*. Vol. XVIII (1920–22). Ed. James Strachey. London: Hogarth, 1955. 273–4.

Gobeil, Madeleine. "Interview with Michel Leiris." *Sub-stance* 11/12 (1975):44–60.

Goujon, E. "A Study of a Case of Incomplete Hermaphroditism in a Man." In Barbin, above. 128–44.

Grosz, Elizabeth. "Inscriptions and Body Maps: Representations and the Corporeal." *Feminine, Masculine and Representation*. Eds. Terry Threadgold and Anne Cranny-Francis. Sydney: Allen and Unwin, 1990. 62–74.

—. "Notes Towards a Corporeal Feminism." *Feminism and the Body*. Eds. Judith Allen and Elizabeth Grosz. Special issue of *Australian Feminist Studies* 5 (1987):1–16.

Gusdorf, Georges. "Conditions and Limits of Autobiography." Trans. James Olney. *Autobiography: Essays Theoretical and Critical*. Ed. James Olney. Princeton: Princeton UP, 1980. 28–48.

Heath, Stephen. *The Sexual Fix*. London: Macmillan, 1982.

Henriques, Julian, Wendy Hollway, Cathy Urwin, Couze Venn, and Valerie Walkerdine, eds., *Changing the Subject: Psychology, Social Regulation and Subjectivity*. London: Methuen, 1984.

Hertz, Neil. "Medusa's Head: Male Hysteria under Political Pressure." *Representations* 4 (1983):27–54.

Laqueur, Thomas W. "Amor Veneris, vel Dulcedo Appelatur." *Fragments for a History of the Human Body. Part Three*. Ed. Michel Feher with Ramona Naddaff and Nadia Tazi. New York: Zone, 1989. 90–131.

—. *Making Sex: Body and Gender from the Greeks to Freud*. Cambridge: Harvard UP, 1990.

Leiris, Michel. *L'Age d'homme*. Précédé de *De la littérature considérée comme une tauromachie*. 1939; rpt. Paris: Gallimard, 1973. Trans. Richard Howard. *Manhood: A Journey from Childhood into the Fierce Order of Virility*. San Francisco: North Point P, 1984. Translations of *L'Age d'homme* are generally my own; where I have followed Howard, I have cited page numbers from *Manhood*.

Lejeune, Philippe. *Lire Leiris: Autobiographie et langage*. Paris: Klincksieck, 1975.

Malouf, David. *12 Edmonstone Street*. London: Chatto and Windus, 1985.

Mehlman, Jeffrey. *A Structural Study of Autobiography: Proust, Leiris, Sartre, Lévi-Strauss*. Ithaca: Cornell UP, 1974.

Panizza, Oscar. "A Scandal at the Convent." Trans. Sophie Wilkins. In Barbin, above. 153–99.

Pontalis, J.-B. "Michel Leiris ou la psychanalyse sans fin." *Après Freud*. Paris: René Julliard, 1965. 300–24.

Porter, Roger. "Figurations and Disfigurements: Herculine Barbin and the Autobiography of the Body." *Autobiography and Questions of Gender*. Ed. Shirley Neuman. London: Frank Cass, 1991. 122–36.

Roudinesco, Elisabeth. *La Bataille de cent ans: Histoire de la psychanalyse en France*. 2 vols. Paris: Seuil, 1986.

Schou, Lene. "A propos *L'Age d'homme*: note sur le rapport 'critique littéraire' et psychanalyse." *Prepub* 24:25–44.

Schwenger, Peter. *Phallic Critiques: Masculinity and Twentieth-Century Literature*. London: Routledge and Kegan Paul, 1984.

Sedgwick, Eve Kosofsky. *Between Men: English Literature and Male Homosocial Desire*. New York: Columbia UP, 1985.

Silverman, Kaja. "Masochism and Male Subjectivity." *Male Trouble*. Eds. Constance Penley and Sharon Willis. A special issue of *Camera Obscura* 17 (1988):31–66.

Smith, Paul. "Vas." *Male Trouble*. Eds. Constance Penley and Sharon Willis. A special issue of *Camera Obscura* 17 (1988):89–111.

Turner, Bryan S. *The Body and Society: Explorations in Social Theory*. Oxford: Basil Blackwell, 1984.

Weeks, Jeffrey. *Sexuality*. London: Tavistock; Chichester: Ellis Horwood, 1986.

Poet and Patriarch in Maxine Hong Kingston's China Men

JOSEPH FICHTELBERG

Few recent American writers have enjoyed such extraordinary success as Maxine Hong Kingston. Her autobiographical *The Woman Warrior* (1976) has achieved near-canonical status – hailed not only by mainstream readers but by Third World critics and feminists who see in her mordant portraits of Chinese-Americans a protest against patriarchal culture. But it is her neglected *China Men* (1980)[1] that is truly exemplary of Kingston's quarrel with patriarchy. Henry Louis Gates, Jr. uses the term "signifyin(g)" to describe the antithetical position Kingston adopts – the reproduction of dominant literary models with a distinct, often ironic difference. Marginalized writers, Gates argues, use "antiphonal structures" to reverse dominant meanings (67, see also 44ff.), dispersing tropes as a jazz artist disperses musical themes. But there is an even more radical way to address an oppressive discourse. Truly revolutionary writers, Julia Kristeva asserts, do not merely reverse their culture's tropes but *traverse* them – "explore all the sources of signification, that which posits a meaning as well as that which multiplies, pulverizes, and finally revives it" ("Oscillation" 165). The importance of *China Men* is that it self-consciously displays that process of pulverizing and reviving meaning. By examining *China Men* through Kristeva's insights, one discovers how culturally marginalized writers may recast discursive norms.

I

Although she has often been called a feminist,[2] Kristeva's syncretic thought is not easily categorized. An amalgam of structural linguistics, psychoanalysis, Hegelian philosophy, and dialectical materialism, her work strives to be self-consciously "non-systematic"[3] – "a space for contestation and self-contestation: a circle that never closes" (Kristeva, *Sémiotiké* 31). Particularly in her earlier essays of the 1960s and 70s, the object of that self-consciousness was what Kristeva called the "0–1" system of Aristotelian logic – a "monological" pursuit of truth through the "exclusion of contradictions" (*Sémiotiké* 183), founded ultimately upon the subject–predicate relations of Greek syntax (151). The notion of sign itself, she observes in "Word, Dialogue, and Novel," "is a product of scientific abstraction (identity–substance–cause–goal as structure of the Indo-European sentence), designating a vertically and hierarchically linear division" (*Desire* 69). Poetic discourse, Kristeva claims – particularly that associated with the avant-garde of the last hundred years – subverts that logic by generating an ambiguous, "paragrammatic" structure, a network of references capable of simultaneously negating and affirming:

> Poetic language is a dyad inseparable from the *law* (that of normal discourse) and of its *destruction* (specific to the poetic text); and this indivisible coexistence of the "+" and the "−" *is* the constitutive complementarity of poetic language [*langage*].[4] (*Sémiotiké* 179)

Rather than the system of binary oppositions structured by the law of the excluded middle, the "0−2" logic of paragrammatic discourse demands the "inseparable cohabitation" of opposites (183):

> That is to say: definition, determination, the sign "=" and the very concept of sign, which supposes the vertical (hierarchical) rupture [*découpage*] signifier–signified, cannot be applied to poetic language, which is an infinity of ruptures [*découpages*] and combinations. (*Sémiotiké* 150)

For Kristeva, poetic language is one of rigorous subversion.

Kristeva grounds discourse in psychoanalytic process. Drawing in part on the work of Melanie Klein, she views the acquisition of language as dialectical, the rupture of an initial identification with the mother by the symbolic law of the father. That presymbolic matrix Kristeva calls the *chora* (receptacle), after Plato's designation in the *Timaeus* of a "Space, which is everlasting, ... providing a situation for all things that come into being, but itself apprehended without the senses, by a sort of bastard reasoning, and hardly an object of belief" (52b). Kristeva's receptacle is equally amorphous, less a fixed structure than a modality associated with the rhythmic, "musical" character of preverbal utterance (*Revolution* 29). Since the *chora* "has no thesis and no position" (26), it cannot be grounded in discourse; rather, it grounds, much as the unconscious does consciousness. Amorphous, too, is the infant's sense of self, "fragmented" by the competing oral and anal drives that "connect and orient the body to the mother" (28). Indeed, it is the mother's intermediation that establishes what Kristeva calls the "semiotic" modality, "articulating (in the largest sense of the word) a continuum: the connections between the [child's] (glottal and anal) sphincters in (rhythmic and intonational) vocal modulations ... " (28–9). The ambiguous "0–2" logic thus has a somatic basis in the mother's nurturing role.

But language itself is acquired through a countervailing process of separation from the mother. Exclusionary impulses are already contained within the semiotic *chora*, in the sadistic drives aroused by the infant's sphincters (148–52). With the onset of the mirror phase, in which a unified image supplants the body's diffuse drives, the process is accelerated; and with the Oedipal phase it is complete. Here Kristeva largely accepts Lacan's account of the phallus as the primary signifier.[5] The child, who had formerly relied on the mother for gratification, now perceives a lack, "*separates* from his fusion with the mother, *confines* his jouissance to the genital, and transfers semiotic motility onto the symbolic order" (47). But if the symbolic function – language itself – is constituted through rupture from the semiotic *chora*, the latter is not entirely suppressed. In acts of protest against the dominant order – neurosis, psychosis, avant-garde art – the semiotic re-emerges. One sees this preverbal behavior in fetishism or glossolalia, or in the calculated linguistic subversions of Mallarmé and Joyce, evoking pre-Oedipal orality (153). The semiotic *chora*, then, is not a stage to be superseded but a potential ever in dialectical tension with the dominant symbolic mode. It nurtures disruption.

This sense of revolutionary optimism associated with the return of the repressed is the quality distinguishing Kristeva's work from Lacan's. For Lacan, the acquisition of language is an essentially tragic event, an Hegelian fight to the death that ends in enslavement.[6] Kristeva, by contrast, sees poetic language as a ground for regeneration. Symbolic structure, in Kristeva's thought, is always linked to social structure, an order driven by its revivifying ruptures. Just as the socially disruptive carnival became Bakhtin's textually productive carnivalesque,[7] so the semiotic ruptures of revolutionary art force social change. The "site of social relationships but equally of asocial relationships," the revolutionary text "introduces ... the dynamic of the socio-historical process, at the same time that it helps to create this process by formulating its subject across [*à travers*] a new structure of language" (*La révolution* 371, my translation). By recapitulating the rupture that brought symbolic discourse into being, the artist can reverse the process, freeing the social by disrupting linguistic structure. Moreover, as Kristeva has often noted, this process is independent of gender. The very notion of the subject in process/on trial (*le sujet en procès*) suggests that all speakers are equally challenged. Revolutionary writers, Kristeva asserts, "traverse" rather than deny sexual difference:

> The word "traverse" implies that the subject experiences sexual difference, not as a fixed opposition ("man"/"woman"), but as a process of differentiation. ... only the truly great "literary" achievements bear witness to a traversal, and therefore, to sexual differentiation. In this way, the subject of the writing speaks a *truth* proper to any speaking subject, a truth that the needs of production and reproduction censure. ("Oscillation" 165, my translation)

Great art, Kristeva asserts, challenges the very structure of language by resisting the domination and loneliness at its core. Such art asserts life in the face of death.

These three concepts, then – traversal, rupture, *chora* – form the basis of a Kristevan reading. By traversing meaning, revolutionary texts multiply linguistic structures, subjecting them to extraordinary stresses that cause them to explode or fragment. But the truly innovative writer is not satisfied with mere rupture. Rather, she reabsorbs those shards of discourse into a larger and older unity represented by the *chora* – a receptacle far more diffuse yet more powerful than the phallic signifier of language. The *chora* is the locus of poetry itself, the creative, rhythmic, and musical matrix underlying all discourse. It is both the context and the substance of meaning. To define that elusive context is the task of *China Men*.

II

Kingston opens *China Men* with a resonantly ambiguous image. The questing Tang Ao, seeking the Gold Mountain, stumbles instead upon a Land of Women, in which he is summarily enslaved. Forced to submit to the degradation reserved for women, he has his ears brutally pierced, his toes broken and bound, and his face painted, to transform him into a tottering dainty. But the traditional tale offers more than simple wish fulfillment; it is a coded appropriation of phallocentric discourse, a textual aggression conducted by women. Hence the appearance of phallic instruments scarring an androgynous body: an old woman's "long nail" scrapes the victim's neck (4); a needle repeatedly punctures his earlobes, probing the "layers of skin" like so many sheets of paper (4). And yet the needle is not the only prominent instrument. Equally prominent is the feminine "eye" directing the thread – a crone's "bright eye" squinting as she threads a needle (3), the "wide eye" of the needle

"('needle's nose' in Chinese)" widening the hole (4), the mouth that the crone threatens to sew shut; the "loops of thread," and the "gold hoops" (4). As if in conformity to Kristeva's "0–2" logic, Kingston here announces her appropriation of opposites in a deconstruction of symbolic gender. As she can claim this typically male quest myth, she can also make it feminine.

But what Kingston offers in the first vignette, she dismisses in a second. Now the narrator recollects an afternoon when she saw her father coming home. The sharply-dressed man had all the right attributes – an expensive suit, fine shoes, even the same tobacco smell, but he was not her father. When the real father arrived, she ran to him with the same eagerness, seeking out the "Rainbo notepads and the gold coins that were really chocolates" (6). If writing here is associated with the father's notepad, it is also counterfeit, a means not to change but to abandon identity. In effect, Kingston has reversed herself here: a laboriously produced androgyne becomes an amorphous male whose features are effaced. Rupture (signified in the puncture wounds and broken bones), by which the narrator appropriates male fantasy, is immediately shadowed by the uncertain continuity of the father, of symbols, of writing. Kingston's subversion of the father is itself subverted.

The text thus challenges patriarchal discourse by fragmenting it, rendering it ambiguous. The same disruption surrounds the narrator's first portraits of BaBa. Confronting his silence, the narrator offers several scenarios in which her father's birth – in 1891 or 1903 or 1915 – provokes rupture. "'Your little brother is different from any of you,'" a grandmother explains to BaBa's brothers. "'Your generation has no boy like this one'" (16). His distinguishing mark is the ability to hold a pen, to "'prepare for the Imperial Examinations'" (16). And yet the literary tradition that BaBa represents is moribund. Although the examination site is suffused in a generous atmosphere of "rhymes, metaphors, puns, and radicals" bandied by boys who draw "invisible calligraphy" on their hands (25), BaBa's experience recapitulates Tang Ao's travail. In the cell accommodating him during the examination, he huddles in fetal position beneath a blanket, propping open his eyelids as he desperately tries to stay awake. "He understood the blue-eyed Buddha-who-cut-off-his-eyelids" (26), and hears the disembodied screams of his predecessors as he drives an awl into his thigh to fight drowsiness. But the monumental examination with its seven-hundred-word essays secures him nothing more prominent than a post in the village school, where his dedication to text quickly decays. Those exalted "parallelisms" with which his literary world was filled –

correspondences between "the elements, the humors, the architecture of emperors' palaces and commoners' houses, the weather, the trees, the members of families, ... the centuries, the dynasties of China" (34) – crumble before the squirming farmers' sons whose highest ambition is to journey to the Gold Mountain. In a scene repeated at the end of the text, the narrator graphically captures the decay: "he saw a writer splotch his paper; another took dab after dab to form one stroke; another outlined a word and colored it in; another dribbled ink in the wide part of a word, then spread it out. Heavy hands moving from right to left smeared columns of writing" (35) that paradoxically "destroy[ed] ... literacy" (39). Only when BaBa's senses have completely deadened can he break with tradition and head for America.

III

If Western literature has enshrined the journey as a labor of self-discovery, BaBa's flight to America is decidedly ambiguous: both a rupture promising renewal and a renewed lapse into despair. Characteristically, the very account of the passage is counterfeit, Kingston offering versions of the "legal" and the "illegal" father but leaving the matter undecided. In each of them, though, one notes the presence of the *chora*, suggesting a crisis in signification. BaBa's first step is to adopt a fictional lineage, a trail of "paper" relatives established by former emigrants, complete with nominal house, farm, and village. The village men would "chan[t] these facts to a beat," or "rhym[e]" them (46) – an indication of semiotic rupture. The journey itself is marked by receptacles – barrels, boxes, crates – signs of the semiotic *chora*. In one of the more ornate versions, BaBa is concealed in a crate and conveyed to a "dar[k] place" where he is rocked asleep by the sea's rhythm (49), "a new language, ... the water's many tongues speaking and speaking" like Kristeva's preverbal music (51). "Of course," the narrator adds, "my father could not have come that way" (53), and the counterfeit is replaced by the legal journey, ending in the prison-like enclosure of Angel Island. Subjected to medical examination much like Tang Ao's (they "pulled his eyelids with a hook" [53]), the legal father discovers a fragmented world – a setting where writing is both preserved and destroyed, where women walk overhead and men imagine they inhabit a "coffin" (56). The walls are covered with poems of protest and lament, yet writing is treacherous; a woman drops a telltale note and is saved when the men tear it up and eat it. BaBa does not sign a poem about freedom for fear he might be deported. Yet when he finds freedom, as a dashing New York laundry worker, he does so through the alienated form of screen images, his texts now *City Lights* and *Little Miss Marker*, watched "again and again" all day in darkened theaters (61). Indeed, this portion of the text is awash in counterfeit images. Like the pictures "Ed" has taken beside cars and airplanes, the community of Chinese Sojourners survives as a series of empty signifiers.

Significantly, Kingston follows this long tale of decay with an intertext recapitulating – but reversing – "Edison's" experience. "The Ghostmate," an allegory of the questing male, presents a youth far from home, who "may have passed the Imperial Examinations ... or failed" (74), and who enters a Circean world filled with pulsing music again suggestive of the *chora*. The beautiful muse who greets him promises creative freedom – the best materials, time to study and work – and the youth responds by glimpsing an agenda of masterworks: "the possibility of the lightest, smallest shoe, the true poem, the embroidery or painting of the phoenix" (78–9). But like Odysseus, he longs for the familiar; and when he finally returns home, an emaciated wretch, he finds that centuries have elapsed. The conventional ending, the chastened hero happily restored to his family, belies the tale's complexity, for in its undoing of quest and creation, it poses a textual impasse. If the lonely BaBa imagined himself a gallant student nostalgic for Parisian lovers, the allegorical youth's satisfaction only increases longing. Moreover, the tale calls attention not only to the instability of the quest myth itself, but to the absurdity of all heroic artistry, that "creative onanism," as John Irwin puts it, "in which through the use of the phallic pen on the 'pure space' of the virgin page ... the self is continually spent and wasted" (qtd. in Gilbert and Gubar 6). The quest tale thus dissolves itself in a play of opposites recapitulating a successful quest – a rupture that preserves. "The Ghostmate" traces the 0–2 logic of poetic ambiguity.

But the quest is not only an individual matter; it has political implications that Kingston explores through a pair of narratives linked to the ambiguous father, "Great Grandfather of the Sandalwood Mountains" and "The Grandfather of the Sierra Nevada Mountains." Once again, the narrator seeks links with a dead tradition on another ambiguous terrain, the cane fields of Hawaii standing "east, that is, west" of her origin, and seeded with the "murdered and raped bodies" of Filipinos and Chinese (88). Here, too, tradition has nothing to say: the cane tassels make "no ... outlines" to be construed "as a message" (88); the wind-blown leaves whisper no words. Thrown back upon her imagination, the narrator is free to construct a space where ambiguity becomes a revolutionary instrument.

Associated with that ambiguity is a sense of cosmic rupture. So great had been the trauma forcing Bak Goong overseas that the Yellow River itself "had reversed its course overnight; it reared up, coiled in the air, and slapped down backwards to run the other way, south instead of north" (92). But escaping the "century-size upheaval" in China merely thrust him upon new barbarism abroad (93), symbolized by the queer Chinese dialects and the English who talked a slippery prose from sadistic, sphincter-like mouths. Domination and discourse intertwine.

Indeed, once Bak Goong settles into the life of forced labor in this worker's paradise, his struggle becomes almost entirely defined by language. It is a sign of his initial impotence that he is unable to defy the plantation's rule of silence, designed to prevent collusion among disgruntled workers. As he hacks without effect at thick trunks, he imagines the speeches he would make: " 'You go out on the road to find adventure,' he wanted to say, 'and what do you find but another farm where the same things happen day after day. Work. Work. Work. Eat. Eat. Shit and piss. Sleep. Work. Work' " – each syllable punctuated by the dull thud of his axe (100). British imperialism has reduced discourse to a deadened uniformity in which the Hegelian master is more damaged than the slave. "Shut up. Go work. Chinaman, go work .... You stay go work. Shut up" is the oppressor's response to Bak Goong's pent-up arias (101). And surrounding them all are the ghostly voices of despair, "the lamentation of old men and children, thousands of souls wailing in separate voices" (110–11). The deadening sameness of imperialism isolates as it betrays.

Bak Goong's remedy literally involves the liberation of repressed speech. After suffering a respiratory attack in which he is consumed by sadistic fantasies – "Cut – you – into – pieces. Chop – off – your – legs .... Chop – you – down – stinky – demon" he splutters as he coughs (114) – he recalls the Chinese version of the Midas tale, and induces the China men to bellow their secrets into an eye-like hole. Since they were the "founding ancestors" (118), they could establish such customs, so terrifying to the British that the men are left alone. But this reappropriation of a Western myth is structurally less revolutionary than the presence of the semiotic *chora*, a rupture evoked repeatedly in the chapter. It first appears in Bak Goong's opium vision of "an amazing gold electric ring connecting every living being," breaking down the binary oppositions between "sleeping and waking, work and play, yours and mine" (95). "[M]eanings are for decoration," Bak Goong decides, as he rejects the patriarchal dyads underwriting imperialism (95). Hence his subsequent vision of "two rainbows across the sky, the colors of the top one in the opposite order of the bottom one" (97), which replaces BaBa's phantom Rainbo pad with a more pliant text. A third vision suggests the *chora* even more graphically. Above the sea one night Bak Goong witnesses two dancers "revolv[ing] in ... brightness," "their random movements repeated in series, a dance.... . He heard music draw out into one long note. The waves going in and out forever was the same as no motion at all" (109). Rhythm, movement, music – all embody Bak Goong's revolutionary message. If he has been unsuccessful in overthrowing patriarchal dominance, he has at least become a "founding ancestor" of a new, visionary order.

And yet, once again, Kingston does not allow this essentially Taoist vision to stand unchallenged. For if in his ecstasy Bak Goong imagines himself "Lao Tse's great thinker" (95), the following intertext, "On Mortality," offers a Taoist disciple punished for speech. Tu Tzu Chun is promised immortality if he can endure the nine hells without uttering a word. In this reverse quest he sees his wife tortured and endures horrible mutilation, comforting himself by recalling that all he saw was illusion. Entering a long black tunnel he emerges, like Tang Ao, reborn as a deaf-mute female. In time she, too, gives birth, still suffering in silence; but when her husband threatens to kill the baby, she cries out, thus forfeiting immortality for the human race. And lest the reader blame the failure on male questing, Kingston retells the tale in a second intertext featuring a Polynesian trickster. Demanding silence from all creatures, he descends into the ocean in search of Hina of the Night, surrounded by signs of the *chora* – "a chant that could hardly be discerned from silence" (122) – as he enters the goddess's vagina. But emerging with Hina's heart, he is spotted by a bird, who breaks silence with laughter, another sign of semiotic rupture.[8] Once again, then, language has reached an impasse, a crisis of implication.

The companion narrative of Ah Goong, the railroad builder, deepens that impasse. At times the heroic worker seems to embody rupture itself. A daredevil dynamiter, he recapitulates the descent of Tu and the trickster, upending the world as he sets tunnel charges: "Hills flew up in rocks and dirt. Boulders turned over and over.... . The terrain changed immediately. Streams were diverted, rockscapes exposed" (136). With these explosions, the hierarchy of signifier and signified itself disappears: the sound of the blast is "a separate occurrence, not useful as a signal" (136); and when Ah Goong hangs suspended over cliffs setting charges, he becomes a bird, or, urinating, a waterfall (132). Yet although the China Men leave their mark on the land (" 'The track sections are numbered,' " Ah Goong would tell the dying, " 'your family will know where we leave you' " [138]), the land

consumes them. After the project and their heroic strike are over, they
are summarily dismissed, excluded, and murdered, a fortune signified
by Ah Goong's climactic visit to a San Francisco jeweller. Wanting to
bestow a Sojourner's gift upon his wife, he had a jeweller "refine" his
hoard of gold into a ring he designed himself – "two hands clasping in a
handshake" (150). The ring, a counterfeit, would become a battered
heirloom, a sign that the Gold Mountain really existed (127–8). That
the eye-like ring commemorated impotence as well as virility, death as
well as resourcefulness, is an irony only a battered Sojourner could
understand.

IV

One episode during Ah Goong's narrative suggests Kingston's
emerging textual strategy. During the railroad strike, artists from local
newspapers come to sketch the men, and the same scene yields contradictory images. In some sketches, the strikers are "perfect young gods
reclining against rocks, wise expressions on their handsome noble-
nosed faces." In others they are "faeries with antennae for eyebrows
and brownies with elvish pigtails," dancing in the moonlight (141–2).
The ironic opposition does more than expose racial stereotypes; it
points to the universal and simultaneous presence of opposites in our
images of the world – an ambiguity disrupting the oppressive conformity of language. But this Taoist vision also puts Kingston's
text itself at risk, for the constant ruptures of continuity, the shifting perspectives in storytelling, expose all language to its own deconstruction. In undermining patriarchal discourse, Kingston may well
undermine her own text.

Kingston makes the threat explicit in the opening vignette of "The
Making of More Americans." The narrator, recalling a childhood visit
to her grandfathers, spots a large toad. " 'A field chicken,' " cried her
grandfather Say Goong, as if the creature "had detached itself from the
living earth" (165). " 'Sky chicken. Sky toad,' " the man insisted to the
wondering child. " 'Heavenly toad. Field toad' ":

> It was a pun and the words the same except for the low tone of *field*
> and the high tone of *heaven* or *sky*. He put the toad in my hands – it
> breathed, and its heart beat, every part of it alive – and I felt its
> dryness and warmth and hind feet as it sprang off. How odd that a
> toad could be both of the field and of the sky. It was very funny.
> (166)

In this summer scene bursting with creative energy – the child enters a latticework festooned with "gourds, beans, tomatoes, grapes, and peas, winter melons like fat green prickly piglets" (166) – the narrator almost literally recoups thetic rupture, the moment when symbols are generated, as a dual, indeterminate structure presided over by patriarchs. The grandfather's odorous manure pile was magnificent: it "hummed" as it fueled the entire garden; it swarmed with blue-black flies "like excess sparks"; "it smelled good." Even the dirt was "clean and not dirty at all" (166). But if signifiers contain alternatives, they also conceal absence. Hence the narrator portrays the ephemeral delight of another discovery, a "wide brown eye" in the dark stable (167), "waves of dark skin over a hot and massive something that was snorting and stomping" (166) – an immense creature called horse, paradoxically "contained ... in a word" (167). Yet a few years later, the horses were gone, as were the manure pile, the grandfathers, the house and garden. Such vastness "could not possibly have disappeared so completely" (168); but all that remained were absent landmarks, like the signified in a game of *fort/da*.[9] "This is the ancestral ground" (171), said BaBa, taking photographs of vacancy as the child wondered. Language, apparently so substantial, becomes the record of progressively effaced traces after all, the repository of Lacanian deaths. From the metaphors that reverse common sense, to the horses emerging from nothingness and back again, to the grandfathers similarly appearing and disappearing, Kingston suggests the dangers in undermining discourse. Behind the spectral genealogy lies a subversion of creativity itself.

Kingston explores these perils in the tale of Mad Sao, the successful Chinese-American punished by visions from home. Resisting his mother's importunities, he is besieged by scolding letters, all suggesting the gradual effacement of signs as the price for overthrowing patriarchs. " 'The arbor we sat under is gone, eaten,' " wrote Sao's mother after the communist takeover, evoking a landscape similar to that of the American grandfathers: " 'Frogs, beetles, all eaten... . There'll not be harvest again' " (173). " 'We've burned the outhouse for fuel,' " claims another letter, adding that outhouses had become useless. " 'Nothing comes out because nothing goes in' " (174) – a constriction of orifices suggesting the eclipse of language in a return of sadistic anality. Even gender distinctions fade; the dying old are so shriveled that one "couldn't tell whether it was man or woman" (175). When his mother dies, Sao takes the same step that Kristeva mapped out for the failed avant-garde (*Revolution* 82, 182, 214–15; *Desire* 139 ff.). Now deprived of letters he is thrust back into a presymbolic madness dominated by the mother. Like the family admiring the absent farm, Mad Sao begins "talking to the air, making motions to the air, talking to no voice" (176), and can find no rest until he returns to China and properly buries the ghost, satisfying the ancestral line.

But Mad Sao is not alone. The young narrator, hiding in her basement from the fearsome Kau Goong, has a similar reaction: "I thought over useless things like wishes, wands, hibernation. I talked to the people whom [sic] I knew were not really there" (181). And Uncle Bun, so obsessed with overthrowing the capitalist patriarchs that he becomes paranoiac, reduces the world to a series of empty signifiers. For Bun, all discourse collapses as metaphor yields to metonymy in the endless reproduction of the same. Hence his obsession with wheat germ (" 'Stir it into milk and juices. Drink it in soups and beverages .... Mix it with ice cream and strawberries. Combine it with flour. Combine it with rice.' " [190]) becomes a terror of forced feeding. In a parody of presymbolic orality, he fears that a mountain of American garbage is being reserved for him. " 'They're going to feed it to me. They'll capture me and tie me down and shovel it into my mouth. They're going to make me eat it. All of it. It's all for me' " (199). Abandoning the system of differences that constitutes language, Bun, too, disappears without a trace.

But if abandoning difference is disastrous, asserting it is equally so, a point Kingston reserves for the last of these American narratives, that describing the strange fortunes of an uncle and aunt. Their story is a tragicomedy arising from repeated thetic ruptures. A prosperous Hong Kong merchant, I Fu was one day overcome by a feverish vision of the world initially reminiscent of Bak Goong's Taoist illuminations. "Inanimate objects glowed ... the trees and flowers and bugs and dogs were spraying colors. Human beings flared haloes.... . Bands of light connected couples" (212). As the young narrator had suddenly understood metaphor, so now the uncle penetrates essential symbols:

> He explained later how he understood the stopping quality of red light and the go of green. The city was not making a general roar or hum. His ears separated out the sounds of various motors, the gas pipes and water mains under the city, each bicycle wheel, the way the rubber peeled off the asphalt.... . He passed a bookstore ... [and] wanted to stop and see whether *Red Chamber Dream* and Communist books were red, the Clear River poems blue and green, Confucius's writing a white light, and the *I Ching* yellow or saffron.... . He passed a drugstore and saw the little drawers leaking squares of light. (212)

But whereas Bak Goong and the narrator delighted in the collapse of dyads, I Fu reinforces them, in a manner that provokes disaster. Absorbed in the system of differences constituting language, he arrives at the bank, where he withdraws his life savings and gives the money to strangers, as if to be rid of that universal, empty signifier.[10] Alone he feels omnipotent, "choreographing the movements of people and the weather" (212). Recovered, he can only invent tales of post-hypnotic thievery, all the while insisting on difference. " 'I could see everything,' " he explains; " 'the world was the same, but the story behind it was different' " (213). Difference creates disaster.

Indeed, the narrator's entire encounter with these relatives suggests the impotence of difference. Ushered into their tiny San Francisco flat, she notes the different fortunes, habits, expressions of this family, and must submit to the aunt's tale of being "alternately very rich and very poor many times" (207). When she greets her aunt she cannot recall whether the woman is an evangelical or an indifferent Christian (203), and when she leaves she is bothered by her mother's strictures against taking a gift, "throwing it in and out of windows, pushing the windows up and down, pulling the box back and forth until I gave up and took it" (217). Language, too, partakes of the malaise. The narrator's Chinese explanation of the word *science* falters for lack of a synonym better than *magic*; in the street she notes the contemptuous gestures of older women who "do not mean disdain – or they *do* mean disdain, but it's their proper way of treating young people" (202). But the young are equally contemptuous of the old, signified in the disdain of the aunt's older sons and the rebelliousness of the youngest. " 'There's nothing we can do about him,' " the aunt laments (218), voicing the dull fear that echoes throughout *China Men*. Like her sardonic portraits of cultural difference, Kingston's attacks on patriarchal discourse may well yield "nothing significant" (219). Ambiguity has fostered impotence.

V

Kingston has thus come full circle. Opening with a strong assault on patriarchalism and its textual dominance, she allows madness to threaten the narrative, nonsense to shadow deconstruction. If Kingston's subversion is to succeed, she will need to find a way to avoid the excesses of her eccentric characters, to create an independent stance in discourse without abandoning it – a task, as Michel Foucault notes in *The Order of Things*, that is, at best, treacherous (382–5). In a critique of discourse, outright rejection is as useless as uncritical acceptance. Rather, having, in Kristeva's terms, "multiplied" and "pulverized" that discourse, she must now "revive" it by returning to her immediate family.

Appropriately, Kingston begins the operation with two intertexts treating Sojourners. "The Wild Man of the Green Swamp" traces the fortunes of a carnivorous beast haunting a Florida town. As public anxiety grows, so do his terrible feats, until a sheriff's posse hunts him down. The beast turns out to be a diminutive, homesick Chinese sailor who has jumped ship and escaped from a hospital. In the swamp he has lived by his wits, killing small animals with an aluminum club and cooking them in a pot, keeping himself reasonably clean. Yet he can abide neither Americans nor Chinese, and when he is told he will be deported, he hangs himself. Here is yet another of Kingston's solitaries, confronting the enormous force of an alien culture and succumbing, with only a mute, impotent protest.

The reverse is true, however, for Lo Bun Sun, the most self-conscious of Kingston's heroes. This Chinese Robinson Crusoe is distinguished from his English counterpart by his obsession with texts. On his remote island he sustains himself by using ink and paper to keep a diary. When his writing implements wear out he fashions new ones from bark and berries; when he discovers his Friday, Sing Kay Ng, he becomes a teacher, and the two keep school, "reading, studying, writing, recording plantings, harvests, bird migrations, the seasons, the weather ... " (231). Yet Lo Bun Sun's activities have neither the desperation of BaBa's scholarship nor the egotism of the Ghostmate's solitude. His is a conscientious attempt to survive, to use writing for self-preservation. His texts have an intrinsic dignity because of the writer's faith that language can save. Hence, it is appropriate that Lo's very name joins opposites:

> There is drudgery in his name: *Lo* is "toil," what one does even when unsupervised; he works faithfully, not cheating. *Lo* means "naked," man "the naked animal," and *lo* also sounds like the word for "mule," a toiling animal, a toiling sexless animal. *Bun* is the uncle who went to China to work on a commune. And *sun* is like "body" and also "son" in English and "grandson" in Chinese. *Sun* as in "new." Lo Bun Sun was a mule and toiling man, naked and toiling body, alone, son and grandson, himself all the generations. (226)

When one adds that *lo* also connotes a spiritual master, a disciple of Buddha among the lotus eaters, as well as the *dike* and *libation* by which one "transplanted ... young plants by hand" (227), it is clear that this is a redemptive figure meant to restore continuity, to reverse death by "traversing" meaning. Unlike the Wild Man, who died in inarticulate despair, Lo Bun Sun's struggle to "leave a record" is its own resonant meaning (227). Death and life, rupture and continuity coincide in his story. He is a symbol of reconciliation.

Lo Bun Sun's solitary perseverence becomes the model for the text's final chapters, in which the narrator returns to her immediate family. BaBa, the decayed scholar thrown out of work at a Stockton gambling parlor, becomes the very embodiment of autocratic excess, attacking the children, withdrawing into sullenness, shrieking inarticulate nightmares in which he is both villain and victim. "He covers his ears and shuts his mouth tight, but the scream comes out" (251), the narrator notes of his sadistic regression. The reader recalls BaBa's early cursing of "sisters or grandmothers or women in general" (14). Unlike his former misogyny, however, these attacks seem *motivated*; they mark him as a tragic figure, one whose sufferings ennoble. Hence the narrator's encounters with patriarchal discourse are now far more benign. She recalls with pleasure walking with BaBa to work as he read the ideographs of benevolent societies; "he pointed out sights; he named the plants, told time on the clocks, explained a neon sign" (240) – decoded the world. Patriarch has turned educator.

What marks this discourse as different from BaBa's former manner is its contingency, its overwhelming sense of facticity. Whereas the language he inherited from China was hierarchical, a network of correspondences, the language he uses in America is often chaotic, improvised. Hence he was never charged when the gambling hall was raided because he always made up "a new name befitting the situation" (242). The police "never found out his real names or that he had an American name at all"; and although he retained the patriarchal "power of naming" (242), that power now rests on chance – a condition the narrator explicitly links to poetry. For the gambling parlor – a Crusoe's island having "no noise, no people, no sun" (240) – is a locus of language, with all the danger and surprise of revolutionary discourse.[11] "You had to be a poet to win," the narrator remarks, and the winning poems were "plain and very beautiful: 'Shiny water, bright moon' "; "white jade that grows in water," "red jade that grows in earth" (241). Like Sing Kay Ng, the narrator, too, becomes a pupil, and conspirator: "He gave me pen and ink, and I linked words of my own: 'rivercloud,' 'riverfire,' the many combinations with *horse, cloud*, and *bird*" (241). Both patriarchy and its dissolution are part of that covert instruction.

To reinforce this revolutionary tutelage, the chapter begins and ends with evocations of the *chora*. "One of his places was the dirt cellar," she explains, where on occasion he would show her the well, "a hole full of

shining, bulging, black water, alive, alive, like an eye, deep and alive
... the opening to the inside of the world" (238). This "black sparkling
eye of the planet" (239), so resonant with maternal imagery, redeems
that other well poisoned, in *The Woman Warrior*, by the narrator's
nameless aunt. After BaBa's depression, the imagery recurs in the
basement of his new laundry, through whose passageways the children
discover "the secret of cities" (254). " 'This is beautiful' " he remarks of
a Yosemite photograph (255), as the narrator realizes that "males
have feelings" (254). In his facticity, in his suffering, BaBa has been
redeemed.

Redemption is also the theme of the only chapter in *China Men*
treating a contemporary. "The Brother in Vietnam" opens with a
reprise of BaBa's momentous birth. In Stockton, as in China, the
siblings "jumped up and down" when their brother was born, singing
like the "animals in fables: 'Jump like a squirrel. Bob like a bluejay.
Tails in the air. Tails in the air'" (265; cf. 16). But the decay of
patriarchy is far more vicious in the son's generation, as the text is
flooded with images of anonymous casualties – "limbs, and heads in
impossible positions, rib cages barely covered with skin, faces that one
could not stop staring at. Piles of skeletons with teeth and eye sockets
and hair" (266). If, before, Ed had escaped to the maternal warmth of
Little Miss Marker, theaters are now dominated by newsreels of world
war: men peer from a "big hole," scream in explosions, march leadenly
on colorless terrain (263). Chinese cartoons depict mothers with bellies
bloated, like Uncle Bun's, by forced feeding; "tanks and rockets roll
by" in endless parade; "all the talk [is] about war and death" (268).
Under such conditions, the very contradictions of patriarchalism seem
demonic. At home the narrator draws pictures of a nuclear explosion –
"a brain on a column" like a transformed needle and eye – in which she
thinks she hears the angelic "golden music" of a suicidal *chora* (273). To
enable her son to avoid the draft, it was rumored, a "mother stabbed his
eyes out with her two hairpicks" (269), a grotesque version of pre-
Oedipal fixation. Like BaBa shrinking before misfortune, veterans will
not talk, their stories far "worse than guts hanging out, legs and brains
hurtling through the air, cities and countries bombed into insanity ... "
(274). For the narrator, as for her forebears, cataclysm defines the
world.

As the threat of mass destruction renders individual difference
negligible, the narrator witnesses the collapse of all signification. The
"O" on her dog tag stands for blood type, religion, and race, "because
neither black nor white" (276); and grown men drink ink – one of Lo's
"Four Valuable Things" – attempting to fail their army physical. The

brother, a high school English teacher, presides over the destruction of language in a manner far more devastating than did BaBa. In school he finds texts mutilated or jammed behind radiators: *Romeo and Juliet* becomes a genealogy of horror, yet a home movie sent by a former student in Vietnam loses its terror on repeated viewing. In the Navy, the destruction is complete. Given a job tutoring sailors, the brother witnesses the very extinction of meaning. " 'I see words, and the ink runs together,' " says one student. " 'Then it's dark' " (289). " 'The words look like they're melting in water,' " says another; and there are repeated evocations of receptacles: " 'Dark like a tunnel.' " " 'Dark. Claustro.' " " 'Like a tight cave. And I can hardly breathe' " (290). Linked to such phobias is Uncle Bun's brand of paranoia, now alarmingly accurate. When the brother drinks juice, eats candy or bread, rides in a plane or car, he supports "the corporations that made tanks and bombers, napalm, defoliants, and bombs." Objects lose their distinctions in such a system; "Everything was connected to everything else and to war" (284). In this fatal continuity, everyone is coded, cross-referenced, indexed, exploited. There is no escape.

The brother's naval service thus approximates Kingston's struggle to manipulate a murderous discourse. Like BaBa's, his initial response is denial – refusing food, acting strangely, keeping silent. He, too, is tormented by violent dreams in which he "takes up his sword" and slays enemies, whose bodies "come apart in rings and rolls" (291), a parody of Tang Ao's torments. Yet the dream victims remained silent, neither "screamed [n]or wept because their mouths had been gagged and eyes blindfolded" (291), as if in masochistic denial. What saves the brother is a double articulation. Like Bak Goong, he recognizes that his defense against the demons is constant speech. "From morning till night" he mutters (287) – produces texts whose only purpose is to manifest self. Lo Bun Sun had composed long lists of complaints, "fictions about raving death, starvation, and mutilation" (227), but always returned to chronicling his endless chores. So too the brother, whose anxieties leave a record:

> "My brain feels like wet cement. I can't see. Here I'm getting up, and I didn't even go to sleep yet. I didn't even have any dreams. Sorry. No dreams to tell. When I get out of the Navy, I'm never going to make a bed again. They're turning us into housewives. Make beds. Fold clothes. Shine shoes. Sweep. Swab. The Navy is housework." (287)

To oppose an oppressive discourse, one must create a language of one's own.

But even this discourse is vulnerable, and the brother's triumph involves a more principled stance. Invited to study French, Chinese, and Vietnamese in the Navy's language school, he is at first attracted by the offer. Much of his ancestral Chinese, after all, translates well into Vietnamese. But to exploit language under such circumstances is to return to barbarism, to become "a persuasive interrogator–torturer ... [to] force a mother to choose between her baby with a gun at its belly and her husband hiding behind the thatch, to which she silently points with her chin" (301) – to murder the father by eclipsing his perversions. Recognizing that all language of the father involves such choices, but that choice is inevitable, the brother politely declines, feeling alien for the remainder of his tour, but principled, intact. Neither revolutionary nor torturer, he survives by perceiving, without succumbing to, contradiction. The narrator's conclusion might well be the successful poet's epitaph: "He had not gotten killed, and he had not killed anyone" (304). Neither master nor slave, he had at least endured.

If the final chapter reverses the revolutionary implications of BaBa's gambler–poet, the exchange is not unanticipated. For if a culture's discourse is truly oppressive, the poet's only recourse, as Kristeva argues, is a kind of guerilla writing, asserting only long enough to deny, arguing by evasion. One senses Kingston's thoroughgoing commitment to this program in a final vignette. At a party, the narrator meets an older Filipino scholar convinced that his country is the Gold Mountain. In 1603, he avers, Chinese appeared looking for "a gold needle in a mountain." In the noise of the party, his meaning is unclear. " 'A gold needle,' " the narrator wonders. "To sew the sails, was it? A compass needle, was it? ... Because I didn't hear everything, I asked him to repeat the story, and what he seemed to say again was 'They found a gold needle in a mountain' " (307–8). And yet the Chinese could have been anywhere – in Mexico, Cabit, or California. The gold needle could have been a fiction, and the scholar's promise to " 'write it down in a letter' " might have been a lie (308). What remains vivid are "the young men," absorbed, like the narrator, in the tale. Observing as she records them, the narrator glimpses the constituents of self.

NOTES

1. For recent readings of *China Men*, see Sledge; Juhasz; and Rabine. I would like to thank Paul John Eakin for his sensitive criticism of this essay.
2. See Féral; Jardine, *Gynesis*; Jones; and Zepp. For other assessments of Kristeva's work see Adriaens; Jardine, "Theories of the Feminine"; Philip; and Brandt.

3. The phrase is Brandt's, who argues, however, that Kristeva's approach has not evaded system (137 and *passim*).
4. See also Kristeva, "My Memory's Hyperbole" 267.
5. See Lacan, "The Signification of the Phallus" 281–91; and "The Mirror Stage" 1–7.
6. Indeed, when Lacan reaches back to the presymbolic, he finds "death, from which … existence takes on all the meaning it has. It is in effect as a desire for death that [the subject] affirms himself for others; if he identifies himself with the other, it is by fixing him solidly in the metamorphosis of his essential image, and no being is ever evoked by him except among the shadows of death." See "Function and Field of Speech and Language" 105. On Lacan's Hegelianism, see Casey and Woody 77–88.
7. See Kristeva's "Word, Dialogue, and Novel," in *Desire in Language* 78. Cf. Bakhtin 196–277.
8. See Kristeva, *Revolution in Poetic Language*, 80, 205, 217 ff.; Cixous; and Irigaray 163.
9. See Freud 14 ff.
10. See Marx 133, 141.
11. See Rabine 481.

WORKS CITED

Adriaens, Mark. "Ideology and Literary Production: Kristeva's Poetics." *Semiotics and Dialectics: Ideology and the Text*. Ed. Peter Zima. Amsterdam: John Benjamins, 1981. 179–220.
Bakhtin, Mikhail. *Rabelais and His World*. Trans. Hélène Iswolsky. Bloomington: Indiana UP, 1984.
Brandt, Joan. "The Systematics of a Non-System: Julia Kristeva's Revisionary Semiotics." *The American Journal of Semiotics* 5.1 (1987): 133–50.
Casey, Edward and J. Melvin Woody. "Hegel, Heidegger, Lacan: The Dialectic of Desire." *Interpreting Lacan*. Eds. Joseph H. Smith and William Kerrigan. New Haven: Yale UP, 1983. 75–112.
Cixous, Hélène. "The Laugh of the Medusa." Trans. Keith Cohen and Paul Cohen. *Signs* 1.4 (1976): 875–93.
Féral, Josette. "Antigone or *The Irony of the Tribe*." *Diacritics* 8.3 (1978): 2–14.
Foucault, Michel. *The Order of Things: An Archaeology of the Human Sciences*. New York: Vintage-Random, 1970.
Freud, Sigmund. *Beyond the Pleasure Principle. The Standard Edition of the Complete Psychological Works of Sigmund Freud*. Trans. James Strachey. London: Hogarth, 1955. Volume 18. 7–64.
Gates, Henry Louis Jr. *The Signifying Monkey: A Theory of Afro-American Literary Criticism*. New York: Oxford UP, 1988.
Gilbert, Sandra M. and Susan Gubar. *The Madwoman in the Attic: The Woman Writer and the Nineteenth-Century Literary Imagination*. New Haven: Yale UP, 1979.
Irigaray, Luce. *This Sex Which Is Not One*. Trans. Catherine Porter with Carolyn Burke. Ithaca: Cornell UP, 1985.
Irwin, John. *Doubling and Incest, Repetition and Revenge*. Baltimore: Johns Hopkins UP, 1975.
Jardine, Alice A. *Gynesis: Configurations of Women and Modernity*. Ithaca: Cornell UP, 1985.
——. "Theories of the Feminine: Kristeva." *Enclitic* (1980): 5–15.
Jones, Ann Rosalind. "Writing the Body: Toward an Understanding of *l'écriture féminine*." *Feminist Studies* 7.2 (1981): 247–63.
Juhasz, Suzanne. "Maxine Hong Kingston: Narrative Technique and Female Identity." *Contemporary American Women Writers*. Eds. Catherine Rainwater and William J. Scheick. Lexington: U of Kentucky P, 1985. 173–89.

Kingston, Maxine Hong. *China Men*. New York: Random, 1980.

——. *The Woman Warrior: Memoirs of a Girlhood Among Ghosts*. New York: Knopf, 1976.

Kristeva, Julia. *Desire in Language: a Semiotic Approach to Literature and Art*. Ed. Leon S. Roudiez. Trans. Thomas Gora, Alice Jardine and Leon S. Roudiez. New York: Columbia UP, 1980.

——. *La révolution du langage poétique: l'avant-garde à la fin du XIXe siecle: Lautréamont et Mallarmé*. Paris: Seuil, 1974.

——. "My Memory's Hyperbole." Trans. Athena Viscusi. *The Female Autograph*. Ed. Domna C. Stanton. 1984; rpt. Chicago: U of Chicago P, 1987. 219–35.

——. "Oscillation du 'pouvoir' 'au refus'." [Interview by Xavière Gautier.] *Tel Quel* 58 (1974): 99–100; trans. Marilyn A. August. *New French Feminisms*. Eds. Elaine Marks and Isabelle de Courtivron. New York: Schocken, 1981. 165–7.

——. *Revolution in Poetic Language*. Trans. Margaret Waller. New York: Columbia UP, 1984.

——. *Sémiotiké: recherches pour une sémanalyse*. Paris: Seuil, 1969. Quotations are my translations.

Lacan, Jacques. "The Mirror Stage as Formative of the Function of the I as Revealed in Psychoanalytic Experience." *Écrits: a Selection*. Trans. Alan Sheridan. New York: Norton, 1977. 1–7.

——. "The Signification of the Phallus." *Écrits*. 281–91.

——. "The Function and Field of Speech and Language in Psychoanalysis." *Écrits*. 30–113.

Marx, Karl. *Grundrisse: Foundations of the Critique of Political Economy*. Trans. Martin Nicolaus. New York: Vintage-Random, 1973.

Philip, Lewis E. "Revolutionary Semiotics." *Diacritics* 4.3 (1974): 28–32.

Plato. *Timaeus*. Trans. Francis M. Cornford. Indianapolis: Bobbs-Merrill, 1959.

Rabine, Leslie. "No Lost Paradise: Social Gender and Symbolic Gender in the Writings of Maxine Hong Kingston." *Signs* 12.3 (1987): 471–92.

Sledge, Linda Ching. "Maxine Hong Kingston's *China Men*: The Family Historian as Epic Poet." *MELUS* 7.4 (1980): 3–22.

Zepp, Evelyn. "The Criticism of Julia Kristeva: A New Mode of Critical Thought." *Romanic Review* 73.1 (1982): 80–97.

The Autobiographical Manifesto: Identities, Temporalities, Politics

SIDONIE SMITH

Decolonization never takes place unnoticed, for it influences individuals and modifies them fundamentally. It transforms spectators crushed with their inessentiality into privileged actors, with the grandiose glare of history's floodlights upon them. It brings a natural rhythm into existence, introduced by new men, and with it a new language and a new humanity. Decolonization is the veritable creation of new men. But this creation owes nothing of its legitimacy to any supernatural power; the "thing" which has been colonized becomes man during the same process by which it frees itself. (Fanon 28)

All "I's" are not equal. Nor are they conceptualized similarly. There is, for instance, the "we" that is sometimes an autobiographical "I." There is also the Rastafarian "I and I"; and the female "I" that, as Maxine Hong Kingston suggests, in Chinese is the same as "slave." Charged with history, representational imprints, and self-representational politics, "I's" are consolidated, naturalized, centralized or marginalized through certain cultural practices that effectively "regulate" the epistemological, ontological, and hermeneutical implications of autobiographical utterances (Butler, *Gender Trouble* 1–34).

In the postcolonial, global environment, the cultural hegemony of the west comes under question. Imperial gazes become *déclassé* as the old imperial "I" is revealed for what it has been: a locus of normative and exclusionary stabilizations of subjectivity that silence marginalized peoples, thereby occluding specific temporalities of identities, specific heterogeneous histories. Stripping the silver from the back of the mirror that reflects back the imperial gaze, revealing the palimpsestic lineaments of their status as subject rather than object, formerly "subject" peoples begin to resist the totalizing definitional politics of traditional autobiographical practice. But what kinds of auto-biographical strategies lead to what kinds of empowerments? That is the issue I want to explore here, with particular attention to the autobiographical manifesto.

One strategic move we might label the move of mimesis. The autobiographer might position herself as the white male bourgeois autobiographer: that is, she mimes the textual politics of "man" through the law of the same, the white male One. Speaking from this location in discourse proffers authority, legitimacy, readability. It proffers membership in the community of the fully human, the "brotherhood of metaphysical man." For subject peoples, slaves and ex-slaves, subalterns, homosexuals, women, such membership is psychologically and politically expedient and potent. Unselfconsciously embraced, however, mimesis invites recuperation as well as the promise of power, the maintenance of subjection to the self-definitions that bind. It maintains the silver on the back of the mirror.

Yet there is another side to this mirroring, the nitrate of mimicry. For something may be exposed here: an unauthorized speaker positions herself in the locale of traditional selfhood, thereby introducing a menacing suspicion of inexact correlation between representations. "As incomplete mirrors, as the waste of the system that produced the identity of the white male," suggests Linda Kintz, "[an unauthorized speaker] can only reflect back to the male subject a partial representation of himself, a reflection that is askew, flawed, not specular" (131). Such autobiographical miming quietly contests the "natural," "commonsensical," "universal" categorizations of difference. In addition to mimesis's treacherous invitation to recuperation, then, comes its promise of escape from an exclusionary configuration of identity.

A second strategy for a contestatory autobiographical practice involves the engagement in a politics of fragmentation as the means to counter the centrifugal power of the old "self." For it is problematic to maintain a decisive, unified point of departure for identity as the ground of a liberating autobiographical practice since the exclusions of unified points are legion. But shattering the old notion of the individual in favor of the split and multiply fragmented subject cannot always serve emancipatory objectives; rather, it can paradoxically serve further oppressive agendas, as Judith Butler cautions:

> If oppression is to be defined in terms of a loss of autonomy by the oppressed, as well as a fragmentation or alienation within the psyche of the oppressed, then a theory which insists upon the inevitable fragmentation of the subject appears to reproduce and valorize the very oppression that must be overcome. ("Gender" 327)

Any autobiographical practice that promotes endless fragmentation
and a reified multiplicity might be counterproductive since the autobiographical subject would have to split itself beyond usefulness to be
truly nonexclusionary. It is hard to coalesce a call to political action
around a constantly deferred point of departure.

Other strategies for oppositional autobiographical practice are
grounded in conceptions of "experiential" politics. Difficulties nego-
tiating the terrain of "the real" lead, in fact, to opposing orientations to
experience. For some there is an "experience" outside representation
to which the text refers. Since there is an ontological basis to identity, a
potentially emancipatory practice might be one that seeks to uncover
the "true" self and the "truth" about the self's experience, the sources
of oppression and strength, the essential difference in body, psyche,
and modes of knowing and being in the world. For others such a
positivist approach to experience neglects the relationship of experience
to discourse, the artifactual nature of representation, the operations
and apparati of cultural determinations. What I have elsewhere called a
predatory textuality occludes the former transparencies of experience.
As it does so, an autobiographical practice emerges that participates in
a drama of negativity, to allude to Julia Kristeva's theoretical frame,
the drama of the what-I-am-not. Perhaps we can linger in the space
of negativity, consciously resisting the imperializing attempt to uni-
versalize any "us," "we," or "I," but once again we might be caught in
an endless qualification of our individual positionalities that takes us
further away from any community of interest and political action.

Yet autobiographical writing has played and continues to play a role
in emancipatory politics; and so a set of questions circling around the
notion of agency needs to be posited. How can the subject, subjected as
she is by cultural determinations, make change happen? Can there be a
liberating change or merely a change of positions within an always
already "colonized" space? Can any "I" recollocate the marker of
the subject or only capitulate to a predetermined recollocation?
From within the postmodern theoretical territory decolonization itself
proves problematic. How can the forces of determination, whether
linguistic, economic, psychosexual, ideological, or discursive be
eluded? Can there be a free, agentic space; and if so, where in the world
can it be found?

In her recent analysis of gender trouble and feminist theory, Butler
has argued that

> to understand identity as a *practice*, and as a signifying practice, is
> to understand culturally intelligible subjects as the resulting effect

of a rule-bound discourse that inserts itself in the pervasive and mundane signifying acts of linguistic life. (*Gender Trouble* 145)

But she also notes that discourses are many, their temporal consonances and dissonances variable, their impacts unpredictable. While rules govern the cultural intelligibility of an "I" through the operation of repetition, with repetition comes variation. Consequently identity is not determined by the rules; rather, it is a practice of working within and against the rules. And agency is likewise "located within the possibility of a variation on that repetition" (*Gender Trouble* 145), a reading of agency similar in certain ways to Paul Smith's when he suggests that "a person is not simply an *actor* who follows ideological scripts, but is also an *agent* who reads them in order to insert him/herself into them – or not" (xxxiv–xxxv).

Autobiographical practices become occasions for the staging of identity, and autobiographical strategies occasions for the staging of agency. Thus within what Butler labels "this conflicted cultural field" the autobiographer can lay out an agenda for a changed relationship to identity. We see this agenda in recent texts by women which participate in self-consciously political autobiographical acts. I call these texts autobiographical manifestos. Purposeful, bold, contentious, the autobiographical manifesto contests the old inscriptions, the old histories, the old politics, the *ancien régime* by working to dislodge the consolidations of the Eurocentric, phallogocentric "I" through an expressly political collocation of a new "I." In service to a new "social reality," what Donna Haraway describes as "our most important political construction, a world-changing fiction" (191), the manifesto offers an arena in which the revolutionary can insist on identity in service to an emancipatory politics, even if, as Robert K. Martin argues, that identity is "assumed."

* * *

Definitions suggest that a manifesto is a proof, a piece of evidence, a public declaration or proclamation, usually issued by or with the sanction of a sovereign prince or state, or by an individual or body of individuals whose proceedings are of public importance, for the purpose of making known past actions, and explaining the reasons or motives for actions announced as forthcoming (*OED*). Within this definitional context six constituent aspects of manifesto affect our discussion.

1. To appropriate/to contest sovereignty:
In the imperial gaze of the old "I" – that "transcendental rational

subject outside of time and space, the subject who is the speaker in
Enlightenment philosophy" (Hartsock 160) – peoples at the margins
are totalized and stabilized as "not-an-individualized-'I,'" a "lack"
whose humanity is "opaque," and whose membership in the human
community is negated by relegation to what Nancy Hartsock describes
as "a chaotic, disorganized, and anonymous collectivity" (160–1).
The autobiographer of the margins thus enters the generic arena as an
alienated speaker, but not an alienated speaker in the postmodern
sense. This alienation, as Susan Stanford Friedman has argued,

> is not the result of creating a self in language, as it is for Lacanian
> and Barthesian critics of autobiography. Instead, alienation from
> the historically imposed image of the self is what motivates the
> writing, the creation of an alternate self in the autobiographical
> act. Writing the self shatters the cultural hall of mirrors and breaks
> the silence imposed by male speech. (41)

And we need to add, also, of "white" speech. Autobiographical
manifestos reject vigorously the sovereignty of this specular *ancien
régime*, and the hegemonic collocation of the old "I" of Western
autobiographical practice.

In her quarrel with the old sovereign, the autobiographer grapples
with what Paul Smith terms the ideological "I," that fixed "subject
position" of discursive and cultural practices, representing culturally
legitimated and authorized performances of identity – gendered,
racialized, sexualized, etc. These collocations (of "woman," "black,"
"lesbian," etc.) linger and labor inside the text, ghosts in the techno-
logical machinery of autobiography. Such ghosts function as templates
for repetition. Repetition, however, breeds contempt; that is to
say, repetition brings with it alterations precisely because, as Smith
suggests, "imaginary identifications ... are continually vulnerable to
the registration of ever renewed and contradictory interpellations"
(106). The autobiographical manifesto confronts this process directly:
the tensions set in motion by contradictory collocations of subject
positions and identities incite, to use revolutionary rhetoric, self-
conscious encounters with the politics of identification and catalyze
identity around specific and oppositional contours of "I-ness." Resisting "the taken-for-granted ability of one small segment of the popula-
tion to speak for all" (Hartsock 171), the autobiographer purposefully
identifies herself as subject, situating herself against the object-status
to which she has been confined.

2. To bring to light, to make manifest (literally, struck with the hand):

Since awareness of the pressures to repetition and certain cultural identifications is the ground of resistance to repetition, the difficult road to a liberatory autobiographical practice lies through the terrain of cultural critique. And so, when Cherríe Moraga comments in her autobiographical manifesto, *Loving in the War Years*, that "the Third World lesbian brings colored female sexuality with all its raggedy edges and oozing wounds – for better or for worse – into the light of day," she captures colloquially the political agenda of the autobiographical manifesto: to force issues "into the light of day" (138). Intent on bringing marginalized experiences out from total occlusion in the shadows of an undifferentiated otherness with its embodiments, its opacities, its anonymities, the autobiographical manifesto anchors its narrative itinerary in the specificities and locales of time and space, the discursive surround, the material ground, the provenance of histories.

To bring things "into the light of day," to make manifest a perspective on identity and experience, affects an epistemological breakage in repetition: it asserts the legitimacy of a new or alternative "knowledge" located in the experience of the margins.[1] The autobiographical manifesto thus attempts to develop what Nancy Hartsock describes as

> an account of the world as seen from the margins, an account which can expose the falseness of the view from the top and can transform the margins as well as the center ... an account of the world which treats our perspectives not as subjugated or disruptive knowledges, but as primary and constitutive of a different world. (171)

The individual story becomes the occasion for what Hartsock calls "'standpoint' epistemolog[ies]" (172), analyses of specific confluences of social, psychological, economic, and political forces of oppression; and the trajectories, strategies, and tools of the analyses take various forms, some of which we will explore below as we consider the enabling myths and motivating metaphors of resistance.

3. To announce publicly:

Autobiographical writing is always a gesture toward publicity, displaying before an impersonal public an individual's interpretation of experience. The very impetus for contemporary autobiographical manifestos, however, lies in the recognition of a vexed relationship between what too easily becomes the binary opposition of the political and the personal. "The personal is political" rang the early rallying cry of the white, middle-class feminist movement; and through the last two decades the politics of personal relationships, the economics of reproduction, and the politics of psychosexual development have been central to feminist analyses in many fields. In challenging the hegemony of white middle-class feminism, however, theorists of multiple differences have differentiated the personal stakes and psychological impacts of systems of colonization, focussing on the personal experiences of multiple oppressions, of class, caste, race, gender, sexuality, nationality. In this more heterogeneous context, "the private" requires reconceptualization, as Aida Hurtado suggests when she emphasizes that

> the political consciousness of women of Color stems from an awareness that the public is *personally* political. ... There is no such thing as a private sphere for people of Color except that which they manage to create and protect in an otherwise hostile environment. (849)

And so a cautionary gesture is necessary here. Different autobiographers come at the private/public duality from different experiences of oppression, from different locales. As a result, the topography of private/public politics may proceed along different axes.

Hurtado argues that we need to foreground the relative positionality of specific women vis-à-vis the "middle-class white man" who stands for the figure at the "center" of the "public" space: "his" gaze maps out the places of power, the margins of meaning, the geographies of knowledge. As a result, the cartography of private space takes its contours from multiple spaces of adjacency. For instance, the white middle-class woman exists alongside "public man," sharing his private spaces. But the woman of Color exists separately from that "man," generally at a distance from his private space. Different alignments toward the hegenomic "private space" condition different cultural constructions of "woman," different cultural practices for women (848–9).[2] The autobiographical manifesto asserts unqualifiedly, even exuberantly, both the politicization of the private and the personalization of the public, effectively troubling the binary complacencies of the *ancien régime* of selfhood with its easy dichotomization of private and public (Haraway 205). But the trajectory of its mappings must be considered in the specific cultural locations of the woman who issues the manifesto's call to action.

4. To perform publicly:

While it might seem strange to repeat the former aspect of the autobiographical manifesto with a change of one word, it seems important to note separately the performative aspect of the autobiographical manifesto. Expressly a public performance, the manifesto revels in the energetic display of a new collocation of identity. The manifesto engages directly the cultural construction of identities (of gender, race, *et al.*) and their sanctioned and legitimated performances, fore-grounding the systems of identification pressing specific collocations on specific persons. It takes a public stand on behalf of purpose-ful deflections, intervening in previous oppressive performances of identity, "troubling" culturally authorized fictions sustaining regimens of repetitions.[3] Historicizing identity, the autobiographical manifesto implicitly, if not explicitly, insists on the temporalities and spatialities of identity and, in doing so, brings the everyday practices of identity directly into the floodlights of conscious display.

5. To speak as one of a group, to speak for a group:

Much, though not all, of women's autobiography assumes a collective orientation. In the manifesto, however, group identification – "an awareness of the meaning of the cultural category WOMAN for the patterns of women's individual destiny" (Friedman 41) – is the rhetorical ground of appeal. During her public performance the mani-festo speaker positions herself expressly as a member of a group or community, an autoethnographer so to speak (Lionnet 99). The "I" anchored in collectivity is the "I" of what Rita Felski à la Jurgen Habermas labels a "counter-public" sphere (166). Counter-public spheres are multiple, invoking collocations around various experiences of oppression and exclusions from the "central" or "centripetal" bour-geois public sphere. While Felski's particular interest focusses on the dynamics of the feminist counter-public sphere, which she says "does not claim a representative universality but rather offers a critique of cultural values from the standpoint of women as a marginalized group within society" (167), for the purposes of this discussion we need to foreground the existence of multiple counter-public spheres which operate along analogous lines, proffering their specific critiques of universalizing spheres of influence.[4]

In the manifesto, communitarian ethnography functions as a kind of "nationalism." Bernice Reagon captures the "nationalism" inherent in communitarian politics when she suggests that a liberating space

> should be a nurturing space where you sift out what people are saying about you and decide who you really are. And you take the time to try to construct within yourself and within your community who you would be if you were running society ... [This is] nurturing, but it is also nationalism. At a certain stage,

> nationalism is crucial to a people if you are ever going to impact as
> a group in your own interest. (qtd. in Hartsock 163)

Nationalism motivates the specific navigational moves the manifesto
takes through the landscape of identity. Postulating a contestatory
discursive "nationalism," the manifesto quarrels with centering
agendas and, through its narrative itinerary, stages a breakage in
repetitions. As it does so it resists the universalizing discursive practice
of "man" and proclaims the viability of the non-universal position.

6. To speak to the future:

The generic contracts of Western literary practices promise something, but what exactly they promise is subject to various theoretical
interpretations. Traditionally, Western autobiography involves a
contractual obligation in which the autobiographer engages in a
narrative itinerary of self-disclosure, retrospective summation, self-
justification. Thus critics of autobiography, including such contemporary theorists as Philippe Lejeune, emphasize the retrospective
aspect of autobiography. Postmodern theorists have shifted the trope
to the autobiographical text as the site of a deadly specularity.
Paul de Man, for instance, argues that "autobiography veils a defacement of the mind of which it is itself the cause" (930). As a result,
"the autobiographical project" becomes, according to Paul Smith, "a
privileged kind of impossibility, always given over to uncertainty,
undecidability, and, finally, to death" (103). But other theorists resist
what they consider the dead end of death in autobiography. For
instance, Kathleen Woodward talks of the writing of autobiography as
taking place not under the sign of death, defacement, or desire but
under the sign of anxiety, "a state of expecting a danger and preparing
oneself for it, although the danger may be unknown to oneself, that is,
not consciously known" (108). Attempting to suggest a difference
between male and female narratives, Woodward suggests that where
men may write under the sign of desire and its "emphasis ... on past
loss," women write under the sign of anxiety for future loss (108–9).

The "I" of the autobiographical manifesto does not write under the
sign of desire or the sign of anxiety. Rather the "I" writes under the sign
of hope and what Hélène Cixous calls *"the very possibility of change"* (249
my emphasis), emphasizing the generative and prospective thrust
of autobiography. Calling the "self" into the future, the manifesto
attempts to actively position the subject in a potentially liberated
future distanced from the constraining and oppressive identifications
inherent in the everyday practices of the *ancien régime*. Thus, while the

manifesto looks back in what Teresa de Lauretis terms "the critical negativity" of theoretical critique, it also gestures forward in "the affirmative positivity of its politics" to a new set of spaces for identity (26).[5]

Since new interpretations and hopeful futures are "crucially bound up with power" (Modleski 136), the manifesto always foregrounds the relationship of identities to power. It insists on new interpretations, new positionings of the subject as a means of wresting power, resisting universalized repetitions that essentialize, naturalize, totalize the subject. In service to that political cause, the autobiographer issues the call for a new, revolutionary subject, offers an agenda for "I"- transformations. Ultimately, then, the manifesto pursues a utopian vision, "a 'waking dream' of the possible," writes Françoise Lionnet, "which might inspire us to see beyond the constraints of the here and now to the idealized vision of a perfect future" (110).[6]

* * *

I have tried to elaborate some descriptive markers of the auto- biographical manifesto as a way of stimulating certain ways of reading the self as manifesto. Like theory generally, they are meant not to rigidify and specify all the workings of the autobiographical manifesto but to suggest some lines of inquiry and some originating points for considering variations and problematics. I turn now to a brief con- sideration of three autobiographical manifestos.

In a recent semester I taught a graduate course in feminist theory. When we turned to the French feminists and specifically to Hélène Cixous's "The Laugh of the Medusa," the students breathed a sigh of thankful relief. After the sometimes turgid and inelegant prose of certain Anglo-American theorists, they found Cixous's prose vibrant, provocative, always troubling but never dull. As our discussion pro- gressed we found ourselves focussing on the rhetorical strategies of Cixous's flamboyant self-presentation. For "Laugh" offers a thrilling and gutsy performance of gender (à la Butler), enacts what Friedrich Nietzsche describes in *The Will to Power* as "*the magic of the extreme*, the seduction that everything extreme exercises" (qtd. in Lionnet 74).

Cixous's provocative "Laugh" is certainly a manifesto. The language that establishes its tenor is the language of revolution – future-oriented, explosive, subversive. Its expressed gesture is toward both the break- ing up of the old and the positing of the new: "as there are no grounds for establishing a discourse, but rather an arid millennial ground to break," she proclaims, "what I say has at least two sides and two aims: to break up, to destroy; and to foresee the unforeseeable, to project" (245). The prose abounds in the terminology and metaphors of revolutionary warfare. There are "sovereigns" to fight, an "empire" to "seize" by a "militant" (253) who goes on "scouting mission[s]" (248).

For Cixous the enemies are two: man the oppressor and woman without a body. The former is the entirety of patriarchal culture and its fantasy of the normative human/male. Thus she metaphorizes the male body as a state dick-tatorship (259). The latter enemy is "a woman without a body, dumb, blind," who can never be "a good fighter" because she functions only as a "servant of the militant male, his shadow" (250). Man is the sovereign to be deposed, woman without a body, the specular peasantry holding up the state dick-tatorship. To fight the war of liberation, Cixous's freedom fighter must capture the female body, the lost territory of subjectivity, releasing it from its status as lack, its relegated negativity.

In order to carry out a revolutionary plot, the speaking "I" must become an agent provocateur, infiltrating herself doubly, inside her body and inside history. The two agendas, the one individual and the other collective, are effected through the revolutionary medium of language since writing will "give her back her goods, her pleasures, her organs, her immense bodily territories which have been kept under seal" (250) and it will facilitate her "shattering entry into history, which has always been based *on her suppression*" (250). For Cixous only the writing "I" has the potential to become the revolutionary "I," since writing enables woman to come into agency and to escape the confinement of objectification.[7] The battleground for the freedom fighter is thus the battleground of state representationalism, of language itself. Since language is the revolutionary's arsenal, to be "a good fighter" (250) is to wield "the antilogos weapon" (250), "scoring [her] feats in written and oral language" (251). Hers is a revolutionary mouth, an oral insurgency:

> If woman has always functioned "within" the discourse of man, a signifier that has always referred back to the opposite signifier which annihilates its specific energy and diminishes or stifles its very different sounds, it is time for her to dislocate this "within," to explode it, turn it around, and seize it; to make it hers, containing it, taking it in her own mouth, biting that tongue with her very own teeth to invent for herself a language to get inside of. (257)

Language must become the revolutionary palace, the symbolic, in the double sense of the term, Bastille to be seized: "Writing is precisely *the very possibility of change*, the space that can serve as a springboard for subversive thought, the precursory movement of a transformation of social and cultural structures" (249). And this text, this instance of writing, this "laugh" is such a space of revolutionary seizure and transformation.

To explode the stabilities of phallic history and assassinate authoritarian historians the revolutionary writing subject must deploy a "feminine practice of writing," a writing whose materiality derives from the recovery of the female body. The relationship between revolutionary practices and the female body coalesces in the manifesto around the two figures of Dora and the Medusa. Of Dora first: Cixous positions Dora as a heroic precursor of the new revolutionary woman, a figure of the formerly repressed woman of "the poetic body" (257), a woman who resisted the inscriptions of Freud's hystericization of her. In this way Dora is identified with Freud's later reference to female sexuality as "the Dark Continent." The manifesto's speaker then links the revolutionary agenda of her emancipatory psychosexual politics to the Black Nationalist movement pressing its anticolonial, anti-imperialist agenda during the late 1960s and 70s, thereby linking independent but partially analogous processes of colonization and decolonization. Like "the colonized peoples of yesterday, the workers, the nations, the species off whose backs the history of men has made its gold" (258), woman is positioned under the sign of oppression/repression. *"The Dark Continent is neither dark nor unexplorable,"* the speaker declares: "It is still unexplored only because we've been made to believe that it was too dark to be explorable. And because they want to make us believe that what interests us is the white continent, with its monuments to Lack" (255). In fact, the speaker goes so far as to identify women with black nationalists: "We the precocious, we the repressed of culture ... we are black and we are beautiful" (248). Thus the revolutionary potential of "woman" is magnified by her positioning as surrogate black African: "You can incarcerate them, slow them down, get away with the old Apartheid routine, but for a time only" (247). Blurring the apparently stable boundaries between the personal/conjugal "subjective economy" (259) and the political economy, she links the psychosexual drama of the repressed to the political/economic exploitation of the oppressed: the personal is political, the political personal.

If Dora is the foremother of the New Woman, the Medusa is her mythical mentor. While mythically Medusa figures as a deadly threat to male power and destiny, in the utopian space of new women she functions differently: "You only have to look at the Medusa straight on to see her. And she's not deadly. She's beautiful and she's laughing"

(255). Literally laughter breaks up the assembled and calm planes of the face; and as it does so, it aligns the human with the animal, with the grotesque body. The effect of laughter on the body elides the gap between species and gestures toward the instability of boundaries separating one "species" from another, unhinging secure placements in hierarchies of meaning. It also breaks up the elegant, cool, controlled planes of statuesque representationalism, forcing the irrational through the lucid planes of reason and control. The sound itself breaks through the language of phallocentrism, a call from beyond, from the body, from elsewhere. Ultimately, laughter "break[s] up the 'truth'" (258) of a universalized, rational, unified subject, destabilizing foundational notions of truth by traducing the boundaries of binary opposites: control and abandon, reason and the irrational, body and mind.

As the vatic representative of the oppressed, the seer of the dark continent, the narrator both calls for and practices a revolutionary writing practice that "laughs." Of a feminine practice, she writes: "It is impossible to *define* a feminine practice of writing, and this is an impossibility that will remain, for this practice can never be theorized, enclosed, coded – which doesn't mean that it doesn't exist. ... It will be conceived of only by subjects who are breakers of automatisms, by peripheral figures that no authority can ever subjugate" (253). While definitions confine and delimit, writing can explode old practices, disrupt old patterns. Throughout, the narrator's analyses of the conditions of women's silence and women's alienation from their bodies proceed by turns indirectly and directly. As Linda Singer suggests, in her analysis of the comparative politics of the texts of Michel Foucault and Cixous,

> to establish her differences from hegemonic forms of authority, Cixous dispenses with or conspicuously transgresses much of the textual etiquette and many of the conventions of academic discourse. Her texts are constructed eclectically. ... By transgressing disciplinary and paradigmatic boundaries, Cixous positions her work within a different economy of legitimation. Dispensing with conventional footnotes and attributions, she constructs her authority as separate and apart from validation through the chain of fathers. (150)

She also destabilizes the notion of narrative progression, moving forward through allusion and language rather than through idea, analysis, and development.

Moreover in the flamboyant performance of this revolutionary "woman" certain stylistic strategies are deployed exuberantly. Iconoclastic statements common to the manifesto abound. "Let the priests tremble, we're going to show them our sexts!" (255). Excesses of language signal a revolutionary playfulness and cavalier rebellion against the conservative regimes of common coinage. Thus new words are formed – erotogeneity (246), frigidified (247), sexts (255). Forceful imperatives explode on the page: "Write your self. ... Inscribe the breath of the whole woman" (250). Pronominal boundaries are breached as the narrator intermingles the interlocutor and the self, fluidly moving through the "I," "you," "she," and "who" as a way of disrupting the certain differentiations separating object and subject, the "I" and the "you." Moreover, the narrator often shifts her interlocutor – to the "you" of the other woman, to the "You" of the oppressor. Within a particular passage the narrator shifts perspectives and pronominal locations, breaches the boundaries between the "I" and the other so that the relative positioning of narrator and interlocutor seems undecidable. She dismantles the old pronominal relationships as part of her revolutionary agenda to explode the old engendering of language.[8] "Blaz[ing] *her* trail in the symbolic," the narrator destabilizes the old certainties separating pronouns and the old symbolic configurations of gender, creating what she herself calls "the chaosmos of the 'personal' " (258). She has herself "flown/stolen" in "the gesture that jams sociality" (258).

In jamming sociality with the language of the body the narrator inaugurates the utopian regime of the New Woman, that newly coined sovereign. Cixous thus heralds the new age, one in which the New Woman's "libido will produce far more radical effects of political and social change than some might like to think" (252). The new subject is constituted of a "vatic" bisexuality that "doesn't annul differences but stirs them up, pursues them, increases their number" (254). In her there is present "both sexes" which are "variously manifest and insistent according to each person, male or female"; and in her is present the "nonexclusion either of the difference or of one sex," with the result that the new subject contains the "multiplication of the effects of the inscription of desire, over all parts of my body and the other body" (254). This newly constituted subject will join with others, men and women, "to render obsolete the former relationship and all its consequences, to consider the launching of a brand-new subject, alive, with defamilialization" (261). Radical change lies ahead as Cixous ends her revolutionary manifesto with an almost scriptural call to love:

In the beginning are our differences. The new love dares for the other. ... She comes in, comes-in-between herself me and you, between the other me where one is always infinitely more than one and more than me, without the fear of ever reaching a limit. (263–4)

With limits, the New Woman "finds not her sum but her differences" (264). With the Law "blown up," violence, volcanic eruption, destruction subside into the aftermath of a pronomial revolution of love. The revolution finds its utopian conclusion by ushering in a new history.

* * *

The rhetoric of Gloria Anzaldúa's autobiographical manifesto is not a rhetoric of revolutionary explosiveness and exuberant or excessive performance. Anzaldúa's manifesto progresses through the rhetorical focus on the geographical subject signalled in the title *Borderlands/ La Frontera*. For Anzaldúa the topography of the borderland is simultaneously the suturing space of multiple oppressions and the potentially liberatory space through which to migrate toward a new subject position. The geographical trope is at once psychological, physical, metaphysical, spiritual, since it functions as a space where cultures conflict, contest, and reconstitute one another. Like Cixous, Anzaldúa presents and consolidates a revolutionary subject through metaphor – here the "*mestiza*" who "has gone from being the sacrificial goat to becoming the officiating priestess at the crossroads" (80).

Anzaldúa's autobiographical essays work to dislodge the ontological and epistemological imperialism of the "sovereign self" of western rationalism, an exclusionary "self" consolidated through racist and heterosexist as well as patriarchal identity practices. Since these practices determine the cultural positioning of peoples on the borderlands and the hierarchical relationship of one people to another, "the answer," Anzaldúa argues,

> to the problem between the white race and the colored, between males and females, lies in healing the split that originates in the very foundation of our lives, our culture, our languages, our thoughts. A massive uprooting of dualistic thinking in the individual and collective consciousness is the beginning of a long struggle, but one that could, in our best hopes, bring us to the end of rape, of violence, of war. (80)

Dualistic practices determine what histories are recorded, what voices are heard, what epistemological projects succeed, what ontological status people bear.

Anzaldúa fights the collective amnesia the colonial situation engenders in borderlands people by engaging in a project of anamnesis: a recollection or remembrance of a past efficiently occluded by the forces of oppression and acculturation. But here the anamnesis is not so much personal, albeit the personal punctuates the analysis, as it is collective. The narrator looks through the opacities of colonization for cultural remnants with which to reinterpret history. She finds in certain myths the possibilities of a new "nationalism of the *mestiza*" that will encourage breakages in the repetition of what Lionnet describes as "historically and Eurocentrically determined racial metaphors of the self" (116).

To pursue a new nationalism of transformative "hybridization," Anzaldúa's narrator elaborates a countermythology. Pressing backward and ever backward through the history of the Mexican and Aztecan people, she finds, through gaps in the efficient but not total erasures of colonization, a mythical source of inspiration in the "complete" figure of the pre-Azteca-Mexica great goddess. Recovering a precolonial history, the narrator finds that the Goddess *Coatlicue*, "Lady of the Serpent Skirt," "contained and balanced the dualities of male and female, light and dark, life and death" (32). Explicitly linked to the Medusa of Greek mythology and of Cixous's manifesto, Coatlicue is "a symbol of the fusion of opposites: the eagle and the serpent, heaven and the underworld, life and death, mobility and immobility, beauty and horror" (47). Her serpent state refuses a dualistic ontology, captures imaginatively that "something more than mere duality," that "third perspective."

Inspired by the recovery of Coatlicue, the narrator proceeds to rewrite the history of the Azteca-Mexica nation. She refuses the common story of La Chingada's (Malinche's) culpability, setting forth instead another interpretation of Cortez's victory over the Aztec peoples: "the ruling elite had subverted the solidarity between men and women and between noble and commoner" (34). Once the Coatlicue "state," in both senses of the word, had been undermined and superseded by a hierarchical/dualistic state, defeat by colonizing armies followed inevitably. Cultural reorganization accounted for colonization, not woman's treachery. Adding greater complexity to the cultural history of her peoples, integrating an analysis of the oppressions of gender to those of class and race, the narrator multiplies the sources of colonization. Doing so, she begins to transform the experience of oppression into the call for a new consciousness. The recovery of an alternative cultural myth empowers her to both critique the sovereign regime and to countervalorize an alternative nationalism.

In contradistinction to the old terrorist state, the new state is a state of consciousness. For the narrator Coatlicue effectively becomes

> the mental picture and symbol of the instinctual in its collective impersonal, prehuman. She, the symbol of the dark sexual drive, the chthonic (underworld), the feminine, the serpentine move-ment of sexuality, of creativity, the basis of all energy and life. (35)

Consequently the recovery of the Coatlicue state means the recovery of body/soul, spirit/matter, that "other mode of consciousness" which "facilitates images from the soul and the unconscious through dreams and the imagination" (37). The insinuating serpent is the figure for the animistic recovery of a larger consciousness, one fuller than the rational self of the European cultural scene. Such a state uproots the source of violence in the west, the specularization of things and people and the consequent erasure of spirit from the physical realm (37). Thus the strategic significance of the "serpent skirt" individually and collectively derives from the intervention it promotes in the repetition of the performance of the "terrorized" self, a self that blames, hates, and divides into the "accusatory, persecutory, judgmental" on the one hand and "the object of contempt" on the other (45).

Movement toward the new consciousness, the new nationalistic state, is a geographical move which becomes the "crossing," or *travesía*, into a "new territory" (48). Crossing to this new "state," the old identities crack, shed and give way to a new "state," a newly consti-tutive knowledge that exposes the "falseness of the view from the top":

> Every time she makes "sense" of something, she has to "cross over," kicking a hole out of the old boundaries of the self and slipping under or over, dragging the old skin along, stumbling over it. It hampers her movement in the new territory, dragging the ghost of the past with her. It is a dry birth, a breech birth, a screaming birth, one that fights her every inch of the way. It is only when she is on the other side and the shell cracks open and the lid from her eyes lifts that she sees things in a different perspective. It is only then that she makes the connections, formulates the insights. It is only then that her consciousness expands a tiny notch, another rattle appears on the rattlesnake tail and the added growth slightly alters the sounds she makes. Suddenly the repressed energy rises, makes decisions, connects with conscious energy and a new life begins. (49)

A new identity practice dislodges the old practice of "autonomy" which the narrator describes as "a boulder on my path that I keep crashing into" (50). The old notion of the sovereign self of western auto-biographical practice fades away from consciousness as she surrenders her conscious "I" to the "power" of her "inner self, the entity that is the sum total of all my reincarnations, the godwoman in me" (50). Surrendering to her mythical and cultural inheritance, she recovers a new sense of self, a self multiplied in more than "one" person:

> And someone in me takes matters into our own hands, and eventually, takes dominion over serpents – over my own body, my sexual activity, my soul, my mind, my weaknesses and strengths. Mine. Ours. Not the heterosexual white man's or the colored man's or the state's or the culture's or the religion's or the parents' – just ours, mine.
>
> And suddenly I feel everything rushing to a center, a nucleus. All the lost pieces of myself come flying from the deserts and the mountains and the valleys, magnetized toward that center. *Completa.*
>
> Something pulsates in my body, a luminous thin thing that grows thicker every day. Its presence never leaves me. I am never alone. That which abides: my vigilance, my thousand sleepless serpent eyes blinking in the night, forever open. And I am not afraid. (51)

The new consciousness leads to a state of openness, not self-closure; it is not individual but transindividual, not unitary but multiple. Thus the narrator of *Borderlands* configures the Coatlicue-state in its psycho-logical and political dimensions as a space through which to negotiate ambivalence and oppositional politics.

The new state is achieved through the representational politics of language. Like Cixous, the revolutionary subject of *Borderlands* must claim her own language. While Anzaldúa specifies three predominant identities constitutive of her own experience – Anglo, Mexican, Indian – she also multiplies the matrices of identifications, the serpent eyes, when she explores the multiplicity of languages spoken throughout her experiential domain. The tongue is the tongue of a linguistic border-land, a wet surface where multiple languages meet and mix, slip and slide. Thus at the beginning of her manifesto, Anzaldúa issues a challenge to the Anglo reader, and to the sovereignty of English as the language of self-representation in the United States:

> The switching of "codes" in this book from English to Castillian

> Spanish to the North Mexican dialect to Tex-Mex to a sprinkling
> of Nahuatl to a mixture of all of these, reflects my language,
> a new language – the language of the Borderlands. There,
> at the juncture of cultures, languages cross-pollinate and are
> revitalized; they die and are born. Presently this infant language,
> this bastard language, Chicano Spanish, is not approved by any
> society. But we Chicanos no longer feel that we need to beg
> entrance, that we need always to make the first overture – to
> translate to Anglos, Mexicans and Latinos, apology blurting out
> of our mouths with every step. Today we ask to be met halfway.
> This book is our invitation to you – from the new mestizas. (iv)

In not apologizing for the agglomerative linguistic potpourri that
is the language of her project, in resisting the pressure to translate
the Spanish passages for the Anglo reader, the manifesto's narrator
refuses to reconcile her self-portraiture with the dominant forms
of subjectivity in the west. Many languages intermingle with one
another, in a state of non-hierarchical multiplicity, creating a hybrid
language that captures the multiplicity within the speaking subject and
resists the seductive call to recuperation into the power of the one and
the same tongue. The narrator of *Borderlands* embraces her multiple
voices: "I will no longer be made to feel ashamed of existing. I will have
my voice: Indian, Spanish, white. I will have my serpent's tongue – my
woman's voice, my sexual voice, my poet's voice. I will overcome the
tradition of silence" (59). Fighting the "linguistic terrorism" of the
cultural position of Chicanas, she proclaims the nationalistic allegiance
to her specific tongue/s.

    Allied to the power of language is the power of storytelling, including
the power of self-storytelling. Self-reflexively the narrator invokes an
"ethno-poetics" as she performs as "the shaman" (66). Tribal storytelling, her self-representational practice induces a "shamanic state" in
which her " 'awakened dreams' " (70) enable her to play with crossings
of borderlands, with crossings between "my Self" and "the world's
soul" in a great "dialogue" (70). Through the great materiality of
language she "writes the myths in me, the myths I am, the myths I want
to become," and thus feels the power of transformation, the utopian
power of creation:

> My soul makes itself through the creative act. It is constantly
> remaking and giving birth to itself through my body. It is this
> learning to live with *la Coatlicue* that transforms living in the
> Borderlands from a nightmare into a numinous experience. It is
> always a path/state to something else. (73)

"The future will belong to the mestiza," Anzaldúa proclaims, precisely because the future

> depends on the breaking down of paradigms ... the straddling of two or more cultures. By creating a new mythos – that is, a change in the way we perceive reality, the way we see ourselves, and the ways we behave – *la mestiza* creates a new consciousness. (80)

The prose section of this manifesto concludes with a call for the utopian consciousness of the new mestiza, a new way of seeing, not a reconciliation of opposing consciousnesses or perspectives. The new mestiza works to transcend duality through the autobiographical practice of métissage, to use a phrase from Lionnet's theoretical vocabulary. In the spaces of métissage, suggests Lionnet,

> multiplicity and diversity are affirmed. ... For it is only by imagining nonhierarchical modes of relation among cultures that we can address the crucial issues of indeterminacy and solidarity. ... *Métissage* is such a concept and a practice: it is the site of undecidability and indeterminacy, where solidarity becomes the fundamental principle of political action against hegemonic languages. (5–6)

The promisory collocation of selfhood, the utopian identity posited in Anzaldúa's manifesto, is a serpentine performance of the Coatlicue state and mestiza consciousness. The serpent as female im/personation and as agent provocateur insinuates itself throughout the narrator's text in a "quickening serpent movement" (81). Like Cixous's, the rhetorical style and structural arrangement of Anzaldúa's manifesto reflect her new mestiza consciousness in a performance of the very contestatory politics she elaborates. Here too we find a pronominal fluidity as the "I" becomes a "she" and the "she" an "I" and both a "we." The narrator breaks the formal boundaries that characterize the *ancien régime*, that old structure of domination through hierarchization. Multiply voiced in its languages, the text does not work toward a totalized vision but celebrates the multiplicity of eyes, voices, and speaking positions that engage in dialogue with one another. Poems, critical essays, prose evocations, fragments from other poets and writers, fragments of street languages, all combine to capture the vitality of cultural politics, the interdependencies of identities, the collage of new self-collocations. Finally, they coalesce in a defiant call to action: "Stubborn, persevering, impenetrable as stone, yet possessing a malleability that renders us unbreakable, we, the *mestizas* and *mestizos*, will remain" (64).

* * *

Donna Haraway's "A Manifesto for Cyborgs: Science, Technology, and Socialist Feminism in the 1980's" is not an autobiographical manifesto in the ways that Cixous's and Anzaldúa's texts are; but her essay provides a third point from which to consider the possibilities of revolutionary subjectivity. In her "ironic" or, as she suggests, "blasphemous" manifesto, Haraway argues "for the cyborg as a fiction mapping our social and bodily reality and as an imaginative resource suggesting some very fruitful couplings" (191). Her invocation of the metaphorical cyborg functions as a "postmodern strateg[ic]" move (194) that works to resist any unitary and therefore imperial subject secured by identitarian politics. For Haraway would dislodge all sovereigns, not only the *ancien sovereign* of Western discursive practices but the *nouveaux sovereigns* of Marxism and feminism with their "dream of a common language," since any dream of a common language, any dream "of a perfectly faithful naming of experience, is a totalizing and imperialist one" (215).

Working to undo the old teleology of the western humanist tradition, including its psychoanalytical and Marxist agenda, Haraway deploys the cyborg metaphor in order to subvert the old story of origins, original wholeness, developmental individuation, paternal inheritance, en-genderment: "The cyborg is a creature in a postgender world; it has no truck with bisexuality, pre-Oedipal symbiosis, unalienated labor, or other seductions to organic wholeness through a final appropriation of all the powers of the parts into a higher unity" (192). All these narratological templates for identity politics look backward to a natural point of origin; and for Haraway, points of origin need to be exposed for the fictions they ultimately are. Points of origin are politically suspect precisely because they map a totalizing uniformity onto diverse peoples and experiences through a specified locus of identification. And identity politics are exclusionary, fractured, partial (197). The problem with any "we" is that its deployment innocently colludes in the colonizing naturalization of categories such as "woman." The con-temporary project must be to make the category of "woman," as the category of "man," evaporate altogether.

The cyborg is a metaphor for its time. Recognizing the importance of historicizing epistemology, of accounting for the metaphorical specificities of particular moments in time, Haraway's manifesto is

> rooted in claims about fundamental changes in the nature of class, race, and gender in an emerging system of world order analogous in its novelty and scope to that created by industrial capitalism; we

are living through a movement from an organic, industrial society to a polymorphous, information system. (203)

The scientific-technico world, governed by the "domination of informatics," renders obsolete the old epistemological certainties of a dualistic world, one naturalized by the semiotics of dichotomies ("between mind and body, animal and human, organism and machine, public and private, nature and culture, men and women, primitive and civilized" [205]). In the current postmodern surround of a postcolonial global world the old naturalized categories rearrange themselves into denaturalized categories of meaning. Now the operative organizational mode is that of "coding" at all levels, of the atom, the cell, the information circuit, the multinational economy. And so we must recognize that women live and operate in an "integrated circuit."[9] While the integrated circuit may be constraining and colonizing in new ways and render former oppressions nostalgically preferable, it can also provide "a source of power" through which "fresh sources of analysis and political action" can illuminate "subtle understanding of emerging pleasures, experiences, and powers with serious potential for changing the rules of the game" (215).

Thus the cyborg – "a kind of disassembled and reassembled, postmodern collective and personal self" (205). As an assemblage of "networks" in a surround of "structural rearrangements related to the social relations of science and technology" (214), cyborgs inhabit multiple spaces, present multiple identities that expose "the permeability of boundaries in the personal body and in the body politic" (212). In the "utopian tradition of imagining a world without gender, which is perhaps a world without genesis" (192), Haraway embraces the ironic possibilities presented by the cyborg. While, as she suggests, "the main trouble with cyborgs ... is that they are the illegitimate offspring of militarism and patriarchal capitalism, not to mention state socialism," they nonetheless provide liberatory possibilities because "illegitimate offspring are often exceedingly unfaithful to their origins. Their fathers, after all, are inessential" (193). Imagining cyborg politics requires imagining "unnatural" borders. Thus, like Anzaldúa, Haraway explores a "border war," but the topography of her revolutionary skirmish is not geographical. Rather, her border dispute, her border rearrangement, takes place in the space "between organism and machine" (191). Multiple borderlands are breached by the cyborg: between human and animal; living organism and machine; the physical and nonphysical realms (195). Through the breaches, Haraway suggests, "we can learn from our fusions with animals and machines how not to be Man, the embodiment of Western logos" (215).

Haraway's manifesto calls for cyborg performances of "permanently partial identities and contradictory standpoints" upon which to build epistemologies (196). "Monst[rous]" and "illegitimate" collocations of animal, human, and machine, cyborgs promise a new kind of politics contestatory of identity politics. This new politics she calls "affinity" politics (196). Denaturalizing the old certainties of identity, the cyborg functions as a de/naturalized locus of affinity. And the politics of affinity promises an escape from exclusionary impact of identitarian standpoints:

> The theoretical and practical struggle against unity-through-domination or unity-through-incorporation ironically not only undermines the justifications for patriarchy, colonialism, humanism, positivism, essentialism, scientism, and other un-lamented -isms, but all claims for an organic or natural stand-point. (198)

Like other revolutionary subjects, cyborgs – such affinity groups as "women of color" who represent "a potent subjectivity synthesized from fusions of outsider identities" (216) – must seize the very technology of preference in the late twentieth century, that is, writing:

> Cyborg politics is the struggle for language and the struggle against perfect communication, against the one code that trans-lates all meaning perfectly, the central dogma of phallogo-centrism. That is why cyborg politics insist on noise and advocate pollution, rejoicing in the illegitimate fusions of animal and machine. (218)

Critically, the cyborg does not chase a dream of a common language but rather deploys "a powerful infidel heteroglossia" (223) through which "she" "recod[es] communication and intelligence to subvert command and control" (217), through which she posits and deconstructs one boundary after another, through which she constantly crosses borders. Concluding with a call to a new revolutionary subject, Haraway places her utopian confidence in affinity with the cyborg: "Although both are bound in the spiral dance, I would rather be a cyborg than a goddess" (223).

*   *   *

The autobiographical manifesto is a revolutionary gesture poised against amnesia and its compulsions to repetition. It is not quite anamnesis (or reminiscence) so much as a purposeful constitution of a future history, the projection of anamnesis into the future. Moreover, the manifesto offers a point of departure for the current generation (of women, of the people from the borderlands, of cyborgs) in its resistance to the former dispensation. In various ways these three manifestos help us map alternative futures for the "I" in the late twentieth century. They point to blurred boundaries, crossed border-lands, differences and divergences, political possibilities and pitfalls.

I want to conclude on a slightly cautionary note. The collective identification of the manifesto's speaker is perhaps the most problematic aspect of this autobiographical form precisely because the postulation of a counter-public sphere of "women" or "Mestizas" or "cyborgs," etc., functions yet again as a gesture of universalization, if a universalization whose application is narrower than the hegemonic center's universalization. As recent therorists have argued, com-munity is a problematic utopian ideal.[10] Posited on exclusivities, or blindnesses to complex material realities, an idealized community erases differences and contradictory experiences.[11] Thus, however attractive the ideal of "a unified collective subject" might be, we must constantly remind ourselves that the price we pay for celebrating collectivity may be "the actual activities and self-understanding of women, in which gender-based divisions frequently conflict with a whole range of other alliances, such as those based on race or class, and work against any unproblematic notion of harmonious consensus" (Felski 169). Haraway's notion of "affinity politics" attempts to break the power of a too rigid communitarian identity politics.

The dynamics of identity politics and the metaphors deployed in service to that politics are most complex in Cixous's manifesto. Cixous promotes a communitarian identity politics based on a foundationalist notion of "woman." Her metaphor of the Medusa's laugh has a way of consolidating and unifying gender identification. Now if the goal of her manifesto is to foster effective revolution, the means to victory may indeed be a "strategic" essentialism, a strategic universalization of Woman (although not biological woman) operating at a specific historical juncture with a "common or shared epistemological stand-point" (Butler, *Gender Trouble* 14). Cixous herself seems aware of the difference between strategic and ontological essentialism when she declares: "I do not deny that the effects of the past are still with us. But I refuse to strengthen them by repeating them, to confer upon them an irremovability the equivalent of destiny, to confuse the biological and the cultural" (245). But the effect of such a universal "we" is that exclusionary politics intrude once again to the degree that "woman" becomes normative and dehistoricized. Even more problematic is her jarring recourse to the rhetoric of the black nationalist movement and the figure of Africa as the dark continent. Deriving from Freud's essay on female sexuality, the metaphor is central to her deconstruction of phallic specularizations of woman. But her position as a white woman speaking as and for "woman" becomes suspect as soon as she introduces the rhetoric of black nationalism. Since she cannot erase her position as a speaker from a white continent, her deployment of the metaphor insinuates a racial subtext into a manifesto. This subtext only foregrounds the way in which Cixous establishes a prioritization or hierarchization of oppressions, with the oppressions of gender asymmetry taking precedence. Metaphors, while provocative in one direction, have a way of foreclosing options in other directions by participating in imperialistic identity practices.

Both Anzaldúa and Haraway try to resist a reified identity politics. While both of them deploy metaphors as counter-mythologizing vehicles, they try to invest the metaphors with destabilizing effects. Haraway keeps insisting on the energy of a revolutionary "irony" which she says "is about contradictions that do not resolve into larger wholes, even dialectically, about the tension of holding incompatible things together because both or all are necessary and true" (190). And Anzaldúa, in her recourse to the serpent as a generalized ancestor of the *mestiza*, tries to keep particularizing her experience. As she does so she refuses simplifications and keeps multiplying languages and identities, those thousand serpent eyes through which she consolidates/ disperses a visionary politics.

In the end these manifestos offer us fascinating performances of the revolutionary subject, performances which, as Frantz Fanon noted, effectively "transform spectators crushed with their inessentiality into privileged actors, with the grandiose glare of history's floodlights upon them." Such performances help us to hope by insisting on the possibility of self-conscious breakages in the old repetitions.

NOTES

1. "Knowledge" is, as Edward W. Said argues in his study of Orientalism, "essentially the *making visible* of material." See Said 127 and Probyn 178.
2. Hurtado argues that "for white women, the first step in the search for identity is to confront the ways in which their personal, individual silence endorses the power of white men that has robbed them of their history. For women of Color, the challenge is to use their oral traditions for specific political goals" (848–9).
3. See Butler's discussion of the relationship of acts to ideas: "Because there is neither

an 'essence' that gender expresses or externalizes nor an objective ideal to which gender aspires," argues Butler, "and because gender is not a fact, the various acts of gender create the idea of gender, and without those acts, there would be no gender at all. Gender is, thus, a construction that regularly conceals its genesis; the tacit collective agreement to perform, produce, and sustain discrete and polar genders as cultural fictions is obscured by the credibility of those productions – and the punishments that attend to agreeing to believe in them; the construction 'compels' our belief in its necessity and naturalness. The historical possibilities materialized through various corporeal styles are nothing other than those punitively regulated cultural fictions alternately embodied and deflected under duress" (*Gender Trouble* 140).

4. What Felski says of the internal and external dynamics of the feminist counterpublic sphere applies to these multiple spheres: "*Internally*, it generates a genderspecific identity grounded in a consciousness of community and solidarity among women; *externally*, it seeks to convince society as a whole of the validity of feminist claims, challenging existing structures of authority through political activity and theoretical critique" (168).

5. De Lauretis calls these future spaces the "space off" – "those other spaces both discursive and social that exist ... in the margins ... of hegemonic discourse and in the interstices of institutions, in counterpractices and new forms of community" (26).

6. As Lionnet via René Dumont has suggested, "utopian thinking is perhaps the only way out of the impasse created by the neocolonialist strangulation of nations and peoples" (247).

7. Linda Singer argues that for Cixous "the absence of a female-identified discourse adequate to representing women's sexuality in its difference is both a symptom of and instrumental to the continued subjugation of women within the patriarchal order" (139).

8. See also Wittig, "The Mark of Gender."

9. Haraway acknowledges the phrase from Grossman.

10. See Young 171.

11. Felski notes that "the ideal of a free discursive space that equalizes all participants is an enabling fiction which engenders a sense of collective identity but is achieved only by obscuring actual material inequalities and political antagonisms among its participants" (168).

WORKS CITED

Anzaldúa, Gloria. *Borderlands/La Frontera*. San Francisco: Spinsters/Aunt Lute P, 1987.

Butler, Judith. *Gender Trouble: Feminism and the Subversion of Identity*. New York: Routledge, 1990.

——. "Gender Trouble, Feminist Theory, and Psychoanalytic Discourse." *Feminism/Postmodernism*. Ed. Linda J. Nicholson. New York: Routledge, 1990. 324–40.

Cixous, Hélène. "The Laugh of the Medusa." *New French Feminisms: An Anthology*. Eds. Elaine Marks and Isabelle de Courtivron. Amherst: U of Massachusetts P, 1980. 245–64.

De Lauretis, Teresa. *The Technologies of Gender: Essays on Theory, Film, and Fiction*. Bloomington: Indiana UP, 1987.

de Man, Paul. "Autobiography as De-Facement." *Modern Language Notes* 94 (1979): 919–30.

Fanon, Frantz. *The Wretched of the Earth*. Trans. Constance Farrington. Harmondsworth: Penguin, 1967.

Felski, Rita. *Beyond Feminist Aesthetics: Feminist Literature and Social Change*. Cambridge: Harvard UP, 1989.

Freidman, Susan Stanford. "Women's Autobiographical Selves: Theory and Practice." *The Private Self: Theory and Practice of Women's Autobiographical Writings*. Ed. Shari Benstock. Chapel Hill: U of North Carolina P, 1988. 34–62.

Haraway, Donna. "A Manifesto for Cyborgs: Science, Technology and Socialist Feminism in the 1980s." *Feminism/Postmodernism*. Ed. Linda J. Nicholson. New York: Routledge, 1990. 190–233.

Hartsock, Nancy. "Foucault on Power: A Theory for Women?" *Feminism/ Postmodernism*. Ed. Linda J. Nicholson. New York: Routledge, 1990. 157–75.

Hurtado, Aida. "Relating to Privilege: Seduction and Rejection in the Subordination of White Women and Women of Color." *Signs* 14 (1989): 833–55.

Kintz, Linda. "In-Different Criticism: The Deconstructive 'Parole.' " *The Thinking Muse: Feminism and Modern French Philosophy*. Eds. Jeffner Allen and Iris Marion Young. Bloomington: Indiana UP, 1989. 113–35.

Lionnet, Françoise. *Autobiographical Voices: Race, Gender, Self-Portraiture*. Ithaca: Cornell UP, 1989.

Martin, Robert K. "Is Anybody There? Critical Practice and Minority Writing." MLA Convention. Washington, December, 1989.

Modleski, Tania. "Feminism and the Power of Interpretation: Some Critical Read-ings." *Feminist Studies/Critical Studies*. Ed. Teresa de Lauretis. Bloomington: Indiana UP, 1986. 121–38.

Moraga, Cherríe. *Loving in the War Years*. Boston: South End P, 1983.

Said, Edward. *Orientalism*. New York: Random House, 1979.

Singer, Linda. "True Confessions: Cixous and Foucault on Sexuality and Power." *The Thinking Muse: Feminism and Modern French Philosophy*. Eds. Jeffner Allen and Iris Marion Young. Bloomington: Indiana UP, 1989. 136–55.

Smith, Paul. *Discerning the Subject*. Minneapolis: U of Minnesota P, 1988.

Wittig, Monique. "The Mark of Gender." *The Poetics of Gender*. Ed. Nancy K. Miller. New York: Columbia UP, 1986. 63–73.

Woodward, Kathleen. "Simone de Beauvoir: Aging and Its Discontents." *The Private Self: Theory and Practice of Women's Autobiographical Writings*. Ed. Shari Benstock. Chapel Hill: U of North Carolina P, 1988. 91–113.

Young, Iris Marion. "The Ideal of Community and the Politics of Difference." *Feminism/ Postmodernism*. Ed. Linda J. Nicholson. New York: Routledge, 1990. 300–23.

Notes on Contributors

Lynn Z. Bloom, Professor of English and holder of the Aetna Chair of Writing at the University of Connecticut (USA), has published widely on the subject of women's autobiographies and diaries. She has also edited a number of women's diaries and is the Editor of the American Women's Diary Series. She is at work on *Our Stories, Our Selves*.

Trev Broughton teaches Women's Studies at the University of York (England). She is working on issues of gender in Leslie Stephen's *Mausoleum Book*, as well as on the problems of "doing literature" in a Women's Studies context.

Susanna Egan is Assistant Professor of English at the University of British Columbia (Canada) and the author of a number of articles on autobiography and of *Patterns of Experience in Autobiography*.

Joseph Fichtelberg is Assistant Professor of English at Hofstra University (USA) and the author of *The Complex Image: Faith and Method in Autobiography*, and articles on Dos Passos, Gosse, and Crèvecoeur.

Leigh Gilmore is Assistant Professor of English at the University of Southern Maine (USA), where she was one of the organizers of "The Subject of Autobiography" conference. She has published on women's literature and is at work on a book from which her essay in this collection is taken.

Rebecca Hogan is Assistant Professor of English at the University of Wisconsin-Whitewater (USA). She is co-editor of the journal *a/b: Auto/Biography Studies* and edited the Summer 1986 special issue on diaries.

Cynthia Huff is Director of Women's Studies at Illinois State University (USA). The recipient of a Fullbright Research Grant, her publications include *British Women's Diaries* and articles on women's autobiography, the diary genre, and feminist theory. She is currently working on women's childbirth accounts and on the Carlyles' letters.

Shirley Neuman, Professor of English at the University of Alberta (Canada), has written essays on autobiography, women's writing and Canadian literature as well as monographs on the autobiographies of W. B. Yeats and Gertrude Stein. Her edited volumes include (with Smaro Kamboureli) *A Mazing Space: Writing Canadian Women Writing*, the first collection of essays on the topic. She is completing a book on representations of bodies in autobiography.

Jeanne Perreault is Assistant Professor of English at the University of Calgary (Canada). She has published essays on feminist autography and on North American native women writers and has co-edited the anthology *Writing the Circle: Native Women of Western Canada*.

Roger J. Porter is Professor of English at Reed College (USA). He has published extensively on autobiography and is preparing a collection of his essays on the subject. He has taught in Greece, Cairo and Paris, and has directed for and founded a theatre in Portland, Oregon.

Sidonie Smith is Professor of English and Comparative Literature at the State University of Binghamton. She has published two books on autobiography: *Where I'm Bound: Patterns of Slavery and Freedom in Black American Autobiography* and *A Poetics of Women's Autobiography: Marginality and the Fictions of Self-Representation*. She is presently co-editing with Julia Watson an anthology titled *De/Colonizing the Subject: Politics and Gender in Women's Autobiography* and completing a series of essays on twentieth-century women's autobiography.